UNIVERSITIES AT MED

DRILL

A HISTORY OF SUSSEX

Market Cross,
Chichester

Bury church and village. The village lies on the upper greensand belt and almost all the buildings, including the church, are built with this greyish limestone or with the brown sandstone from the lower greensand quarries above Pulborough, conveniently accessible by boat (p. 119).

THE DARWEN COUNTY HISTORY SERIES

A History of Sussex

J. R. ARMSTRONG

Cartography by J. BROUGHTON *and* ROY MOLE
Drawings by CAROLINE LOCKWOOD

PHILLIMORE

First published 1961
Third edition 1974
Published by
PHILLIMORE & CO. LTD.
London and Chichester

Head Office: Shopwyke Hall,
Chichester, Sussex, England

ISBN 0 85033 185 4 ✓

SET BY GLOUCESTER TYPESETTING CO. LTD.
PRINTED AND BOUND BY W. AND J. MACKAY LTD.

Contents

*Brass, Margaret
Camoys Trotton,
c. 1300*

Maps and Plans

Note: The broken coastline in the early maps indicates the line as it may have been some 2,000 years ago. Portions—such as the Selsey Peninsula—are purely conjectural. It is possible that the outlet of the Arun was diverted to the east by a long shingle bar (see 'The Waters of the Arun' by Hadrian Allcroft), in which case the valley from Pulborough to the coast would have been already closer to its present form through the accumulation of silt. There has been no attempt to vary the coastline either on these (or any of the later maps), although changes have been continuous. There is insufficient evidence to define the situation at any particular time.

Brass, Wife of Sir
Ed. Gage, 1595

List of Illustrations

Acknowledgements

The illustrations 13, 31, 35 and 37 are reproduced by courtesy of the British Museum; nos. 16, 38–40, and 45 by courtesy of Worthing Public Library; nos. 3–5, 27 and 32 by courtesy of the Sussex Archaeological Trust; no. 36 by courtesy of the Victoria and Albert Museum; no. 44 by courtesy of Brighton Public Library; nos. 47 and 48 by courtesy of Crawley Development Corporation; nos. 7, 22 and 28 by courtesy of the Weald and Downland Open Air Museum; no. 15 by courtesy of Woodmansterne Ltd. Watford; the frontispiece and nos. 14, 18, 24 and 33 are reproduced from photographs by Noel Habgood, F.R.P.S.

Nos. 1 and 10–12 are Crown Copyright; nos. 6, 17 and 29 are reproduced from photographs by J. K. St. Joseph and are the copyright of the University of Cambridge; nos. 8 and 9 are from *The Bayeux Tapestry* by Sir Frank Stenton and are reproduced by permission of the publishers, Phaidon Press Ltd., London. No. 30 is from a photograph by Photo Precision Ltd., and those numbered 2, 19–21, 23, 25, 26, 34, 41–43 and 46 are from photographs by the author.

Preface

The history of any area, whether parish, county or country, is incomplete if consideration is not given to the way in which ordinary people lived, the kind of houses they lived in and their furnishings, the crafts they plied and the tools they used. Little space could be given to all this in the 'History of Sussex' when it was first published. It was therefore very gratifying when I was asked by the publisher to consider a new and very much enlarged edition with the possibility of many marginal illustrations and additional plates and maps.

The first requirement was to bring the text, written in 1961, up to date; but only a fraction of the additional space was needed for this. The rest has been devoted to tracing the history of the buildings in which the majority of the population has lived and worked, rather than the castles, mansions, churches and civic buildings which already receive adequate attention in the many local guides and publications. Sussex is fortunate in having preserved more tangible evidence of these humbler buildings from different periods of the past than perhaps any other county in England; and possesses great regional variety in building materials locally available—whether timber, clay or stone. Below ground fresh archaeological evidence is being found every year, and, above ground, an increasing number of farms, cottages and houses, some dating back to the thirteenth century or earlier are being recognised. For example, since the receipt and correction of the galley proofs of Chapter XIII, another medieval house of the 'Wealden' type has been discovered in Robertsbridge, bringing the total number of these fine medieval houses still surviving in that small market town to nine instead of the eight given in the text. This new dimension to the county's history has been dealt with in seven additional chapters integrated with the rest of the text in such a way, it is hoped, as to help rather than hinder the general narrative.

These chapters, like all the other chapters of this history, are necessarily condensed. What are often extremely complex processes and developments have continually to be simplified by broad generalisations. The specialists who read this volume will be very conscious of this, and I can only ask their forbearance. Simplification is essential if we are not to miss the wood for the trees, but I hope that most of such generalisations will stand up reasonably well to informed criticism, particularly since it is not possible in a brief history such as this to include the notes and references which would be expected in a more extended work.

I should like to acknowledge my debt to the work of members of the Wealden Building Study Group and the Robertsbridge and Battle Archaeological Society, and particularly to Mrs. Saunders Jacobs for allowing me to see in manuscript her survey of the parish of West Chiltington, and to Mr. and Mrs. Lacey for their comprehensive survey of Steyning, both of which I hope may soon be published.

Above all I am indebted to Caroline Lockwood for her patience and persistence in undertaking the line drawings and plans, the stream of which, with all their revisions and modifications seemed at the time unending. Also I should like to thank Lord Darwen for his patience and help in so many matters of lay-out and presentation in which I have little knowledge but rather definite ideas.

March, 1973. J.R.A.

Brass, Sir Ed. Gage
Firle, 1595

I The Geographical Setting

An imaginary traveller with no particular objective in view, finding himself in the centre of the Sussex Weald at some point not too far from Wych Cross or Turner's Hill might look to the north or to the south, wondering which direction to take. From one point of view it would, in fact, make little difference. In both cases he would find himself walking for some miles through steep wooded valleys, with many streams and prosperous farms built of half-timber or local yellow-brown stone, and small fields of rich pasture and ploughland—sometimes across sandy heathland plateaux, with little but pine and birch and bracken, where he might chance on a low outcrop of weathered sandstone.

Oast House, High Weald

After five or six miles he would gradually descend to a low wooded plain. Here the oak is characteristic, the remains of a dense oak forest, which for some two thousand years covered the wealden clay. The farms are oak-framed and often roofed with a large, heavy, grey-brown, moss encrusted sandstone tile, the fields often separated or edged by dense oak and hazel coppices. After six or seven miles through the rutted, sticky ways of this weald clay, he would approach a series of low hills of quite a different kind, rising in places to two or three hundred feet. Here are many small villages rather close together with a landscape not unlike that from which he started—light sandy soils and stretches of heavier loam, with the older buildings mainly of a grey-brown local sandstone.

Finally, after crossing another narrow plain of heavy clay almost devoid of buildings, he would find himself facing the steep escarpment of the chalk Downs. Here he would enter on a region very different in its trees, flowers and wild life, and in the character and size of its farms. Strung along the slightly raised shelf below the escarpment are many farms and small hamlets. The buildings are mainly of flint or a whitish-grey stone called Malm stone, which outcrops just below the chalk. Climbing to the top of the Downs he would see the chalk hills sloping gradually away. From the North Downs, London and the Thames valley would lie on the horizon; from the South Downs, the coastal plain of Sussex and the English Channel.

Today these southern slopes of the Downs are amongst the least populated parts of Sussex, an area of large farms and few villages. Traditional buildings, from churches to garden walls, are of flint, and many villages preserve something of the unique quality they possessed a century ago. These downland slopes, now partly ploughed, were, less than a generation

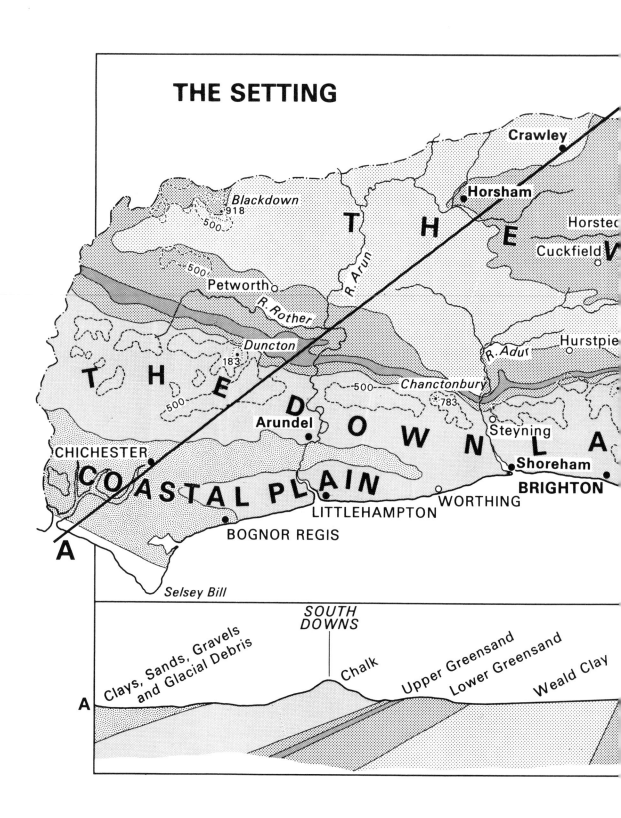

THE SETTING

Crawley

Horsham

Horste[d]

Cuckfield

Blackdown
·918
··500··

T H E V

··500··

Petworth

R. Rother

R. Arun

Duncton
·183

R. Adur

Hurstpie

T H E D O W N L A

··500··

··500·· *Chanctonbury*
·783

Arundel

Steyning

CHICHESTER

Shoreham

COASTAL PLAIN

BRIGHTON

LITTLEHAMPTON WORTHING

BOGNOR REGIS

A

Selsey Bill

SOUTH DOWNS

Clays, Sands, Gravels and Glacial Debris

Chalk

Upper Greensand

Lower Greensand

Weald Clay

A

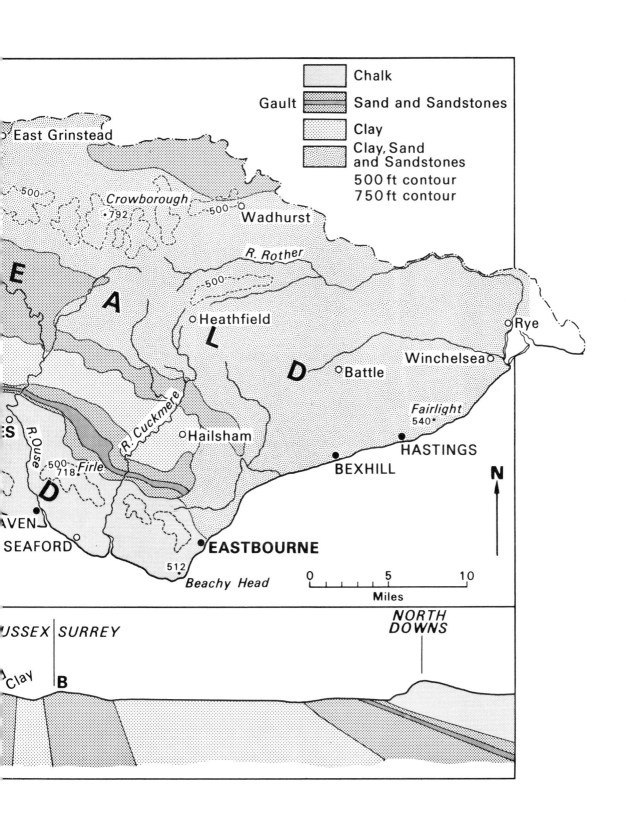

Chalk

Gault — Sand and Sandstones

Clay

Clay, Sand and Sandstones

500 ft contour

750 ft contour

East Grinstead

Crowborough
•792

500
Wadhurst

R. Rother

500

E

A

Heathfield

Rye

L

Winchelsea

D

Battle

Fairlight
540•

(R.) Cuckmere

R. Ouse

Hailsham

HASTINGS

D

500
718• *Firle*

BEXHILL

AVEN

SEAFORD

EASTBOURNE

512
Beachy Head

N

0   5   10

Miles

USSEX SURREY

NORTH
DOWNS

Clay   B

Flint mine Downland Area

ago, open sheep pastures, and had been so for six centuries or more; before that, abandoned scrubland; before that an area of small cultivated fields, cattle enclosures, and hilltop towns; still earlier a region of scattered flint mines, settlements of miners and flint tool makers; before this the main highway between the upland farms and causewayed camps of colonists from the west. Climate played its part in some of these changes, invasion and the introduction of new farming techniques in others, and in recent years an economy determined by war or the threat of war. Changes such as these form the basis of local history. The chapters which follow will, it is hoped, help towards their visualization and understanding.

Assuming our traveller has climbed the Downs somewhere between Ditchling Beacon and Chanctonbury Ring, he will, to the south-west, see the flat coastal plain widening gradually until, at Chichester, it is over ten miles across, whilst to the south-east the chalk formation reaches to the sea, and forms an undulating sequence of valley and cliff, terminating at Beachy Head. Some of the richest farm-land in Sussex is found in the coastal plain, which for the last two thousand years has been the most populated area. Here again our traveller will find, for the most part, the same mixed clays, sands and gravels as he would, had he travelled north and descended into the Thames valley, for if a line is drawn from Hastings along the ridges of the central Weald, through Crowborough and Hand Cross to Horsham, the landscape on either side of this line is rather like a mirror image of that on the other side. It is this basic symmetry which makes the Sussex and the wealden landscape a fascinating area to geologists and geographers. As for its history, a clear picture of these varied and roughly parallel regions is fundamental to an understanding of Sussex, especially of the changes and sequence of human settlement there.

There is however one feature which the traveller, however observant, will not realise. The coast line (see footnote), with its bays and estuaries, shingle bars and promontories, which appear so defined and stable, has in fact been and still is, in a condition of continuous flux. This is due to a number of causes—erosion by the sea, the silting of estuaries and rivers, and at times the slow but gradual alteration in the level of sea or land. These changes, slow in terms of the lifetime of the individual but rapid in the wider context of history have had an incalculable effect on trade, the rise and decline of ports and market centres, and on the distribution and movement of population.

In Neolithic times, some four to five thousand years ago, the coastal plain must have extended several miles further to the south. Since then the rate of erosion has been most continuous at the western end of the county, where the great flat triangle of the Manhood peninsula extends from Chichester to Selsey. Here, even in Roman times, land stretched

16

1. Cissbury looking N.E. The width across the Iron Age enclosure is approximately 1,000 feet, the present height of the ramparts 20 feet. Depressions indicating earlier flint mine shafts are clearly visible (p. 20).

2. Money Mound: a bronze age burial in the central Weald showing the site just before the removal of the last of the stones, which formed two large concentric circles round the grave. The site is now levelled and returned to farmland (p. 22).

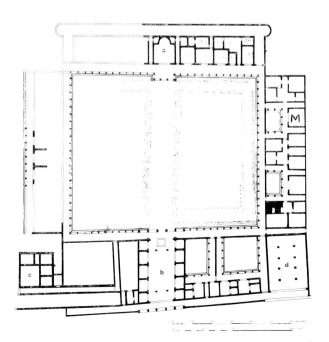

3. Top: Detail of the Dolphin Mosaic in the room marked M in the plan below.

4. Middle: Model of conjectural reconstruction of the Palace looking west; the main entrance is in the middle foreground. The audience chamber or hall of justice faces the entrance on the far side.

5. Left: Plan of the Palace. Details of the lower half can only be conjectural since it is still unexcavated, lying under gardens, houses and the main road from Chichester to Portsmouth.

perhaps three miles further to the sea than it does today, and the denudation still continues. Here, engulfed by the sea, lie Belgic as well as Saxon towns and settlements.

At the other end of the county the process has been reversed. South westerly storms and currents have carried debris from the west to build shingle bars and sand banks across the river estuaries to the east blocking harbours and accelerating the silting up of river valleys. Pevensey, Winchelsea, and Rye, once great sea ports now lie stranded miles from the present coast, while safe and adequate harbours such as once existed at Fishbourne, Steyning (S. Cuthmans port), Old Shoreham, Meeching, Bulverhythe and Hastings have been so long completely silted up that they are now built over and virtually unidentifiable.

Eastern Rother
16th Century map

17

II The First Inhabitants

Palaeolithic implement, Slindon

Evidence of the first men in Sussex dates from the warm spell before the last Ice Age. No human bones have been found, but large flint implements which belong to the earliest part of the Old Stone (Paleolithic) Age have been discovered at various sites. A particularly interesting and important site is in Slindon Park, on the edge of what was once a raised beach some hundred feet above the present sea level; about thirty-five worked flint tools have been found here, and the remains of various animal bones suggest a warm, almost subtropical climate. Here primitive men lived by hunting and fishing. They did not, however. belong to the species from which humans are descended but to a similar species later to be ousted by Homo Sapiens.

With the onset of the last Ice Age, during which the ice sheets crept as far south as the northern sides of the Thames valley, subarctic conditions drove these people far to the south. Nothing whatever belonging to the later periods of the Old Stone Age—a matter of thirty thousand years or more—has so far been found in Sussex. Ten thousand years ago, however, conditions had so far improved with the retreat of the ice sheet again, that hunters following game from the east crossed what is now the North Sea, but which was then dry land, to Britain. They moved from one temporary encampment to another in various parts of England, including a number in Sussex. These people we can definitely think of as our own remote ancestors, but like the earlier Paleolithic hunters they were still nomadic, and did not practise agriculture. They made delicately fashioned arrow- and spearheads, and carved bone harpoons and fish-hooks, and for some five or six thousand years wandered in search of game over the Weald. Very large numbers of their knives, scrapers, arrow-heads and other tools have been found in Sussex, mostly in the central wealden area to the north of the Downs. Notable sites are those at Chithurst and West Heath in the western Rother valley, near Midhurst, and at Selmeston near Firle. At Selmeston one pit yielded over 6,400 worked flints.

During this period, which is known as the Mesolithic Age, the ice sheets over Scandinavia and the North were melting rapidly, and gradually raised the levels of seas and oceans—whereas during the onset of the last Ice Age, the sea level had dropped until the British Isles, and even Iceland, had been linked to the Continent by the drained land. At the beginning of the Mesolithic period, therefore, there was no division between Sussex and Northern France, only a rather flat plain with a river

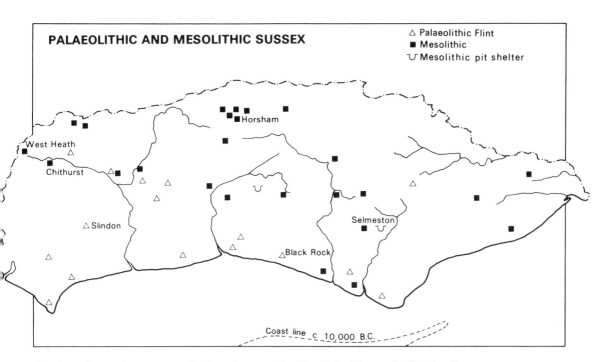

PALAEOLITHIC AND MESOLITHIC SUSSEX

△ Palaeolithic Flint
■ Mesolithic
⋃ Mesolithic pit shelter

Horsham

West Heath

Chithurst

△ Slindon

Selmeston

△ Black Rock

Coast line c 10,000 B.C.

flowing down the centre of what is now the English Channel. Gradually this river widened from the west, and the estuary where it entered the sea encroached further and further to the east. We must imagine those Mesolithic groups, who possibly migrated from north to south following the seasons, having to make, over the centuries, a longer and longer detour to the east when crossing this river. At some point, possibly about seven or eight thousand years ago, the estuary had reached as far as Dover, and there must have been some dramatic event—the result of storm and high tides—when the encroaching sea from the north joined the widening channel from the east, thus forming the Straits of Dover. Once this breach had taken place, the rapid flow of tides and the effect of rough weather would quickly widen the strait, cutting off the Mesolithic people of the Weald from the Continent. Perhaps for two or three thousand years there was little or no contact and during this time the English Channel and the Sussex coastline slowly approached their present form.

Towards the middle of the third millenium B.C. the first true invasion and colonization occurred. Peoples, originally from the Mediterranean, landed first in Ireland and the south-west of England, and then pushed eastward along the hills and chalk plateaux of the south. These wiry dark-haired people possessed the basic crafts of civilisation—pottery, weaving, agriculture and the domestication of animals. They were very different from the nomadic hunters of the Weald and were capable of a highly organised social life; witness the great temples erected at Avebury

*Neolithic vessel,
Cissbury*

Bronze Age beaker

in Wiltshire, and later at Stonehenge. Though the centre of this 'Neolithic' civilization was on the chalk hills of the Salisbury Plain area, it spread along the Downs. Of the twelve hill-top settlements or 'Causewayed camps' built by these Neolithic people in the south of England, four are in Sussex. These are at Whitehawk above Brighton, on the Trundle north of Chichester, at Barkhale above Bignor, and on Coombe Hill above Eastbourne. They are called 'causewayed' because the surrounding banks and ditches are broken by undefended gaps. Two of these 'camps' (the Trundle and Whitehawk) have been partly excavated, and some light has been shed on the life of the communities. Important burials were in long mounds or 'barrows', and of these, seven have been found in Sussex; one, called Bevis's Thumb, near the summit of the Downs at North Marden, measures approximately 150 feet in length by over twenty in breadth.

Perhaps the most interesting feature of this Neolithic culture in Sussex is the mining of flints for implement making. These mines are all located on the upper chalk strata, the only part of the chalk containing flint in any quantity. Not only was this known, but it was also known where the most suitable form of flint was likely to be found. Flint mine-shafts are found fairly close together. On Cissbury Down above Worthing there are over 150 within a radius of a few hundred yards. They are usually fifteen to twenty feet deep and about the same in width. Models of the mines can be seen in the Worthing Museum and in the excellent Museum of the Sussex Archaeological Society at Barbican House, Lewes.

It seems probable that the Neolithic invasion of Southern Britain was stimulated by a rapid improvement in the climate, and there is evidence that for a time it may have been both warmer and wetter than it is today. The Neolithic settlements seem to have been concentrated on the Downs, where many of the now dry valleys may then have contained springs. A relatively small change in the prevailing wind currents, or in the course of the Gulf Stream could cause dramatic changes in our climate. Major alterations in the pattern of invasion, colonisation and settlement have probably been largely determined by such climatic changes.

Such a change of climate appears to have taken place during the next phase in the early history of Sussex—the Bronze Age. This was associated with a new group of immigrants from across the Channel, known as the Beaker Folk from the particular shape of their flat-bottomed drinking vessels, which are quite unlike the round-bottomed pottery of the Neolithic peoples. One of these is illustrated on this page, and is quite unlike the round-bottomed pottery of the Neolithic period. The latter was convenient for placing in the hot ashes of a hearth or in the hollow of an uneven floor, whereas the flat base would only rest securely on a flat surface. What may seem difficult to understand is why the round forms

20

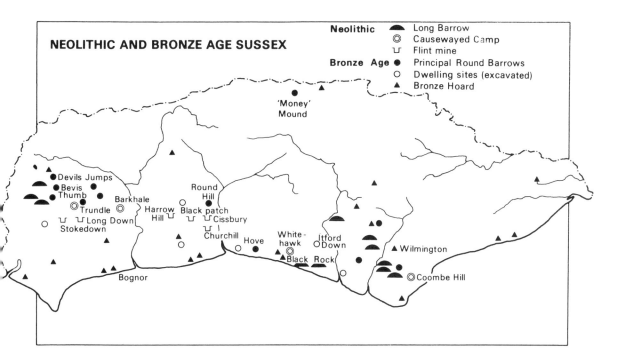

NEOLITHIC AND BRONZE AGE SUSSEX

Neolithic — Long Barrow
◎ Causewayed Camp
⊔ Flint mine
Bronze Age ● Principal Round Barrows
○ Dwelling sites (excavated)
▲ Bronze Hoard

gave place so completely to the flat-bottomed form. The answer, which is equally applicable to small objects such as jewellery or large structures such as houses is the general tendency to follow the fashions set by a ruling class or group whether established by conquest from without, or assimilation from within. The transition from the Neolithic to the Bronze Age could be either.

The Bronze Age is also linked with a return to colder, drier conditions; the downland became less hospitable, while the forests of the Weald, which had flourished during the Neolithic period, provided a more attractive shelter. Whatever the reasons the Bronze Age population spread itself more widely over the Weald, and there is rather less evidence of occupation of the now bleak and windswept Downs. Flint mining, however, continued since bronze implements were few and highly prized. The general way of life was not very different in the Bronze Age from the Neolithic. In both cases we must imagine small, isolated farms, such as two partly excavated (one just before, the other since the war), on the side of Black Patch, near Findon. Both had extensive livestock enclosures for cattle, sheep, goats and pigs. Besides the single farms there were a few hamlets such as that uncovered in 1955–56 on Itford Down, with as many as ten to twenty separate households.

Other groups led a semi-nomadic existence, following their herds from place to place. The standard form of house was a round conical hut, about twenty feet across, with a central hearth and opening in the roof for the

21

Amber cup, Hove

smoke to escape. Cremation took the place of burial. and the remains were interred in round tumuli in contrast with the long mounds of the Neolithic period. Some were very large, such as the one destroyed at Palmeira Avenue, Hove, in the nineteenth century. The amber cup and polished double headed axe and whetstone from this burial and illustrated on this page are now amongst the most treasured objects in the Brighton Museum. The amber cup suggests trade contacts across the North Sea, and the axe and whet-stone were probably symbols of high office, such as the mace and sceptre of a later age.

Other large examples survive on Bow Hill, and there are six in line—known as the Devil's Jumps—on Monkton Down near Treyford. Mostly, however, they were small, and altogether nearly a thousand have so far been identified in the area, chiefly on the higher slopes of the chalk, and on the lower Greensand hills that surround the Weald clay. Occasionally a Bronze Age burial site has been discovered accidentally, as when a farmer ploughing near the summit of the Round Hill, Steyning, sliced through the tops of some twenty burial urns. Although bronze tools were scarce and valuable, and flint continued to serve for most purposes, some large hoards of bronze—mostly socketed and flanged axes and spear-heads—have been found, notably at Black Rock, near Brighton, at Bognor, and at Wilmington. These were probably buried by Bronze Age smiths for safe keeping, and for some reason never recovered.

Since the first edition of this history, a remarkable Bronze Age burial site has been excavated in the heart of the Weald, on a sandstone ridge, midway between Horsham and Crawley. It proved to be unique in the south east of England. Within a circular mound, measuring nearly a hundred feet across, two concentric circles of massive stones were un-covered. These were all that remained of circular drystone walling denuded by centuries of ploughing and twice broken into by grave robbers, or by amateur archaeologists—once in the Roman period, and again in the eighteenth century. A significant feature was that nearly two hundred Roman coins were found scattered at various levels in the earth cover. It is clear that this burial mound, built perhaps fifteen centuries earlier, commemorating some chieftain of the early Bronze Age, had continued as a place of veneration into Roman times—treated perhaps not unlike the wishing wells associated with Christian saints of a later period. Unfortunately, a condition of excavation was that the site should be cleared for agriculture, and not a trace now remains.

In this same region a number of other Bronze Age sites have been identified, and there are some grounds for assuming that the central Weald was more generally settled and utilised in this period than it has previously been supposed. There is in fact, more evidence of Bronze and Iron Age settlement within the Weald than of later Saxon.

III Iron Age Hill Forts and the Roman Conquest

The general way of life of the Bronze Age, which lasted for well over a thousand years with little change, was disturbed by the coming of the Celts from the south-east. This was certainly no sudden event, such as the Roman conquest five hundred years later, or that of the Normans over fifteen hundred years later. It was a rather slow infiltration into a fairly sparsely populated country. The first settlers may have come peaceably as coastal colonists prepared to trade with the existing peoples on the Downs and in the Weald. They came from the south-east and the first settlements were in the eastern part of the county. It may be significant also that at about this time a damper and warmer climatic period returned.

Corn drying oven, Thunders barrow

During the two centuries from about 600 to 400 B.C. other Celtic groups followed. Traffic with the Continent became much more general. Flint, the material from which tools had been made for more than eight thousand years, was now largely replaced by iron, and farming became more concerned with the growing of crops, less with seminomadic herding. This led to a more closely knit population with an increasing number of village communities. It is to this period that there is the earliest evidence of corndrying kilns such as that illustrated on this page. A large number of these have been found in connection with agricultural settlements on the Downs. In all cases the domes which covered the drying chambers have disintegrated, but the furnace chambers underneath the large stone slabs, which form the floors of the drying compartments, remain intact with soot encrustation and usually a great deal of half incinerated grain. The latter has provided some clues as to the type of corn grown. Many pits for the storage of the dried grain have also been found, and on the basis of the evidence now collected, an attempt to reproduce an Iron Age Farm is being made at Butser Down just beyond the Sussex/Hampshire border. This will help us to estimate the agricultural yield, and therefore the size of the population which might have been maintained within any given area known to have been cultivated in this period. The experiment is to include not only cereal growing using the iron-age type plough, but also livestock—early breeds of sheep, cattle and pigs.

The strongly-built Celts were warlike and although there is no reason to believe that they drove out the existing inhabitants, they soon became

23

*Cissbury ramparts,
300 B.C. and today*

the dominant element. With their coming, new areas were opened up for settlement, particularly in the Weald. Here in the remoter forests the descendants of the original mesolithic hunters probably still survived, trading such things as skins for the products of the farmers. Some of these no doubt adapted themselves to changed conditions, becoming charcoal burners to supply the furnaces of the newly established iron-smelting industry in the Weald north of Hastings; in this way their descendants may have continued as forest nomads until comparatively recent times.

These developments culminated, in the third century B.C., in the building of relatively large hill-top cities enclosed by defence works that can still impress us by their scale and massive strength, as at Cissbury, the Trundle and Mount Caburn. Here we find the beginning of a genuine division of labour between town and countryside. Excavations carried out at Mount Caburn in 1932 suggest the existence of some seventy or more households, and of crafts such as iron-working and cloth-making, catering for the needs of the surrounding villages. Again, the size of the fortifications—at Cissbury enclosing sixty acres, with an enclosing wall over a mile long—indicate that these places must have been defence points for the whole of the surrounding area. Seventy families could not possibly have adequately manned even the quarter-mile-long ramparts of Caburn. These banks and ditches are impressive enough today, but the elaborate character of the original fortifications with their revetments of massive timber is illustrated in the marginal drawing on this page. In one at least of these Iron Age forts—that at Highdown—the revetments were re-inforced with flint walls. This grouping of hill-top cities implies a social organisation on a tribal basis similar, no doubt, to that described by Julius Caesar as existing in Gaul two hundred years later. Sussex may therefore have been an area of occasional intertribal war during the time these great forts or 'cities' were built and occupied.

Smaller Iron Age fortified sites exist in other parts, not only in the downland, but also in the Weald. Several of these, such as the Promontory Fort at Henfield have not yet been excavated, or their dates verified: others have only recently been discovered, such as the Promontory Fort near Iping, recognised from an air photograph taken when woodland was cleared in 1957. That the central Weald at this time was by no means uninhabited forest is clear from the great Iron Age fort at Oldbury, just across the Kentish boundary. This lies beside an important track which runs north from the coast near Hastings, past the new iron smelting areas and on through the heart of the Weald into Kent.

During the last century B.C., contacts with the Continent became still closer. In 75 B.C., people called the Belgae, of mixed Celtic and Germanic stock, invaded and occupied most of what is now Essex, Hertfordshire, and part of Kent. This was followed twenty years later by the two expedi-

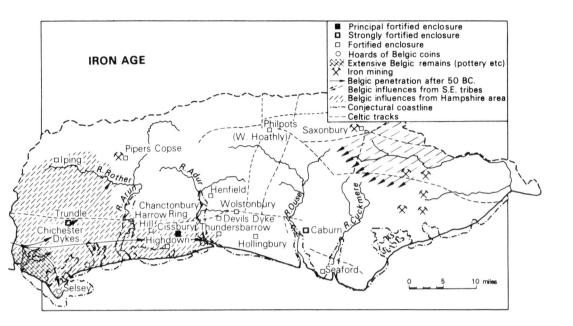

IRON AGE

- ■ Principal fortified enclosure
- ❑ Strongly fortified enclosure
- □ Fortified enclosure
- ○ Hoards of Belgic coins
- ✕✕✕ Extensive Belgic remains (pottery etc)
- ✕ Iron mining
- —► Belgic penetration after 50 BC.
- ↙ Belgic influences from S.E. tribes
- ⁄⁄⁄ Belgic influences from Hampshire area
- ·—· Conjectural coastline
- - - Celtic tracks

Philpots
(W. Hoathly) Saxonbury

Pipers Copse

Ilping

R. Rother

R. Adur

Henfield

Chanctonbury Wolstonbury

Trundle Harrow Ring

Chichester Cissbury Thundersbarrow Caburn

Dykes Highdown Devils Dyke

Hollingbury

R. Ouse

R. Cuckmere

Seaford

Selsey

0   5   10 miles

tions of Julius Caesar, and the temporary occupation of the south-east by Roman Legionaries. Though neither of these events touched Sussex directly, the indirect consequences were considerable. Iron Age strongholds such as Mount Caburn were strengthened, and there would certainly have been an influx of refugees from the north and north-east. Four years after Caesar's second expedition, an invasion by the Belgic tribe of the Atrebates, landing first in the Isle of Wight and Hampshire, had within a few years overrun the Manhood Peninsula of Sussex—the Manhood Peninsula is the name given to the area extending south from the Trundle to Selsey. Leading this invasion was Commius, an Atrebatian, who had been sent to Britain as an envoy before Caesar's first expedition in 55 B.C. Commius therefore knew Britain well, and no doubt had useful contacts in the area.

Soon after the Belgic occupation of the Manhood Peninsula, a Belgic centre of some importance seems to have been established a few miles to the south of where Chichester now stands. Judging by the amount of pottery, coins and jewellery, which at various times have been found on the beaches between Selsey and Wittering, it is likely that this town was later washed away by the sea. This would explain the lack of any trace of the actual site. To protect it and the rich farm-land of the coastal plain against the still unconquered peoples centred on the hilltop city of Trundle, lines of earthworks running from east to west, north of Chichester—one of which is called the Devil's Ditch—were constructed. In the past,

25

Dug-out boat, Arun

various theories have been advanced to account for these earthworks, but excavations in 1958–59 strengthened the view that some at least were Belgic work, with the defences facing north. For how long after this the Trundle continued its independent existence we do not yet know, but it was certainly abandoned before the turn of the century.

When, therefore, the conquest of Britain was finally planned by the Roman Emperor Claudius in A.D. 42, the situation was roughly as follows: Sussex to the West of Brighton was part of a Belgic state under a ruler called Cogidumnus, with a local centre somewhere south of Chichester. Agriculture was widely practised, not only on the coastal plain, but also on the downland. A survey, for instance, of the remains of Celtic field boundaries on the Downs behind Brighton between the Adur and the Ouse has revealed more than thirty Iron Age hamlets, most of which would certainly have been established by the time of the Roman Conquest. Very many of these ancient field boundaries, revealed so clearly in air photographs, have, in the last few years, been completely obliterated by deep ploughing—in most cases the first disturbance for fifteen hundred years.

Further to the east, beyond the Pevensey Levels, which then formed a wide inland estuary separating the hilly region between Bexhill and Rye from the rest of Sussex, the population was relatively sparse, except for the iron-working districts to the north of Hastings. There is no evidence of a port of any importance at that time in eastern Sussex although the Caburn itself must have sloped down directly to the wide, navigable estuary of the Ouse. In 1965 during work on the banks of the Arun to mitigate flooding the remains of six boats hollowed from the trunks of large oaks were found between Burpham and Pulborough. One must have been well over thirty feet long. Their dating has to be confirmed by carbon 14 tests, but it seems probable that some at least date from the pre Roman period, although this technique of boat making may have continued into a later age.

The focus of trade, after the Belgic invasion, seems to have been the Manhood Peninsula, from whence boats trading so far as the east Mediterranean would carry furs and skins in return for cargoes of fabrics and the rarer metals. Sussex traders themselves would be dressed, like their kindred on the Continent, in substantial garments, brightly coloured tunics with breeches and, over all, a woven cloak, fastened by a brooch or buckle, perhaps of silver. These are the people popularly thought of as naked, woad-painted 'Ancient Britons'.

Sussex, or at least that part which was included in the kingdom of Cogidumnus, played a significant role in the actual conquest of Britain. The Romans had a number of friendly contacts amongst the British leaders. Whenever possible they pursued the policy of 'divide and rule',

26

and Cogidumnus from the beginning was an ally of Rome. For the help which he gave, he was rewarded by the grant of a measure of independence as local governor, and the area is referred to in Roman documents as 'The Kingdom' (Regnum). Tacitus, writing some fifty years later the biography of his uncle, Agricola, the first great governor of the new Roman province of Britain, says: 'Certain states were presented to King Cogidumnus, who maintained his unswerving loyalty down to our own times— an example of the long-established Roman custom of employing even kings to make others slaves.'

It was presumably Cogidumnus who founded Chichester, as the local capital, conveniently astride the coast road from Havant to Portslade Stane Street being constructed to link it directly with Londinium, the new commercial centre of Britain. Significantly, the Roman name given to Chichester was Noviomagus or 'Newmarket'.

One of the most interesting discoveries from this early period of the Roman occupation is the so-called 'Minerva Stone', let into the wall under the arcade of the Assembly Rooms in North Street. This was dug up in the eighteenth century, not far from its present position. Part of the lettering was destroyed, but sufficient is left to reconstruct the inscription which, translated, reads: 'To Neptune and Minerva this Temple is dedicated for the welfare of the divine House by the authority of Tiberius Claudius Cogidumnus, King and Legate of Augustus in Britain, by members of the Guild of Craftsmen.' The Latin word is *fabrorum* and probably refers to shipwrights, since Chichester was a port in which shipbuilding would, from the beginning, be the most important industry.

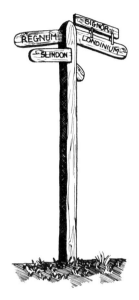

Signpost, Stane Street
Bignor Hill

IV The Roman Occupation

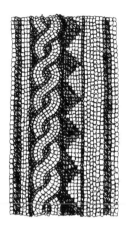

Mosaic border, Bignor

We cannot be precise about the sequence of events in Sussex during the first years of the Roman occupation. The excavation since 1961 of a great Roman palace at Fishbourne suggests that here was an important administrative and supply base which must have played a considerable part in the earlier phases of Roman conquest and consolidation. Certainly the foundation of Chichester and the construction of the roads radiating from there to Clausentum (Southampton) in the west, to Calleva Atrebatum (Silchester) to the north, and Londinium in the north-east, took place very soon after the conquest of the south and south-east. Sussex escaped the ravages of the rising led by Boudicca, and later, while the extreme north was being subdued and the northern defence system in the lowlands of Scotland perfected by Agricola, development was rapid in the south. The amphitheatre for example, at Chichester, was almost certainly built between 80 and 90 A.D. This amphitheatre was identified in 1935 when a depression in the ground was noticed some hundred yards to the south-east of the city wall. Excavations revealed a stone wall, in places ten to twelve feet high, plastered and painted to resemble marble, and enclosing an area measuring 185 × 150 feet. It is now built over, and to quote S. E. Winbolt: 'The vandals could not find it in their hearts or purses to spare the only known Roman amphitheatre in the County of Sussex. '

Excavation of the town itself has been intermittent and often frustrating, since the present city lies exactly over the Roman site, and with Chester preserves better than any other existing English city the basic Roman plan. A few bombed sites have contributed some useful information since the war, but many of the important Roman buildings, such as the Forum and the Basilica, lying under later buildings such as the cathedral, are unlikely ever to be completely revealed.

It is just outside the city that, during the last ten years, there has been uncovered the foundations of the largest Roman building other than fortifications, to be found in Britain. This is on the site of the early invasion base at Fishbourne. Although only half the site which it occupied can at present be explored, the rest being under a number of houses, gardens and a main road, it is clear that it consisted of a great central court symmetrically planned with at least three secondary small courtyards, the whole constituting what can only be described as a palace or administrative centre rather than a great house. It was evidently planned soon after Fishbourne had served its purpose as a military supply base, and it

28

is reasonable to assume that it may have been built for or by Cogidumnus, who, according to a reference in Tacitus' biography of his uncle Agricola, continued to rule under Roman protection for at least another three decades. The palace was completed well before the end of the first century and like the planning of Chichester was part, no doubt, of the Roman policy of impressing the native population by the magnificence of their urban culture and technology.

What happened to this building in the second century is rather less clear. Various modifications were made, some implying a decline in importance, such as the splitting up of larger into smaller rooms. Re-adjustments of this kind were in fact being carried out when the fire occurred which destroyed the building and apparently led to its almost total abandonment in the third century. The palace at Fishbourne has now become one of the best known and most patronised archaeological sites in Britain and thousands of people come to look at the many mosaic pavements and the formal garden which is now being gradually restored to something of its original appearance. This restoration of a Roman garden is based on a careful excavation of bedding ditches, fragments of ornamental fountains, and the examination of pollen remains.

Roman bastion,
Chichester

Evidence from the hundreds of Roman coins found in Chichester also points to the latter part of the first century A.D. and to most of the second century as the period of greatest activity and prosperity, which fits in with the general pattern of Imperial policy. This was to develop towns as quickly as possible as centres for the dissemination of Roman culture, and as embodiments of Roman ideals and authority. It was, however, like its kindred town of Silchester, never densely built, and a population of per-haps two thousand in the second century would be a reasonable estimate, bearing in mind a tendency to decline in the third and fourth centuries. This compares with a population of rather less than three thousand living within the walled area today. The existing walls are medieval, but rest on Roman foundations. The first Roman defences date from the end of the second century, and were probably hastily built when the Caledonians (Picts) first broke through the defences of the North in a large-scale attack and penetrated deeply into Britain. The sense of security and Roman invincibility had been challenged, and during the following two centuries there was a continual undercurrent of uncertainty and insecurity. At the end of the third century the city walls were rebuilt and strengthened with strong bastions at regular intervals, this time not so much against a possible incursion from Scotland but against raiders from the North Sea. Thus control of the seas, which Rome had previously enjoyed, was now also subject to question.

The strengthening of Chichester's defences was part of a carefully conceived system of garrison forts, built at this time round the south-east

29

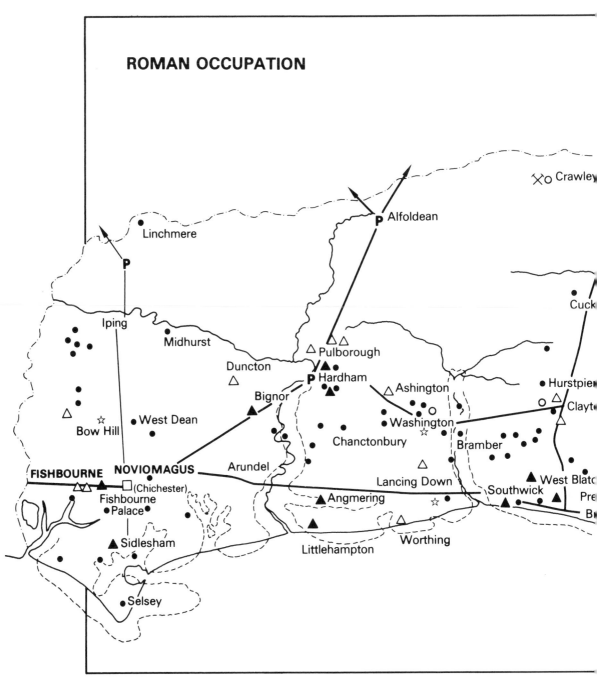

ROMAN OCCUPATION

from Caister in Norfolk to Carisbrook in the Isle of Wight. These coastal defences were placed under a new officer entitled *Comes Litoris Saxonici* (Count of the Saxon shore). The main garrison post in Sussex was at Anderida, (Pevensey). Whereas Chichester was a fortified town occupying

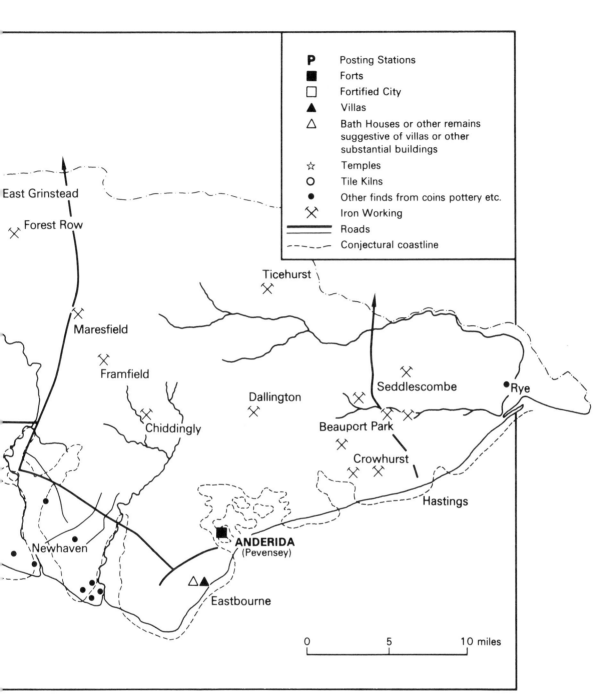

East Grinstead

Forest Row

Ticehurst

Maresfield

Framfield

Dallington

Seddlescombe

Rye

Chiddingly

Beauport Park

Crowhurst

Hastings

Newhaven

ANDERIDA
(Pevensey)

Eastbourne

0   5   10 miles

90 acres, Pevensey was a fort enclosing approximately nine acres and
protecting a town the site of which has been lost, possibly in later inunda-
tions by the sea, but no one visiting the Roman fort today can fail to be
impressed by it. There is certainly no sign yet of faltering workmanship

31

Roman pantiles,
Angmering

or failure to match a sense of design with monumental strength. The walls form an oval, and to that extent the plan differs from those of all the other forts in this coastal series. This was no doubt dictated by the site, which was an irregular peninsula stretching into the estuary which came close to the walls on three sides. In later centuries the sea actually eroded and destroyed the southern side: still later it began to recede, assisted, in the Middle Ages, by the gradual enclosure of the mud flats by sea walls, and by drainage. Today Pevensey lies stranded some four miles from the coast.

The rapid development and prosperity of Sussex in the early days of the Roman occupation is supported by other evidence, such as that of the villas at Bignor and Angmering, portions of which were probably built between A.D. 70 and 80. Both were a long way from any city; both became houses on the grand scale. At Bignor are mosaic pavements, mostly dating from the extension of the house in the second century, which are unsurpassed for their workmanship by anything elsewhere in Britain; while the bath-house wing, excavated at Angmering, with its elaborate sequence of eight rooms, suggests a luxury and magnificence greater, even, than that of Bignor, though the villa itself has not yet been excavated. The reason for building Angmering remains a mystery which may be cleared up by further digging. It lies close to the coastal road which ran from Chichester to Pevensey: and near this road are situated almost half the Roman villas so far discovered in Sussex (some forty in all), including those at Southwick, Preston and Eastbourne. Several other villas were linked to Stane Street, including Bignor, two at Pulborough and one at Wiggonholt.

On the whole the evidence suggests that, apart from the new town at Chichester, and possibly Pevensey, there was no great extension of the Celtic areas of settlement in Sussex during the Roman times. In the central Weald and the locality immediately north of Hastings, the earlier iron industry was, it is true, greatly expanded. The evidence is in the enormous quantities of furnace slag used by the Romans as hard core in the road that crosses the Weald from near Maresfield, north across the Surrey border to Edenbridge: and in the mounds of Roman slag at Beauport Park, near Battle. One of these covered two acres, was fifty feet high, and crowned with trees. In the nineteenth century these mounds were completely levelled when they were used as material for road making. At the time of writing (1972) an area of intensive Roman occupation is being uncovered in a development area within the new town of Crawley. What can only be described as a major industrial complex seems to be emerging including iron working and pottery on a large scale; and this in an area of the Weald where there had been little previous evidence of settlement in Roman times.

These wealden developments, however, were probably comparatively

32

6. Pevensey: Roman fortress and medieval castle from the W. The ruined Norman keep (astride the Roman wall) is enclosed by the medieval castle and moat. The Saxon village lies just beyond (pp. 30–2, 38–9, 41, 51–3).

7. Reconstruction at the Weald and Downland Open Air Museum at Singleton of the evidence consisting of post holes and shallow trenches of a Saxon hall. In the background is a complete reconstruction of a Saxon weavers hut (pp. 44–5).

8. William lands at Pevensey. The ships indicate little change in design from those used by the earlier Saxon and Danish invaders. Note the cavalry horses included in one of the ships.

9. A wooden castle is being built at Hastings on a mound which is being rapidly thrown up. At various strategic points in Sussex *mottes* of this type, housing small garrisons, were built immediately after the conquest (pp. 47, 49).

limited. The coastal plain, the Downs, and the Greensand hills, were already settled before the Romans came; we can assume some improvements in agricultural techniques, and possibly the establishment of some efficiently managed agricultural estates during Roman times. Recent excavations of a villa at West Blatchington revealed a basilica-like building with house and storage rooms presumably under one roof, reminding one of the great composite house and farm buildings of Friesland today. Close to this building, eleven ovens for corn drying were also found, suggesting a large farm centre. Again, buildings of a very large size were added in the second century to the precincts of the villa at Bignor—one almost 200 feet in length. Whether these were barns, or built to house livestock, large-scale agriculture is implied.

Romano-Celtic Temple, reconstruction

Most farming, however, on the Downs and elsewhere, was carried on as before by small farmers owning and cultivating their fields individually, and living in scattered hamlets. Occasionally they would visit Chichester, or the nearest market, to sell their produce, and to buy pottery, farm equipment, or perhaps some exotic import from the Mediterranean, and attend shows which might be staged in theatre or amphitheatre there. Visits might be made to one of the hill-top shrines, such as that on Lancing Down, Bow Hill, or Chanctonbury, but even these small Roman places of pilgrimage were almost certainly on the site of pre-existing Celtic temples. Religious observance, both before, during and after the Roman occupation, combined very satisfactorily a pleasurable outing with the sense of an observance performed.

Posting stations simplified journeys to London or further afield. These were provided with inns and stables where horses could be changed. Two on Stane Street are situated in Sussex, approximately eleven miles apart— the first at Hardham, just south of Pulborough, the second at Alfoldean, two miles south-west of Horsham. Quick transport, or the delivery of letters along such roads was very efficiently organized, and unequalled until the Mail Coach and Turnpike system of the early nineteenth century. A posting station similar to those on Stane Street has been identified on the Chichester–Silchester road at Iping, but it has not yet been excavated. Inhabitants of Sussex felt themselves not only an integral part of the Roman empire, but very closely linked with the peoples across the channel; in the country as well as in the towns Latin was understood, and the urban population was certainly bi-lingual. Both the Celtic speech of Sussex and Latin were spoken by fellow Celts in Gaul. There was, in fact, far less sense of division than there is today.

Yet this Sussex of the fourth century became, within a hundred years, isolated both from the Continent and from the rest of England—a land cut off by forests to the north and a dangerous sea to the south.

33

V Houses and Farmsteads from the Earliest Times to the Saxon Conquest

Alternative interpretations of post hole evidence

Our knowledge of the kind of dwellings in which most of the population lived up to the early Middle Ages is based almost entirely on archaeological evidence. A little can be inferred from the written word and a little from early manuscript illustrations, but only the archaeologist can tell us that such and such a kind of building was to be found in any particular area, or part of an area.

The difficulty about archaeological evidence is that it is found largely by accident, the great Roman palace at Fishbourne, for instance, was first revealed in the digging of a drainage channel through a field in 1960. The second difficulty is that survival in the ground depends largely on the nature of the subsoil. In acid bog conditions, as in the marshes round Glastonbury, or in many districts in Ireland, wood, leather and even cloth can survive for thousands of years, whereas from the lime areas such as the chalk, post holes and pits may be perfectly preserved, but every bit of wood, leather or cloth will have disintegrated long ago; while in the clay and sandy loams which cover the main part of the Sussex Weald and the Coastal Plain, and where the ground has been deeply ploughed throughout subsequent centuries, neither post holes nor material are likely to remain. Here, apart from burial mounds, only the solid deep set foundations of important Roman buildings have any chance of survival, and none but the Romans built foundations of this kind until the Normans arrived.

Another difficulty, particularly where post holes or banks and ditches provide the only evidence, is that there is often more than one possible interpretation of the general plan or even shape of a building. For example, a circular arrangement of post holes may be of posts forming the outer walls of a hut, but they may equally be supporting long rafters which continued to the ground, but left no trace. The second interpretation would more than double the area covered by the hut. There are also many questions of detail. Until recently archaeologists have assumed that a round posthole meant a round post, an assumption recently shaken when it was proved in two recent excavations that the holes had held the untrimmed butt ends which above ground had been squared. This suggests that the whole structure above ground may have been more carefully carpentered than had been assumed. Misinterpretations of this kind may

34

have led to an underestimation not only of the craftsmanship but also of possibly decorative elements in early buildings. This is the kind of problem which should make us accept only tentatively suggested reconstructions whether we are dealing with the remote past or any period before the Middle Ages. With these provisos in mind it can be said that the considerable amount of research done in Sussex during the last few years does enable us to build up some idea of changing house styles in these early centuries.

The nomadic hunters who, for five or six thousand years wandered over the Weald in the mesolithic period left innumerable flint implements to mark their temporary settlements and journeys, but little to help us reconstruct their dwellings. Hollow pits associated with their implements have been interpreted as their dwelling sites, and one such has been preserved just over the northern border of the county at Abinger in Surrey. A reconstruction of a bivouac supported on forked poles based on two post holes seems to be the most probable form of roof. Where archaeological evidence is lacking, however, we can sometimes be justified in assuming that very early ways of building may in fact survive under similar conditions of life into a later age. Charcoal burners, for example, in the Weald, right up to the second world war lived in simple conical huts of turf supported on a wooden frame. Such huts leave absolutely no trace in the ground after even a few decades. It is not unreasonable to suppose that our early ancestors, men of the Middle Stone Age built huts as well constructed, or even that the method of building may have passed down without much alteration from those days until the present day. At the museum at Singleton a charcoal burner's camp has been rebuilt under the guidance of one of the last old-style charcoal burners in Sussex and contains two huts built of turf in this way. Such huts may seem primitive and uncomfortable by twentieth century standards, but they are carefully designed and adapted from materials to hand and give sufficient shelter.

Framework and completed charcoal burner's turf hut

With the colonisation of Sussex by Neolithic farmers we are perhaps on slightly more certain ground, though in Sussex no remains of houses have yet been found. But in Ireland, and on the Continent a number of neolithic sites have been explored in which the foundations, both of stone and timber buildings have been identified. Almost all are rectangular and some are of considerable length; many have supporting aisle posts, and seem to have been divided into a large number of smaller compartments. For this reason it has been assumed that they housed an extended family—three or four generations with married brothers and sisters sharing the one building, and that some part of these buildings may have been used as byres, and to house livestock. Evidence may be produced by archaeologists which will modify the picture for this area, but that this type of house was to be found in Sussex is probable.

35

*Bronze Age
settlement, Itford*

*Bronze Age hut,
Amberley Mount*

For the Bronze Age there is now a good deal of evidence, and a number of recent discoveries have added much to our knowledge. They confirm the general conclusions arrived at in the past—that of scattered farmsteads consisting of small groupings of approximately round huts surrounded by a stockade, but a number of questions still remain unanswered. The most completely explored site in Sussex—on the Downs above Itford near Lewes, consisted of thirteen huts, some of which were almost certainly for storage, but how far the larger huts were occupied by one family is not clear, so that the actual size of the community is conjectural. The second uncertainty is how long such a settlement lasted, since replacement of timbers could be made without noticeable disturbance or the digging of fresh post holes. An excavation of the site of two late Bronze Age houses on Amberley Mount in 1958 proved the existence of another type of house, built on a terrace of sloping chalk and sunk slightly in the ground, anticipating the more deeply sunken huts built by the Saxons more than a thousand years later. A reconstruction of one of these Amberley houses is shown in the marginal drawing. In this reconstruction it is assumed that the posts must have been supports for the rafters, the ends of which would have rested on the ground; otherwise in these sunken houses, if the posts had formed the outside walls the hollowed space outside would, in wet weather have become a quagmire and the house itself a pond. It is also necessary to remember that all our evidence of house design in this period has so far come from the chalk area of the Downs, and it may be quite wrong to assume a similar pattern of buildings in the Weald.

The most important development introduced by the Celtic Iron Age invaders was the building of strongly fortified hill top towns described in chapter 3. The systematic excavation of any of these towns in Sussex has yet to be undertaken. Work on Mount Caburn in 1932 established the fact that seventy or so hollows, clearly identified within the ramparts, were probably all storage pits for corn, those excavated measuring from three to eight feet in depth and diameter. These, it was assumed, were attached to individual houses. Fragments of daub with wattle imprint were found, and some door latches; but the actual size and shape of such dwellings can only be determined by systematic excavation; possibly when this happens both the rectangular and the round house type of dwelling— as in the lake-side settlement near Glastonbury—may be found. Tremendous opportunities, in fact, await the archaeologist in Sussex, but the pressure for emergency operations on sites threatened with immediate destruction necessitates the deferment of large scale projects of this kind.

With the Romans came new techniques of building, and entirely new house plans, both in the town and in the larger country houses or villas briefly referred to in the previous chapter. The two main forms were the corridor house in which the various rooms open off a long verandah or corridor, and the courtyard surrounded on two or three sides, and occasionally on four. Although a house of the corridor form was found on the east cliff at Folkestone to have been built a few years before the Roman invasion, indicating the growing influence of Rome in the southeast of Britain during that period, no building from before the invasion showing Roman influence has been found in Sussex. Of those built soon after the Conquest the villa at Southwick was of the completely enclosed courtyard type illustrated in the marginal drawing, that at Bignor enclosed three sides of a courtyard. At Angmering and Wiggonholt—the excavations at both of which were interrupted by the war, and have not since been resumed—only the bath house in each case was revealed. Since then an emergency excavation in 1966 near the site of the Wiggonholt villa which was carried out prior to the realignment of the adjacent main road, uncovered kilns and the post holes of buildings which may have been connected with industry. Still more recently in the valley leading northwest from Chichester, close to the line of the Roman road from Chichester to Silchester, two Roman villas have been discovered near Chilgrove and the sites of two others are suspected. Probably the majority of the Roman villas were centres of large agricultural estates; almost all have hypocaust systems of underfloor heating, and at least one or two rooms with mosaic paving. Quite clearly they were the houses, whether of natives or immigrants, of a sophisticated and cultured class.

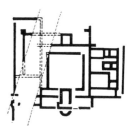

Southwick, Roman Villa

In a town such as Chichester most of the dwellings would have been compressed versions of the courtyard villas of the countryside with a much smaller piazza or enclosed area, in some cases with a shared dividing wall between neighbours. Frequently there would be two, occasionally three storeys, while its country equivalent would have only one. In Chichester only fragmentary research is possible but the marginal drawing shows a conjectural reconstruction of such a house in Silchester, where systematic excavation has been practicable. It gives some idea of the kind of building we should imagine. In the Worthing Museum is a three dimensional reconstruction of one of the rooms in the Roman Villa at Bignor showing in miniature the elaborately painted plaster, window glazing, and furnishing which would have been characteristic of the larger Roman houses, but the bulk of the population in the countryside would continue to build and to live as they had done before the Roman conquest.

Roman townhouse

VI Saxon Sussex

Glass goblet,
Highdown, Saxon Burial

Between the years A.D. 400 and 410 the Roman legions, coastal garrisons and naval forces were withdrawn to defend the Continent against the Teutonic armies which had broken through the northern defences of the Empire. The first exact record of Saxon landings in Sussex occurs in the Anglo-Saxon Chronicle under the year A.D. 477. It reads: 'This year came Ella to Britain, with his three sons, Cymen, Wlenking and Cissa, in three ships: landing at a place that is called Cymenshore. There they slew many of the Welsh; and some in flight they drove into the wood that is called Andred'sley.' (The 'Welsh' here, of course, refers to the Romano-British inhabitants.) What happened in the seventy years between these dates?

It is an obscure period about which there are many conjectures and many traditions, and in recent years a number of widely-read books have been written round such slender evidence as exists so far as Britain is concerned. Sussex is only a small part of this vague jigsaw: although the general pattern is fairly clear, the details are uncertain.

From the close of the fourth century, we must, I think, imagine successive raids and insecurity, leading to the abandonment of the larger villas, and the migration of many of the town dwellers from such places as Chichester to the west, or even across the channel to Brittany. The way would thus be paved for the final invasion and occupation by the Saxons. The actual conquest and settlement was itself extended over a fairly lengthy period. The distribution of known Saxon burial sites suggests that there may have been a good deal of fighting in the area between Shoreham and Pevensey. Grave objects such as the highly wrought brooch illustrated in a marginal drawing display a high level of craftsmanship, however barbaric in design by Roman standards. One of the most prized possessions of the Museum at Worthing is a perfectly preserved incised glass vase with an inscription in Greek. This was found in the early Saxon cemetery on Highdown Hill to the north -east of Worthing. It could have only been made in the eastern Mediterranean, and suggests loot from a Roman site and that such objects were highly valued.

The next entry relating to Ella in the Anglo-Saxon Chronicle is under the year 485 and reads: 'This year Ella fought with the Welsh nigh Mecred's-Burnstead.' Where was this place? No one has yet satisfactorily identified it. Probably it was in the western part of Sussex, or near the Hampshire border. The next entry is five years later, under the year 490: 'This year Ella and Cissa besieged the city of Andred, and slew all that

38

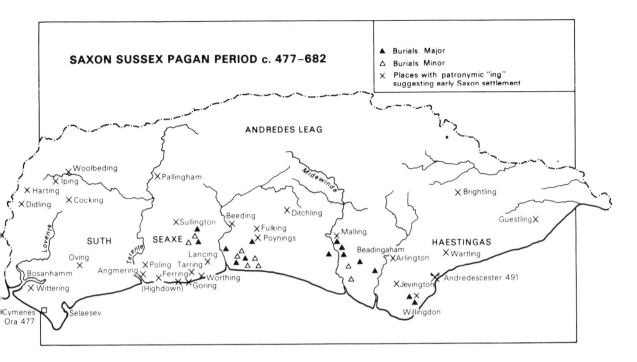

were therein, nor was one Briton left there afterwards.' It had therefore
taken some thirteen years to consolidate the Manhood Peninsula, and from
there to extend control to Pevensey. The pattern of conquest was not unlike
that of the Belgae five hundred years earlier; first the occupation of the
Manhood Peninsula (it is even possible that Cymenshore was, or lay near,
the lost Belgic centre in that area) followed by a slow struggle eastwards.
Just as the Iron Age fortress of Cissbury had been rebuilt five centuries
before, to meet the Belgic advance and later abandoned and ploughed up
during the Roman period, so it was again, hastily but less efficiently,
refortified to meet the new threat.

Beyond Pevensey, estuary and marsh divided the Hastings area from
the west, and what took place there is completely undocumented, but the
area appears to have been invaded and occupied by a separate group of
Saxons—the Haestingas. These gave their name to Hastings, and continued a semi-isolated and independent existence for nearly two hundred
years until the year 771, when it is recorded that Offa of Mercia subdued
the kingdoms of Kent and Sussex, and 'the men of Hastings'.

Ella himself was recognised as a leader of more than local importance,
since he is recorded in the Anglo-Saxon Chronicle as the first 'Bretwalda'
(Broad-Wielder) or vaguely accepted overlord of all the Saxon invaders.
Yet Sussex appears to have remained until the seventh century singularly
isolated from the rest of England. The wealden forest became a more
effective barrier than it had been to Celt or Roman. Stane Street and the

39

*Saxon brooch from
Alfriston*

other wealden highways were abandoned, and there is no evidence even of Saxon iron workings. How then, in view of the rather scanty evidence, should we visualise the changes in Sussex during these two centuries?

First we must conclude that the existing Romano-Celtic population was almost completely driven out of the colonised area. With very few exceptions place names and names of physical features are Saxon: only a few Roman names and words persisted, such as Chichester (Cissa's 'Castra' or fort), or Andredswald (i.e. the forest of Anderida). Secondly the whole pattern and character of settlement was altered. The Saxons were forest plain and valley dwellers, they used a heavy two-yoke plough and worked their fields on a communal basis, sharing the great open fields which surrounded their closely-built and centrally-placed village. Thus the Celtic upland farms and hamlets on the Downs decayed, and settlement was concentrated more completely on the coastal plain, the valleys, and along the Greensand belt under the north side of the Downs. There is little evidence that the Saxons occupied existing towns or villages. They preferred small, compact communities to the more scattered Celtic type of farm and field.

When, therefore, St Wilfred landed near Selsey in the year 681, and by his preaching converted the South Saxons to Christianity, the Sussex landscape was very different from that which a visiting Roman would have observed two or three centuries earlier. Bede, in his *Ecclesiastical History of England*, completed within a few years of Wilfred's death, gives a vivid account of the conversion of the South Saxons, embroidered with some charming and appropriate miracles. The fact that it was over eight years previously that the neighbouring kingdom of Kent had been converted, and that Sussex alone of the Heptarchic (seven) kingdoms remained pagan, shows the extent of its isolation.

Bede speaks of: 'A certain monk of the Scottish nation, whose name was Dicul, who had a very small monastery, at the place called Bosanham, encompassed with the sea and woods, and in it five or six brothers, who served our Lord in poverty and humility; but none of the natives cared either to follow their course of life, or to hear their preaching.' Within the later Saxon church at Bosham is an underground chapel or semi-crypt, which, according to tradition, is on the site of this small monastery. It is probably near here that Wilfred first preached and carried out his mass baptisms. Soon afterwards Bede continues: 'King Ethelwalch of the South Saxons, gave to the most reverend Prelate Wilfred, land of eighty-seven families to maintain his company who were in banishment, which place is called Selsey, that is, the island of the seals. . . . Bishop Wilfred, having this place given him, founded therein a monastery.' This later became the centre of the south Saxon diocese, but nothing remains either of the original monastery, or of the Minster which was built later. The site is now certainly

10. Battle Abbey and town from the S. The arrow indicates the site of the High Altar built where Harold (traditionally) fell. On the plan on p. 48 the dotted lines indicate later roadways. Battle High Street lies along the central section.

11. Site of Robertsbridge Abbey from the S. The foundations of the church can be clearly seen in the crop markings to the N. of the farm buildings (p. 68).

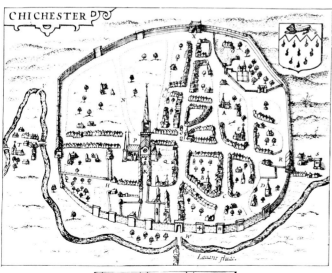

12. Chichester looking N.E. The walls can be seen in the foreground, and their circuit is marked by trees on the N. and E. The main roads meet at right-angles at the Cross and follow the Roman plan. The open space in the N.E. corner is the Priory Park, containing the remains of the Norman *motte*, and the church of the Franciscan friars. Beyond the walls at this point the Festival Theatre in the Round now stands. In the foreground are the Bishop's Palace, the Cathedral and Palace gardens. The inner ring road now cuts across the meadows outside the walls in the foreground.

13. A comparison with Speed's map, drawn in 1610, indicates the relatively small extent to which the walled area has been built up during the last 350 years (pp. 28, 69, 71–4, 155).

14. The Bishop's Palace, Chichester. Between the two projecting wings is an eighteenth-century screen wall which conceals a twelfth-century hall and chapel. The hall itself has been sub-divided into a number of rooms. Behind the wing on the right can be seen the roof and the little triangular smoke outlet of the old kitchen (pp. 62, 71). The two wings date from the sixteenth century.

15. The raising of Lazarus. One of two reliefs which may once have formed part of a series of panels decorating a Norman chancel screen, later replaced by the Gothic Arundel Screen. These reliefs form a perfect contrast in style and spirit to the little early thirteenth-century painted roundel of the Madonna in the chapel of the Bishop's Palace (p. 71).

16. View of Rye from the N. in 1823. The estuary of the Rother is seen still encompassing the eastern slopes of the hill on which the town is built (p. 76).

17. Bodiam Castle from the S.W. In the fifteenth century a harbour was situated in the foreground. The interior, now a hollow shell, was 'slighted' by Waller in 1643 (pp. 80, 107).

under the sea, for the peninsula of Selsey must in Wilfred's day have been several times its present size. Embedded in a modern memorial at the edge of the parish church at Selsey, are two fragments of interlaced decorative stone carving. These may well have formed part of an early Saxon cross— the kind of cross of which many examples survive in the north of England, and which date from the early phase of conversion to Christianity, being set up in the open as centres for preaching the gospel and baptism before the building of more substantial churches. This fragment which is illustrated in the marginal drawing could conceivably have been part of such a preaching cross set up by St Wilfred and his followers.

Saxon carving, Selsey

Selsey, therefore, from the end of the seventh century, became one of the most important places in Sussex, and culturally the most important. During the eighth and ninth centuries other towns began to assume some prominence as market centres. The grass-grown streets of Roman Chichester re-emerged with wooden Saxon houses; while places such as Pevensey, Steyning, Lewes and Hastings developed into towns of craftsmen and traders instead of villages of farmers. In all these towns, mints are recorded by the tenth century—a sure sign of an urban economy.

In the ninth century, however, there was a setback. Just as four hundred years before, life in Roman Sussex had ebbed and stagnated through the continual threat from Saxon raiders, so, in the ninth century, the now settled and Christianized Saxons suffered the same insecurity at the hands of the Danes. It is particularly difficult for a scattered farming community to meet the sudden attacks of mobile forces whose families and lands lie across the water, and who are perfectly equipped for rapid movement. For nearly fifty years, from 852 when parts of Kent were plundered, fear and uncertainty set back any further social and economic progress, though it did lead indirectly to the consolidation of the West Saxon monarchy and the integration of Sussex into this larger unit, which we can begin to think of as England, although it still excluded much of the West Country and the North.

Alfred the Great, King of the West Saxons, who finally checked the Danish conquest, endeavoured to meet these difficulties of defence and it was almost certainly he who inaugurated the building of a series of forts to be garrisoned at the threat of danger by men drawn from the surrounding population. A document of the early tenth century lists these forts and the areas responsible for their maintenance. There were five in Sussex: Hastings, Lewes, Burpham, Chichester and a place called 'Heorepeburan' —possibly Pevensey. Chichester had the largest supporting area, and the Roman walls were its defence. The Anglo-Saxon Chronicle under the year 895 records that: 'The Danish Army went up plundering in Sussex nigh Chichester; but the townsmen put them to flight, and slew many hundreds of them, and took some of their ships.' This must refer to the men who

41

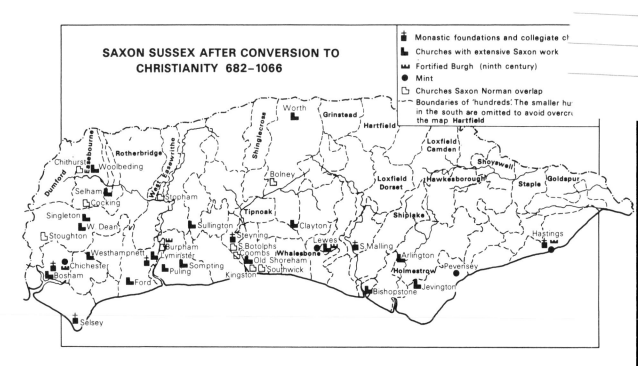

SAXON SUSSEX AFTER CONVERSION TO CHRISTIANITY 682–1066

Legend:
- Monastic foundations and collegiate ch
- Churches with extensive Saxon work
- Fortified Burgh (ninth century)
- Mint
- Churches Saxon Norman overlap
- Boundaries of 'hundreds'. The smaller hu in the south are omitted to avoid overcr the map Hartfield

gathered at Chichester from the surrounding area—it can hardly mean that the actual townsmen were sufficiently numerous to gain a victory on this scale.

A measure of security was restored, for a few decades, in the mid-tenth century. During the reign of King Edgar and the wise administration of the Church by St Dunstan, Archibishop of Canterbury, some of the ravages caused by the Danish raids were repaired. Several of the stone Saxon churches of Sussex may date from this period—built perhaps on the ashes of wooden churches destroyed by Danish raiders.

It was during this period that the territorial division known as the Hundred emerges as the most important unit in local administration. Its origins are obscure, nor is it clear whether the term derives ultimately from a measurement of land or of population. In Sussex there were sixty-one varying considerably in size; their boundaries even by the time of the Norman Conquest appear only approximately settled. What we do know is that the Hundred, from the tenth century onwards, became important not only as a court of justice equivalent at least to the County court and the Quarter Sessions today, but also dealt with many matters which would now be the concern of one of the departments of the county council, such as highways or police. The meeting-places of the courts were at some central point within the Hundred, often recorded in the name of the Hundred, such as the bridge over the Rother—Rotherbridge Hundred, or Tippa's Oak—Tipnoak Hundred.

42

Another division which dates from Saxon times is, of course, the parish. This was an ecclesiastical division, and new parishes were created and older ones subdivided throughout the Saxon period, as new churches were built. But in the more settled areas, most of the parish boundaries would have been defined well before the end of the Saxon period. The pattern that survives today, in spite of some rearrangement in the last hundred years or so, provides a clue to the character and size of the original Saxon communities. The long narrow parishes, for example, which stretch north and south under the ridge of the Downs, indicate the care with which land of different quality—chalk, greensand, gault and weald clay—were included in each settlement, the villages themselves being mostly sited on the dry shelf of the upper greensand, where the springs gush from the base of the chalk escarpment. Centuries late in the Tudor period, the parish rather than the shire, the Hundred or the manor, was to become the fundamental unit in the pattern of local government and administration, and remained so until the nineteenth century.

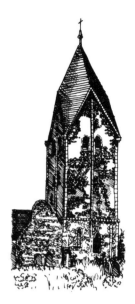

Saxon tower, Sompting

With the reign of Ethelred, the Danish terror returned, and some of the entries in the Anglo-Saxon Chronicle are terse and vivid: 'Thence they advanced, and brought the greatest evil that ever any army could do, in burning and plundering and manslaughter, not only on the sea-coast in Essex, but in Kent and in Sussex and in Hampshire' (A.D. 994); and again: 'and everywhere in Sussex, and in Hampshire, and also in Berkshire, they plundered and burned, as their custom is' (A.D. 1000). At last in 1016, after the death of Ethelred, the Saxon Witan chose the Dane Canute as their king. Peace thus secured, there followed a genuine, though limited, Saxon renaissance. It is to this brief period before the Norman Conquest that most of the stone-built Saxon churches in Sussex belong. Remains of nearly thirty of these survive, incorporated in later Norman or Gothic buildings. We must, however, remember that timber had been for centuries the traditional building material of the Saxons, and there was plenty to hand in Sussex: so it is probable that the rebuilding of so many churches in stone was dictated as much by the vulnerability of wood, as by a belief that stone was necessarily a superior material. Unfortunately, no timber buildings from the Saxon period have survived, and we can only assess their probable quality from other evidence such as jewellery. Much of the Saxon masons' work in Sussex churches does suggest the rather unsure efforts of craftsmen, attempting to translate into stone motives which they were used to carving with mastery in wood. Such examples can be seen in the chancel arch capitals at Selham, or in the tower arch capitals at Sompting. At the same time, in the great roll mouldings of the chancel and tower arches of churches such as Bosham, Sompting and Clayton, we can trace the influence of early Norman buildings such as Bernay. The channel was already becoming a link instead of a barrier.

Capital, Selham

43

VII Saxon Sussex; Farm and Village

Saxon weaver's work hut

The Saxons created the pattern of village settlement which lasted with little change for nearly a thousand years, and which still forms the basic settlement structure through most of the county, except the central Weald. It is, nevertheless, surprising how little certainty there is when any attempt is made to reconstruct the details of their environment—the kind of houses and farm buildings they erected, or how they were planned or furnished. In fact it is mainly because their houses lie buried beneath many layers of subsequent rebuilding, that our knowledge is so limited. The second reason is that, except for a few later churches, they built exclusively in wood, and no secular timber building from the Saxon period survives above ground in Sussex or anywhere else in the country. Recent archaeological research has, however, brought to light some evidence in the Downland area for a particular type of Saxon building often described as a 'grubenhaus'—from the German, 'gruben' to dig. These buildings were sunk one to two feet into the ground, depending on the nature of the subsoil, and they were approximately rectangular with a gabled roof of the simplest kind supported by rafters resting on a central ridge piece, itself supported on upright posts aligned down the middle of the building. This type of building has been found, or rather its foundations have been found, over a very wide area of north-west Europe, as well as in many parts of England. It was a simple, yet very practical method of construction wherever drainage was good, providing maximum internal height with a minimum of walling or timber for roofing. Two such huts have been recently excavated and made the basis for a reconstruction at the Open Air Museum at Singleton. One of these was excavated at Bishopstone near Seaford in 1968 and dates from the fifth century. The other, a working hut for weavers, was excavated at Erringham, near Shoreham, in 1964, and dates from the ninth century. On the floor were two groups of thirty-five loom weights indicating that two large upright looms must have occupied most of the space. The fact that four centuries separated these two huts suggests that it was a form of construction which lasted throughout most of the Saxon period. In the centre of the floor of the Bishopstone house, were the remains of a hearth so it is evident that this type of very simple building also served occasionally as a dwelling, but what proportion of the population lived in such houses, or in larger buildings is not yet clear.

At the time of writing, what may prove to be an extremely important addition to our knowledge of early Saxon settlements in this region is being explored by the excavation of a Downland site just beyond the western boundary of Sussex. It will be the first detailed examination of a Saxon settlement abandoned well before the end of the Saxon period, and therefore free from superimposed later buildings or rebuildings, and which also escaped destruction through subsequent centuries of ploughing. The area of the village covers several acres, of which only a fraction has so far been uncovered. From pottery finds it seems to have been in continuous occupation from the end of the fifth or beginning of the sixth century until the ninth. It lies along the plateau of a Downland ridge well above the valley, close to, but not apparently overlapping, earlier Romano-British settlement. This in itself is very significant, and may involve some revision of the assumption that Saxon settlements in this area were almost entirely in valley and lowland with easy access to water. In this same western Downland region it seems probable that there are at least two other similar early ridge top settlements judging from fragments of pottery which have been turned up in ploughing since the war. The move to the valley, where the church was later built, must have taken place long after conversion to Christianity.

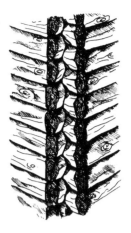

Jointed log construction

The second point of great significance, which the site has already revealed, is that, although there is a sprinkling of 'gruben' or sunken huts, the main domestic buildings conform to a pattern recognisably similar to early medieval farm houses—namely, a central open hall with hearth, and rooms at either end. The dimensions of two of these houses so far uncovered compare very closely with those of larger farmhouses which still survive from the later Middle Ages, or which have been discovered in the early medieval deserted village of Hangleton, described more fully in a later chapter, namely between forty and fifty feet in total length, and between eighteen and twenty in width. Unlike, however, the Hangleton buildings, all of which were built of flint rubble, these all seem to have been built of timber post construction. There is some evidence to suggest that the walls between the posts may have been of horizontal planks or halved logs secured in grooves in the sides of the upright posts. There is another possibility that they were halved logs placed vertically as in the well known church at Greenstead in Essex. There is no evidence of wattle and daub infill. The height of the walls, as well as the roof structure must be conjectural, and whether at either end of the central hall there might have been an upper storey or loft, as in equivalent farmhouses of the later Middle Ages.

A further feature of the village, as revealed at this stage, is the close proximity of building to building combined with a somewhat random arrangement to each other, and along what appears to be the main street. This also matches in with the early medieval site at Hangleton, and altogether suggests there is a greater continuity and a more coherent tradition,

45

Box frame—early drawing

dating from Saxon times, than has been previously assumed. However, until equally undisturbed sites can be found in the eastern part of the county and in the Weald, it would be unwise to generalise.

A method of construction which was general in the forest areas from which the Saxons came, and which it is reasonable to assume would have been practised in Sussex wherever suitable timber was at hand, is that of pine logs laid horizontally and joined together with interlocking joints. This is probably the simplest, the most effective, and the most durable form of building wherever an adequate supply of fir or pine is available. It can range in quality from the frontiersman's log cabin to the highly decorated and beautifully proportioned farm-houses of Scandinavia, or the chalets of the alps, and the Scots pine was certainly indigenous in Sussex in Saxon times, but whether in sufficient quantities in the areas of Saxon settlement to make this method of construction general is not at present known.

A form of building which is frequently referred to as once widespread over the whole of the south of England, is 'cob'. This consists of building walls by ramming together clay and straw, sometimes with a hardcore of stone rubble where available, and building up from a base which may measure as much as three feet in thickness, but tapering upwards. If the tops of such walls are adequately protected by thatch or tiles, they can be very durable and the interiors warm and comfortable. There are just across the border in Hampshire, and further west in Dorset and Devon, cottages and farms in good repair which were built in this manner three or four hundred years ago. But in Sussex apart from a few examples mostly of interior walls, as in a fourteenth-century manor house at Houghton, although suitable materials were just as readily to hand, there is no evidence to suggest that it was ever widely practised; but it must be remembered that, of all forms of building, cob leaves least trace once abandoned or built over.

Almost certainly the majority of Saxon buildings in village and farm continued the use of posts let into the ground as the normal form of construction, but in churches and better quality houses a more sophisticated and durable method, now usually described as the 'box frame' was almost certainly used. For lack of evidence it has been quite unreasonably assumed that this type of construction was only introduced into the south-east after the Norman conquest and was not used by the Saxons although previously practised by the Romano–British. In this method the whole frame work of the building consists of squared and interlocking timbers supported on a horizontal ground plate of timber, very similar in principle to a modern steel frame in which everything else, roof, floors and wall panels, is attached or hung. Unless this type of construction was known and widely used in the more important buildings it is difficult to interpret the pilaster decorations

46

on the walls of Woolbeding, or the tower of Sompting church. Such decoration seems to be so obviously a copying in stone of timber framing.

There is the same lack of certainty as to the internal planning of Saxon cottages and farmhouses. The Saxon house depicted in the Bayeux tapestry burning in Hastings, appears to be a two-storey building, roofed with either tiles or shingles, with the upper storey containing a window and supported by posts over an undercroft. Yet this type of plan one would expect in stone rather than in timber.

It is frequently stated that the Saxons favoured the form of building described as a 'long house', with an ancestry going back to Neolithic times—houses in which the domestic living quarters are situated at one end of the building, the byre and storage in the other, with only the simplest of divisions between the two parts, possibly just a slight change in floor levels, and man and beast using the same entrance door. Such houses would vary in size with the number of livestock, and they could be extended at either end. They are still to be found in parts of Denmark and Holland and north Germany—the area from which the Saxons came, but there is little evidence that combined house and byre was ever usual in Sussex, whatever may have been the case in counties further to the west. Here in Sussex, from such evidence as we have, the arrangement of farms seems always to have been that of dwellings separated from other farm buildings, whether byres, barns or stables. For example, of the thirteen buildings uncovered in the abandoned medieval village of Hangleton, only one could be interpreted as possibly a longhouse. More examples need to be discovered before we are justified in considering the longhouse as anything but exceptional. We should remember, however, that from Aella's landing in Sussex to the Norman conquest was very nearly six centuries—longer than from Chaucer's pilgrims to the present day, time enough for many changes in custom or for adaptations to a milder climate. The very fact that no one can be certain what the Sussex village or farm was like in Saxon times, or what changes may have taken place during these centuries, is some measure of the need for much more intensive archaeological research.

Burning house, Hastings, Bayeux Tapestry

47

VIII Norman Sussex

Chancel arch, Bosham

It was during the Norman period that Sussex attained its greatest importance in relation to other English counties. Not only was it intimately associated with the events leading to the Conquest, and with the Conquest itself, but for 150 years it was the main highway from England to the Continent—a bridge connecting the estates of the Norman nobility in England and Normandy. Its growth therefore in population, in the importance of its ports, in the clearing and colonisation of the Weald after centuries of relative neglect, represented changes as great in their way as those that followed the Neolithic, Celtic, Roman or Saxon invasions.

Before describing these changes something should be said about the events leading to the Conquest in so far as they affected Sussex. From the early years of the eleventh century contacts between England and Normandy had been developing. In 1001, Ethelred 'the Unrede' married Emma, the daughter of Richard the Fearless, Duke of Normandy. In 1013 he took sanctuary in the Norman Abbey of Fécamp when in flight from Danish raiders, and in 1016 he gave the rich manor of Rameslie, which included much of Hastings, to this abbey. There was, therefore, long before the Norman invasion, a close connection between Hastings and Normandy and this may in part have determined the invasion plan of William the Conqueror.

At the other end of the county lies Bosham which a popular, though recent, tradition associates with the story of Canute's chair. Conceivably such a legend might have stemmed from the construction of groins for the protection of an anchorage or of a building such as a palace. The story first appears a hundred years after Canute's death; since then local patriotism has identified it with at least half a dozen places including Wareham and Southampton.

Traditions very often have some real foundation, but there is also a temptation for antiquarians with strong local attachments and vivid imaginations to manufacture evidence to support their theories. Sussex has had its quota. The River Adur, for example, was given this name in the sixteenth century in order to support the identification of the Roman town of Portus Adurni with Shoreham, an identification for which there is not the slightest justification. As recently as 1911 occurred perhaps the most spectacular example of all time—the attempt to supply one of the missing links in the early evolution of man by the deliberate planting in a gravel pit at Piltdown (near Chailey) of fragments of a recent human skull near the doctored jawbone of a modern ape. Perhaps the most widely diffused of all local legends are the relatively harmless stories of underground passages stretching often for miles through (or under!) impossible obstacles and usually, though vaguely, associated with smugglers or monks (or both).

Although it is necessary to dissociate Canute from Bosham, the latter was certainly a favourite residence in Sussex of Godwin, Earl of Wessex, and it was from here that Harold (Godwinson) sailed in 1064, an ill-fated voyage which ended in shipwreck and in his taking service with William Duke of Normandy in the war in Brittany. According to the Normans he then swore an oath of fealty to William, which he broke when, on his return to England, he accepted the crown on the death of Edward the Confessor.

Bosham Church and Harold, Bayeux Tapestry

All this is recorded pictorially in the Bayeux Tapestry. This vivid and dramatic account takes the form of an unbroken series of pictures passing without interruption from one event to the next and measures 210 feet in length by approximately two feet in height. The scenes include Harold praying in Bosham Church before sailing, the elaborate preparation of William's invasion fleet, its voyage and landing at Pevensey, the erection of a prefabricated wooden fort at Hastings, the burning of houses in Hastings, and other incidents, and conclude with the battle and the death of Harold.

This battle which altered the course of English history was fought on the hills behind Hastings in 1066. The Saxon army, wearied by a long march from Yorkshire, where Harold had utterly defeated a Danish invasion from the North Sea, had taken up trenched positions on ground through which the High Street of the town of Battle now runs. In the centre, and protecting the flanks, were some two or three thousand strongly-armed house-carls, but the bulk of the force consisted of poorly-armed levies from the south-eastern counties. Marshy ground separated the Saxon lines from the Normans, who occupied the ridge to the south of where the Abbey now stands. This restricted the use of the cavalry, which William had brought across with his invasion fleet. For hours the Normans failed to break the Saxon lines, and it was not until the evening of this October day that victory was secured by two stratagems—a pretended flight which encouraged the heavy Saxon troops to break ranks and follow, and the shooting of arrows upwards, which, dropping from above, rendered useless the long Saxon body-shields. The victory was absolute. The conflict of perhaps 30,000 men, during eight hours, and at a total cost of a few thousand casualties, set England on a new course, and changed in particular the character and status of Sussex.

Although there seems to have been little further opposition in the south-east, in the north, in the south-west and in the Fens, sporadic resistance

49

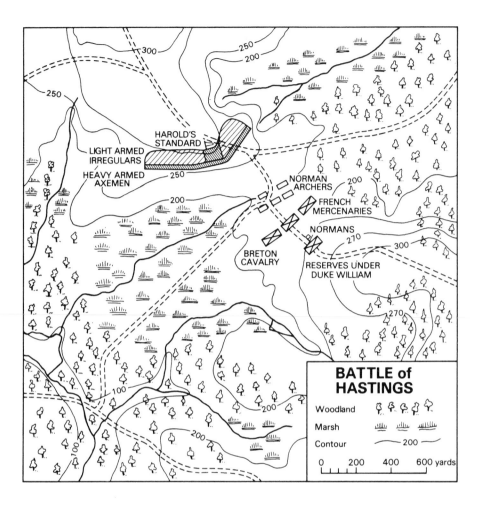

BATTLE of HASTINGS

Woodland	
Marsh	
Contour	—— 200 ——

0   200   400   600 yards

continued for several years. In Sussex, in view of its vital situation across the communication routes with Normandy, immediate measures had to be taken to secure these. For this reason Sussex was subdivided into rapes, or administrative divisions which ran north to south, each based on a port, and controlling one of the highways to the north. These rapes were given by William to five of his most trusted Norman barons. Strong castles were built to defend the harbours and ports, and along the routes which ran north, temporary garrison points of the wooden *motte and bailey* form were erected. The fact that most of these were abandoned some time before the close of the century indicates that any real danger from local risings or attacks, even in the forested areas of the Weald, were no longer feared.

The most powerful of these feudal barons was Roger of Montgomery, who held the combined rapes of Chichester and Arundel. Chichester was both port and fortified garrison point, and the Norman castle mound can still be seen within the city walls in Priory Park. The route inland from

Chichester was protected by the castle on St Anne's Hill, Midhurst, and temporary mottes probably at Selham and Verdley. At Arundel the Normans created what was virtually a new town, protected by a castle on the hills above. The present castle occupies the site of the original motte and bailey, and the drawing in the margin shows the stage reached by the beginning of the twelfth century when the timber structures had been replaced by a massive open 'shell' keep on the summit of the motte and walls of stone replaced the timber palisade round the outer bailey.

Motte & Bailey,
Arundel c. 1150

Within these rapes Roger held in all eighty-three manors, leased singly or in groups to lesser figures in the Norman hierarchy. Very few Saxon names are to be found in Sussex among those holding land in the Domesday Survey compiled twenty years later. Sussex would have been strongly represented at the Battle of Hastings since most of the last-minute reinforcements to the Saxon army must have been drawn from the immediate neighbourhood. The estates of all who fought at Hastings whether they survived or not were forfeited.

To the east of Arundel came the rape of William de Braose. His rape centred on the fortress of Bramber, which commanded the then wide estuary of the Adur, and protected the port of Steyning. Here again, before the end of the eleventh century an entirely new town was created—at New Shoreham. One of the earliest buildings still standing in Sussex is the Marlipins in the centre of the town. Its original purpose is conjectural, but it most probably served as a kind of early customs house in which the port dues, paid in kind to the Lord of the Manor were stored. In the thirteenth century, before the prosperity of the port began to decline, it was given a new and striking checkerboard gothic-style façade of squared stone and knapped flint. The anchorage lay where meadows now separate the Saxon town of Old Shoreham from the new Norman town. Inland was built a line of garrison posts stretching from Edburton Hill to Knepp near West Grinstead, and Channelsbrook near Horsham, protecting the wealden route to the north.

Next to Bramber came the rape of Lewes, the castle there guarding the wide estuary of the Ouse as well as the ports of Seaford and Newhaven, and Lewes itself. For a time a garrison looked down from a temporary motte erected on the summit of the Caburn. To the east of Lewes lay the rape of Pevensey. Here the Normans utilised the great Roman fortress, building a singularly massive Norman Keep against and over the Roman wall. Later in the Middle Ages a moat and inner bailey, incorporating the Norman fortress, were built within the angle of the Roman walls. Pevensey was still an important port. Further to the east came the rape of Hastings. Hastings was already a place of some importance. Like Pevensey it had possessed a Mint since the tenth century, and for a brief period in the twelfth century it became the most powerful port in the

51

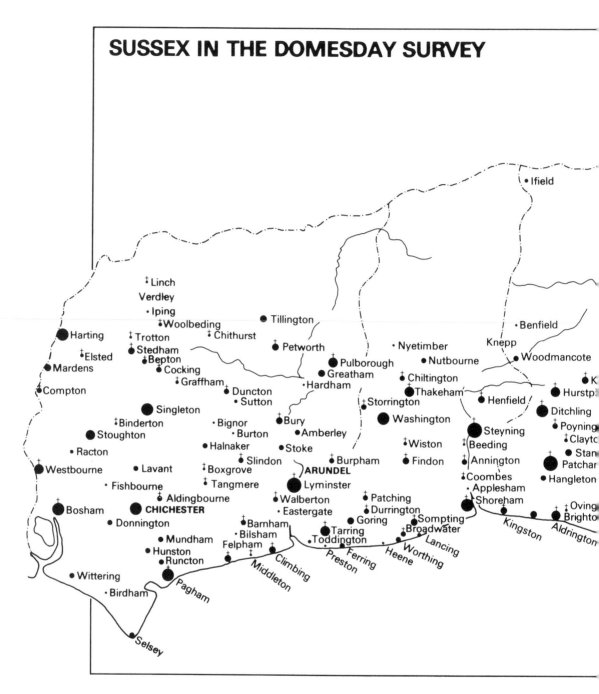

SUSSEX IN THE DOMESDAY SURVEY

Ifield

Linch
Verdley
Iping
Woolbeding
Tillington
Benfield
Harting
Trotton
Chithurst
Knepp
Elsted
Stedham
Petworth
Nyetimber
Woodmancote
Mardens
Bepton
Nutbourne
Compton
Cocking
Pulborough
Chiltington
K
Graffham
Greatham
Hurstp
Duncton
Hardham
Thakeham
Henfield
Sutton
Storrington
Ditchling
Singleton
Bignor
Bury
Washington
Poyning
Binderton
Burton
Amberley
Steyning
Clayto
Stoughton
Halnaker
Stoke
Wiston
Beeding
Stan
Racton
Slindon
Burpham
Findon
Annington
Patchar
Westbourne
Lavant
Boxgrove
ARUNDEL
Coombes
Hangleton
Fishbourne
Tangmere
Lyminster
Applesham
Aldingbourne
Walberton
Patching
Shoreham
Bosham
CHICHESTER
Eastergate
Durrington
Oving
Donnington
Goring
Sompting
Brighto
Barnham
Tarring
Broadwater
Kingston
Aldrington
Mundham
Bilsham
Toddington
Lancing
Felpham
Worthing
Hunston
Ferring
Heene
Runcton
Climbing
Preston
Wittering
Middleton
Birdham
Pagham

Selsey

south-east. The harbour lay inland in the river estuary that then separated Hastings from what is now St Leonard's. The promontory on which the great Norman castle was built stretched some distance out to sea, giving additional protection against storm and tide. Most of this, with the castle,

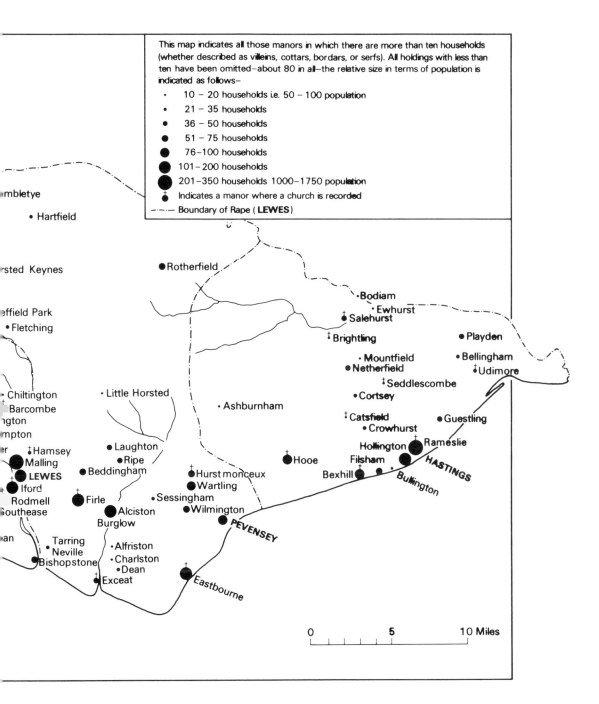

This map indicates all those manors in which there are more than ten households (whether described as villeins, cottars, bordars, or serfs). All holdings with less than ten have been omitted—about 80 in all—the relative size in terms of population is indicated as follows—

- 10 – 20 households i.e. 50 – 100 population
- 21 – 35 households
- 36 – 50 households
- 51 – 75 households
- 76–100 households
- 101–200 households
- 201–350 households 1000–1750 population
- Indicates a manor where a church is recorded
- Boundary of Rape (**LEWES**)

mbletye

• Hartfield

rsted Keynes

●Rotherfield

effield Park

• Fletching

•Bodiam

•Ewhurst

●Salehurst

‡Brightling

●Playden

•Mountfield

●Bellingham

●Netherfield

‡Udimore

‡Seddlescombe

• Chiltington

•Cortsey

‡Barcombe

• Little Horsted

• Ashburnham

gton

mpton

‡Catsfield

●Guestling

• Crowhurst

r ‡Hamsey

● Laughton

Hollington

Rameslie

●Malling

●Ripe

Filsham

HASTINGS

●**LEWES**

●Beddingham

Bexhill

Bullington

‡Iford

●Hooe

Rodmell

●Firle

outhease

●Alciston

●Hurst monceux

Burglow

●Wartling

an

•Sessingham

Tarring

●Wilmington

•Neville

•Alfriston

●Bishopstone

•Charlston

PEVENSEY

•Dean

●Exceat

Eastbourne

| 0 | | | | | 5 | | | | | 10 Miles |

has since crumbled, while the site of the harbour has been built over and paved.

Within twenty years of the Conquest the Domesday survey of the whole country was carried out, and from this record a fairly clear picture of

53

Marlipins, Shoreham

Sussex at the beginning of the Norman period can be constructed. Unless there were many omissions, settlements seem to have been almost completely confined to the coastal area, the downland, and the greensand belts. On the Weald clay, and in the central Weald, only a few settlements are recorded. It does not necessarily follow that these areas were still uninhabited forest, but rather that any settlements which existed were small farmsteads, or the huts of semi-nomadic charcoal-burners and forest workers. Most of the villages situated along the southern edge of the Weald had extensive pannage rights, that is, the right of feeding pigs on fallen acorns and beech mast, and this is occasionally referred to in the survey. Such use of the forest would involve huts for the swineherds. Small communities of this kind, however, with little or no area of cultivated ground, and with feudal relationships which could not easily be defined, would not interest the Domesday commissioners.

In the area where agricultural communities of a recognisable feudal pattern existed, the largest single group—approximately 6,000 out of 10,000—were classified as villani, or villagers. These had a share in the common fields of the village and owed services and payments of various kinds to the Lord of the Manor. The size of their holdings might vary from seven to thirty acres. Although the Normans attempted to introduce an element of order and uniformity, in later centuries, when the customs of various Sussex manors were recorded, there was still a surprising variety in the types of payment or service.

Next in number to the villani came the bordars, who formed rather more than one quarter of the population. These had rather smaller holdings but owed similar duties. Below these came a class of cottars, with little land, and maintaining themselves, for the most part, by working for their neighbours. Right at the bottom came the serfs. Of these 420 were recorded, less than one in twenty-five of the population. The serfs held no property in land and were mostly the household servants of the manorial lord. Only 260 persons were listed as burgesses or townsmen, but most of the town dwellers would in fact be villani in status. Few townspeople at that date would be divorced from the land, towns were still only large villages, and the townsman, even though he might be a specialist craftsman, was also a farmer, although he might delegate to others work on the land. The total population enumerated in the Survey is between ten and eleven thousand. Allowing for certain omissions, such as the forest dwellers, the inmates of Monastic Houses and others, and remembering that those enumerated are the heads of households, which included all generations, grandparents and grandchildren sharing the common hearth, this gives us a total population for Sussex of between sixty and seventy thousand. Although the large towns and coast resorts did not exist in 1066, and a large part of the central Weald was uninhabited (or at least unrecorded in the survey), the popu-

54

lation was not so thinly spread in the rest of the County as it might seem at first sight. It is true to say that there are many villages where the population today is smaller than it was in 1066. In the seventh century Bede estimated the Sussex population at seven thousand families, a total population of some forty thousand. This suggests a remarkable stability during four centuries. The Norman conquest shook Sussex out of this stagnation.

Other significant details of the Domesday Survey include the location of salt-pans where sea-water was trapped in shallow basins and evaporated. Two hundred and eighty-five of these are listed, mainly along the river estuaries; a possible site of one of these survives today, in the 'Dripping Pan' on the south side of Lewes. Salt extraction was certainly an important local industry. It was vital to medieval economy, since the salting of meat and fish was the only form of food preservation known, and the lack of root crops for winter feeding resulted in the autumn slaughter of much livestock and the salting-down of the winter's meat supply. Watermills—157 in all—are recorded in a large number of manors. The fisheries were also important at various centres along the coasts. Tenants at Bristelmestune (Brighton), for instance, paid a rent in kind to the Lord of the Manor of 4,000 herrings—at Southease 38,500! Southease has a church built early in the Norman period with a tall and massive round tower. Both it and others such as those of Piddinghoe and of St Michaels at Lewes, standing at the edge of what was then a wide estuary of the sea were possibly designed to serve as beacon towers to guide fishing boats to their harbour.

Much local material still remains to be extracted from Domesday by careful analysis, and there remain of course many problems and queries. A large number of places, for instance, cannot be identified with certainty, even allowing for considerable change in spelling—places such as Sifelle, Mesewelle or Laneswice.

The map, Sussex in the Domesday Survey page 52–3 shows the general distribution of population, but we must remember that most of the larger manors, such as Malling near Lewes, Harting, Washington, Patcham, Lyminster and Singleton, included large areas which were not coterminous with the Parish or concentrated in the villages bearing these names. In many cases several villages or small hamlets may have been included in one manor, and many of these large manors, described in Domesday, were subsequently divided into separate manorial holdings or sub-manors. The reverse was also true, namely that occasionally a single village was divided between two, or sometimes three, small manorial holdings.

Eighty-five churches were recorded, but again a reservation needs to be made. There is reason to suppose that the mention of a church was only incidental and that only a small percentage of the churches that existed was in fact noted. In several cases churches which contain undoubted

*Round tower,
Southease*

55

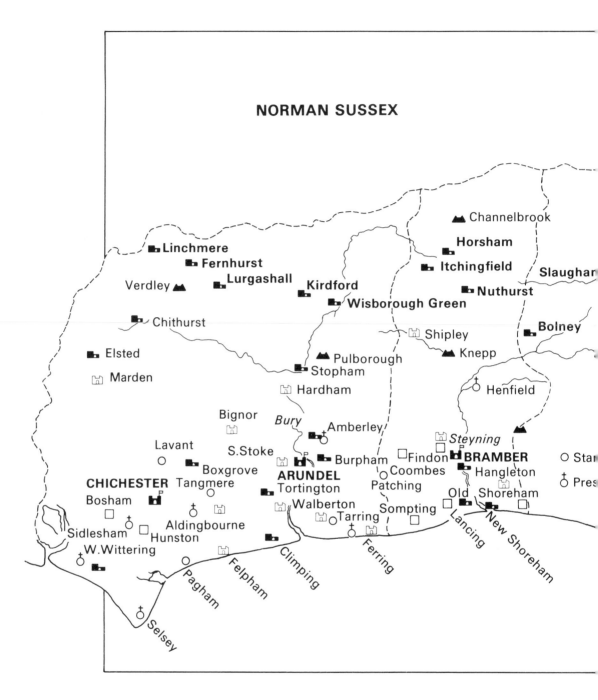

NORMAN SUSSEX

Channelbrook

Linchmere

Fernhurst

Horsham

Itchingfield

Lurgashall

Slaughan

Verdley

Kirdford

Nuthurst

Wisborough Green

Chithurst

Bolney

Shipley

Elsted

Pulborough

Knepp

Marden

Stopham

Hardham

Henfield

Bignor

Bury

Amberley

Steyning

Lavant

S.Stoke

Findon

BRAMBER

Star

Boxgrove

Burpham

Coombes

Hangleton

Pres

CHICHESTER

Tangmere

ARUNDEL

Patching

Bosham

Tortington

Old

Shoreham

Walberton

Sompting

New Shoreham

Sidlesham

Aldingbourne

Tarring

Lancing

W.Wittering

Hunston

Ferring

Pagham

Felpham

Climping

Selsey

pre-Conquest work, such as Selham, Poling, Arlington, Clayton and Singleton are not mentioned. Nor are those mentioned necessarily the largest or most important. Finally, most of those mentioned were entirely rebuilt later in the Norman period, since only a few contain work which

56

† Manor held by Bishop of Chichester

○ Manor held by Archbishop of Canterbury

Principal Castle of Rape

▲ Motte

Church built or rebuilt during Norman Period and with Norman work remaining (selection)

□ Manors possessing Salt Pans (Domesday Survey)

--- Boundary of Rape (LEWES)

— Denotes Manor held by Abbot of Fecamp

Wadhurst Church built in the Norman period where no settlement is mentioned in Domesday

Withyham

thly

Wadhurst

orsted Keynes

Fletching

ld

Burwash

Ewhurst

Heathfield

Playden

Mountfield

Little Horsted

×1066 Battle

Brede

Icklesham

Ashburnham

Catsfield

ooton

Hamsey

Laughton

S. Malling

Ripe

LEWES

Hailsham

Hooe

Rameslie

HASTINGS

Caburn

Bexhill

Rodmell

Burglow

Southease

PEVENSEY

an

Bishopstone

Seaford

Jevington

Eastbourne

E. Dean

0   5   10 miles

can be dated before the Survey. Undoubtedly the great majority of churches at the time of the Survey were of wood, the gradual rebuilding of these in stone being undertaken subsequently.

The map, Norman Sussex includes most of the more important

57

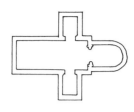

Reconstruction of Worth Church, Saxon style, but Norman plan

Knepp

churches built or rebuilt during the later Norman period, while that on Domesday indicates churches actually recorded in the Survey.

It is in this central Weald that the greatest transformation took place in the century that followed the Domesday Survey. By the close of the twelfth century it was studded with thriving settlements, while three new market towns, Midhurst, Horsham and East Grinstead, were sufficiently important by the thirteenth century to be invited to send representatives to the first Parliaments. The number of churches built, and, in some cases, enlarged before the end of the twelfth century, within the area that was still forest in the time of Domesday, is also some indication of this development. On the other hand there is little evidence of any extensive revival of iron working before the thirteenth century, although there is a rather teasing reference in the Domesday Survey to iron-ore working in the Hundred of East Grinstead.

We might have expected that some part of the Weald, which, at the beginning of the Norman period, constituted the largest area of uncleared forest south of the Trent, would have been declared a royal forest. A good deal of Hampshire and Essex were so designated. That this was not done in the case of the Weald was no doubt due to its position across the main routes to Normandy and any application of the Forest Laws to the Weald would have retarded settlement. Much forest however remained, and local disputes over often ill-defined hunting rights were frequent. In the Middle Ages hunting was not simply a recreation, but an important supplementary source of food. In forested areas hunting rights were therefore jealously guarded. As late as the year 1274 we find, for instance, the Hundreds of Steyning and Poynings reporting the extension by the Earl of Warrenne of rights of 'chase and free warren . . . to the great damage of the country who used to enjoy the right'. Close to the main London to Worthing road at Knepp, an isolated ruin can be seen which is all that is left of a hunting lodge forfeited by William de Braose to the Crown in 1206. King John visited the lodge on several occasions. In 1213 he sent his 'keeper of the Hounds, with eighteen keepers, his fellows, and two hundred and twenty of our greyhounds to hunt the does in the park at Knapp'—a sizeable foray!

Elsewhere the overall pattern of village, field and town was little changed except for increasing size, though any kind of exact comparison is impossible since no survey comparable with Domesday was undertaken again until the first census in 1801.

58

IX Houses and Farms in the early Middle Ages

After the Norman conquest an increasing percentage of ordinary dwelling houses were built in stone, and a number have survived in Sussex, though mutilated or in ruins, from the eleventh, twelfth and thirteenth centuries; for the latter century there are a few timber frame buildings still intact which provide both plans and details of construction. These are all houses of manorial or equivalent status, so that we still have nothing above ground to show what the house of the average villager was like. The archaeologist, on the other hand, as we have seen is hampered in discovering what is in the ground by the continuous occupation of sites so that every village street may represent a succession of buildings one above the other continually modified and rebuilt during a dozen centuries or more. Even when demolition makes it possible to reach the earliest foundations, it is unlikely that anything will be discovered of the earliest buildings. We are forced back, therefore, on to such evidence as can be got from an abandoned village such as Hangleton.

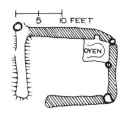

Plan and reconstruction, Hangleton Cottage

One of the smallest cottages among the buildings excavated dates from the thirteenth century, and has been reconstructed in the Open Air Museum at Singleton. It gives some idea of what many of the humbler cottages of the Middle Ages may have been like, both in external and internal space. Below the Downland turf, the walls of this cottage still stood three feet high at one point, and in this corner was an oven sufficiently complete to make possible an exact reconstruction. As the village had, for six centuries been given over to sheep pasture, there had been little or no disturbance of the tumbled flint from the upper part of the walls, so that the height of these walls could be estimated. They were two feet thick at the base, built of solid flint rubble with lime mortar, tapering slightly to the eaves at about four feet six inches above the ground. The interior space measured thirteen feet by twenty-one, and was divided into two rooms by a wattle and daub partition. In the larger room was a central hearth let in flush with the floor, while the smaller room contained the oven. The roof would almost certainly be of simple paired rafters, joined together by collars above head level. Since the walls are only four feet six inches high, and the internal width of the building, thirteen feet, tie beams would not have been necessary and would have been impossibly low. In the Hangleton village another cottage of similar dimensions but less well preserved, was also found.

Window, Portslade Manor

In the Weald, where timber was plentiful, such cottages would have been of timber frame construction with wattle and daub panels, but it is reasonable to suppose that the Hangleton cottages represent in size and accommodation the kind of dwelling in which the humbler villagers lived. At a time when window glass was beyond the resources of small houses, doors and windows were small to keep out the weather. Shutters or oiled cloth could be put up against wind or rain, how far the latter might be left permanently in position we do not know. After dark, the flames from the wood fire would give some light, and the open areas of the roof provided space for smoke to accumulate and percolate through gablets at each end of the roof. Furniture would be of the simplest kind—a table on trestles or on three legs (the advantage of three legs being that they can adjust to an uneven floor), a bench, one or two three legged stools, and, against the wall there would probably be a chest for storage which could also be used as a seat. For sleeping there might be a truckle bed on wheels which could be pushed out of the way when not in use, or else tiered bunks in a corner of the room—round the hearth and on shelves a few storage pots and cooking vessels and wooden platters and bowls. Such furniture provided the bare necessities for living when life was spent mainly out of doors and centred round the open hearth on winter evenings.

If we assume that this was the kind of very simple one or two roomed dwelling of a large part of the population we can be rather more explicit about the houses of the richer members of the community. There is at Pagham a fragment of a stone house dating almost certainly from the eleventh century incorporated in a later building and only revealed during alterations to the latter. This fragment contains a finely cut doorway of Caen stone. At Portslade a manor house of slightly later date still stands, though partly in ruins. It is intact up to the decorated two-light windows of the first floor, one of which is illustrated in the margin. The late twelfth-century halls of the ecclesiastical manor of Amberley and the Bishop's Palace at Chichester are still intact, incorporated in later additions, and the solar wing of the Archbishop of Canterbury's manor of Tarring still stands virtually as it was built. At Swanbourne, near Lewes, at Lodsworth and in Rye are early thirteenth-century halls still, though modified, in good repair and in use as dwellings. Stone houses differ in one important respect from the timber built houses general in Sussex. In the latter the open hall hearth is at gound level, but when building in stone, the hall was often raised on an undercroft, and instead of an open hearth a canopied side chimney was built, the undercroft being used as store or stables. The Lodsworth house has a particularly fine example of such a canopy, now divided between two rooms. The basic plans, however, remain the same whether one is dealing with the cottage or the manor house, and whether the materials are stone or timber, namely, a central

60

hall forming the living space with one or more rooms at one or both ends of the hall, and in the larger houses divided into two storeys at these ends. In the little Hangleton cottage there is simply the open hall and the small room beside it, but in the larger manor houses there was normally at the end of the hall a parlour, and above this a room usually called the solar. This word seems to have meant simply 'a room high up under the eaves' but gradually acquired the meaning of a rather special room, next to the hall in importance, but not necessarily reserved for any particular purpose. At the other end, called the service end, there would be a buttery and a pantry, and possibly a passage between these leading to an external kitchen. A room over the buttery and pantry would also provide storage space or accommodation. Within this basic scheme there was scope for considerable variety—in size, in relative proportion of one part to another, and in decoration. One can truthfully say that no two medieval houses were alike, and by the fourteenth and fifteenth centuries the possibilities of variation were greatly increased in Sussex by the introduction of the jetty.

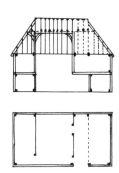

Typical medieval house plan

A few timber-framed buildings survive in Sussex which can with certainty be dated back to the thirteenth century, and because several of these were originally aisled, it has been argued that an aisled plan may have been usual in the larger timber houses of the early Middle Ages in the county. The advantages of an aisle are obvious, since a much wider space can be roofed if rafters and tie-beams can be supported at intervals by posts forming an inner arcade; but whereas an aisle in a building such as a barn or a church is not inconvenient, and may even have some advantages by dividing up the inner space, in a dwelling house this is not so. It is assumed therefore that any device would gain favour by which the same space could be achieved without the intrusive aisle. In the west and north of England this was done by the use of crucks—massive curved timbers rising from ground level to ridge and supporting the entire roof construction. But no true crucks have yet been found in Sussex. What does happen in the thirteenth century is the introduction from across the channel of a quite new technique for supporting adequately the wide roof span; this was the principle of 'crown-post and collar purlin'. One of the earliest and finest examples in the whole of the south-east of England is in St Mary's Hospital, Chichester—illustrated in the marginal drawing. The essential feature is the use of massive cambered tie-beams that support at their centre upright posts called 'crown-posts' which in turn support long beams, called 'collar purlins'. These run the whole length of the building, and in turn support the collars which connect each pair of rafters. This simple but ingenious system of roof construction spreads the weight of the roof and at the same time concentrates it on a relatively few principal units. In Sussex this became, by the fourteenth century, the most usual form of

61

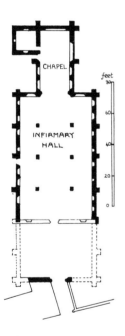

St. Mary's Hospital and plan

construction in all the larger houses, as well as in churches and in farm buildings such as barns. The great hall of St Mary's hospital combines this with aisles and measures nearly forty-five feet in width.

Chichester also has, in the old kitchen of the Bishop's Palace, one of the earliest examples of a method of roof construction which came to be known by the term 'hammer beam'. This was a system of brackets by which the roof timbers could be strengthened and given greater rigidity, and the span increased without either increasing the size of the tiebeam or having recourse to supporting aisle posts. Later it began to be adopted throughout the south-eastern part of England in churches, colleges and many of the open halls of the greater houses. The marginal drawing of a corner of the roof of the old kitchen illustrates how it was found possible to support by a series of brackets the wide span of the rafters.

In the plans of medieval buildings reference is continually made to a 'bay', and one may speak of a hall of one, two, three or more bays—the bays being the distance between the principal supporting posts. In practice it varies enormously, but has an average approximation to about eight feet. It may owe its origin to the space required for a yoke of oxen, and was derived from the basic unit of agricultural measurement, the rod, pole or perch of five and a half yards, or sixteen and a quarter feet. In buildings this measurement tends to be used as loosely as in agriculture, though occasionally as in the surveying and planning of a new town such as Winchelsea in 1284 it was applied fairly exactly. There is no doubt that the medieval craftsmen were influenced by these standard agricultural measurements when setting out a building, just as a farmer was in setting out his field, but they were regarded as approximations—an average, as it were, to which the individual instance seldom corresponds. In the hall symmetry was seldom observed and the bay at the 'dais' or 'high table' end was almost invariably longer than that of the service end—sometimes as much as thirteen feet compared with six or seven feet. At the service end, there was usually a passage across the hall from an outside door to another facing it on the opposite side. These doors might be screened from the rest of the hall by a projecting spur or 'spere'. The upper chambers were sometimes provided with an external stair, and in houses of manorial status this would suggest that the room was sometimes used for a communal purpose such as a courtroom where external access would be an advantage.

Part of the difficulty in describing a medieval house is the fact that although it is known exactly how they were planned, it is not known for certain how the various rooms were used, or how far, for example, sleeping was usual in the hall, or whether only in the winter, the solar being used in the summer, or what kinds of beds and bedding, or what hangings and other furnishings they had. Clearly differences of use would depend very

62

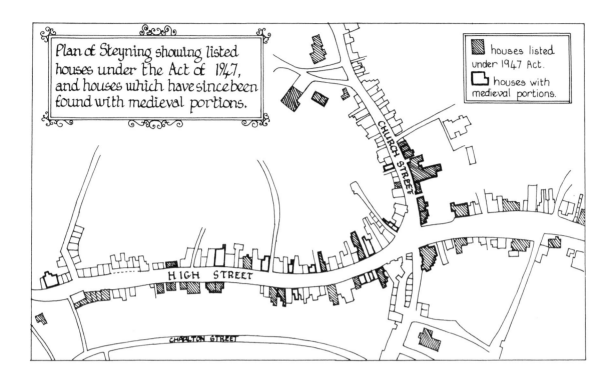

Plan of Steyning showing listed houses under the Act of 1947, and houses which have since been found with medieval portions.

■ houses listed under 1947 Act.

▢ houses with medieval portions.

CHURCH STREET

HIGH STREET

CHARLTON STREET

largely on the size and status of the house. The search for greater privacy certainly influenced the development of the house, and was one of the main reasons for the revolutionary changes of the Tudor period. Even then it is only necessary to think of the open corridors running through almost every bedroom and state apartment of a palace such as Hampton Court, to realise that the idea of privacy was still very different from that of today. It explains the great canopied and screened beds already depicted in paintings of the fourteenth century. But, in the smaller houses, life continued close and communal.

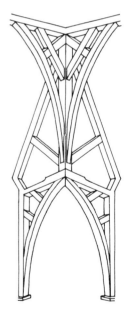

Roof structure, Palace kitchen, Chichester

63

X Monastic Sussex

Tower, Collegiate Church, Hastings Castle

We have seen that, according to Bede, there already existed a small monastery at Bosham when Wilfred converted the South Saxons to Christianity. How long it had been there we do not know: the monks were probably housed in the simplest wooden buildings, possibly scattered huts. At that time the regular monastic plan—church, cloister and communal buildings —was not general. How many other small monastic communities may have existed in Sussex in the two or three centuries that followed we don't exactly know. The foundation at South Malling on the north side of Lewes dates from the eighth century, and there were collegiate churches in the eleventh century at Hastings and Steyning. At Hastings the church was partly rebuilt soon after the Conquest, and incorporated within the wall of the castle; that at Steyning was entirely rebuilt on a grand scale a little later.

These collegiate churches were maintained by groups of clergy leading a semi-monastic life, but engaged in parochial duties. Later such groups were organised under rules akin to those of the Benedictine Order and were called Canons. Of these there were two main Orders, the Austin Canons, based on rules originally elaborated by St Augustine, Bishop of Hippo, and the Premonstratensian Canons who followed a later and rather stricter rule based on that of the Cistercian monks.

It was not, however, until after the Norman Conquest that the monastic Orders began to play that vital part in the social and cultural life of the community which was characteristic of the Middle Ages, and which make this period so different in quality from either the centuries before or those that follow. For some fifty years before the Norman invasion, there had been a burst of religious enthusiasm on the Continent. Part of the drive came from the great monastery of Cluny, which by the beginning of the eleventh century had some hundreds of daughter houses established in various parts of western Europe. In Normandy this religious revival had taken hold of the population at every level, and found expression in some of the finest buildings of the age; but England, on the whole, lay outside the main current and had been little affected. There was sufficient abuse and slackness in the Saxon church for William to be able to use it as a justification for invasion, and the Norman banners were officially blessed by the Pope before William sailed.

In Sussex the number of new monasteries, hospitals and other foundations established during the hundred years following the Battle of Hastings is quite astonishing. If we add to this the new churches built and the

64

18. Mermaid Street, Rye. This street still preserves, with its cobblestones, much of the flavour of the Middle Ages. Most of the houses on either side, including the Mermaid Inn (foreground right), are timber-framed and date from the fifteenth and sixteenth centuries, but many have been concealed by later stucco or brick work (p. 86).

19. This farmhouse in the Weald began as an aisled hall early in the fourteenth century. The aisles were later removed and the nave of the hall with the original doorway set back now occupies the non-jettied part of the side illustrated. The jettied wing on the right was added in the sixteenth century.

20. This wing, with its symmetrical Georgian brick facade, was added in the eighteenth century, and gives no hint of what lies behind, but the gable on the right is in fact the end of the medieval hall clothed in brick to match the Georgian addition.

21. This wing, on the left, was added still later, and the end of the Georgian wing on the right was tile hung to match the tile-hanging of the added wing. Such additions and alterations typify the kind of thing that has happened to the hundreds of houses which still survive from the Middle Ages, truncated, adapted and transformed. Rightly interpreted, they provide perhaps the most tangible record we have of the changing economic conditions, fashions, and life-styles.

Saxon churches rebuilt or enlarged, the activity of the Norman masons and their Saxon apprentices and successors must have been prodigious. The closeness of contact between Sussex and Normandy is very clearly shown in the fact that stone imported from Caen, the chief Norman port, was used in a great many of the buildings within reasonably easy access of the ports and river estuaries. It was even employed in the House of Austin Canons at Shulbrede in the heart of the Weald on the Sussex–Surrey border, many miles from the nearest waterway. This also illustrates how much of the best work went into the monastic foundations, rather than into the churches, which although fine, used only local stone in the inland areas.

A glance at the map will show the wide distribution and variety of the Norman foundations. In Battle Abbey, and in the Cluniac Priory of St Pancras at Lewes, Sussex possessed two of the greatest monasteries in the kingdom. They differed widely both in the character of their administration, and in their contribution to the general life of the community. Battle was a Benedictine Abbey richly endowed by the Crown, and enjoying special privileges. Although situated in the forest eight miles from the nearest town, the enormous guest house suggests that for a time it became a considerable pilgrimage centre. It soon acquired great wealth, and a prosperous town grew up under its shadow and protection, while the growing authority and occasional truculence of its abbots led to many disputes with the greater feudal lords of the area.

In contrast, the great Cluniac Priory at Lewes never became a centre of pilgrimage or a symbol in any way of national consciousness. It was founded by William de Warrenne in 1076 and looked to the Continent for inspiration and leadership—to the network of Cluniac monasteries linked together by triennial convocations held under the supreme Abbot at Cluny. Although, therefore, it was in many ways less a part of the local community, nevertheless its educational work and its hospitals were far more important than anything undertaken at Battle, while its patronage of, and interest in, the arts certainly made a strong local impact. It is possible that we owe the richness and wide range of Norman painting which survives in many of the smaller churches in Sussex to the Priory of St Pancras. They may, in fact, have been done by a guild of artists based on the Priory. At the Reformation, its attachment to a wider continental allegiance drew the particular hostility of Thomas Cromwell, Henry VIII's main agent in the Dissolution of the Monasteries in 1536 and 1539. He was granted this monastery in recognition of his services, and had the great church literally razed to the ground; but, by the irony of fate, he fell from favour and did not live to build the mansion he had planned for the site. Today the railway runs across the choir and nave of this church, of which not a fragment stands above ground.

Mural, Hardham.
Adam and Eve

MONASTIC SUSSEX
FOUNDATION DATES WHERE POSSIBLE

Rusper ◉
C1180

Horsham ⊕

Shulbrede ◯c.1200

Billingshurst ⊕

Cuckfield ⊕

Durford Abbey ◯1160

Easebourne ◻ C. 1210

Shipley ✠ 1125

Midhurst ⊌

Lewe

Harting ✝ late 13th C

Midhurst

Hardham ◯c. 1250

Warminghurst ◖

Hicks ⊌

Wyndham ✝

Storrington

Steyning ⊕ ◖

⊗ ▷ 1493

Boxgrove

Pagham

Arundel

Bidlington (Bramber) ✝

Sele ◻

Saddlescombe ✠

△

⊗ ✠ ⊕ ◖

Arundel

1105
✝ ◻ ◻
Boxgrove

◯ ✝ ⊕
◯ ▽ △ ✝
Chichester

Loddesdown ✝

Pynham ◯

Lyminster ◉

Cokeham
W. Tarring ✝

Old Shoreham ✠

⊕✠✠ 1316
New Shoreham

Tortington
C. 1200 ◯

Poling ⊌

Bosham ⊗ 7th C.

Runcton ◖

Atherington ◖

Ferring ⊗

Selsey ⊗ 7thC.

Note: No attempt has been made to indicate the relative size of establishments, or the gr
and secondary properties which were scattered throughout the country. The patronages c

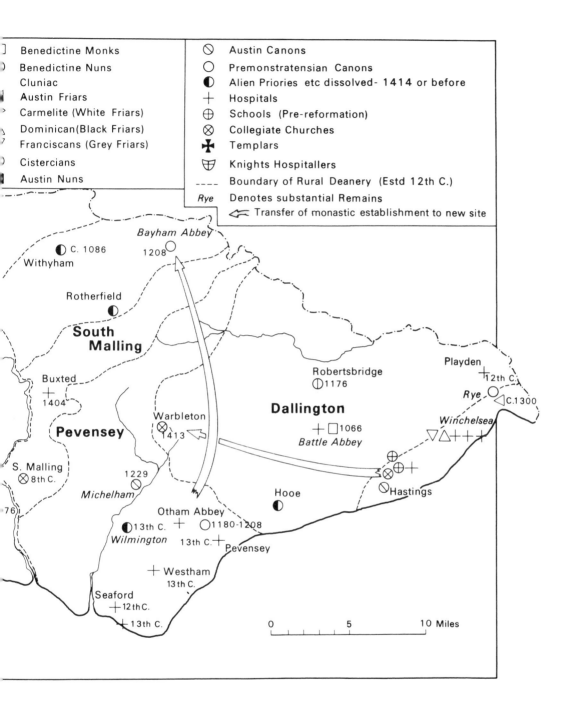

◑ C. 1086
Withyham

Bayham Abbey
1208 ○

Rotherfield
◑

South Malling

Buxted
+
1404

Robertsbridge
◑1176

Playden
+
12th C.

Rye ○
◁C.1300

Pevensey

Warbleton
⊗
1413

Dallington

+ ▢1066
Battle Abbey

Winchelsea
▽ △ + + +

S. Malling
⊗ 8th C.

1229
○

Michelham

Hooe
◑

⊕
⊗ ⊕ +
⊗
⊘ Hastings

Otham Abbey
◑13th C. + ○1180-1208
Wilmington 13th C. +
Pevensey

+ Westham
13th C.

Seaford
+12th C.
+13th C.

0 — 5 — 10 Miles

churches in Sussex were, at one time or another, in the hands of monastic houses, 48 held by the great Cluniac Priory at Lewes.

Bayham Abbey

The only Cistercian Abbey in Sussex was founded at Robertsbridge about the year 1176. The Cistercians followed a more rigorous rule than any of the other Orders, and deliberately chose what, at the time of its foundation, must have been one of the wildest and remotest areas in the Weald. Little is recorded of its history, but it was one of the three 'Greater Monasteries' in Sussex (the others being those of Battle and St Pancras). These were excluded from the Act of 1536 which closed only the 'lesser monasteries'; yet, at the time of the Dissolution, there were only eight monks at Robertsbridge. Today the size and extent of its buildings can only be judged from crop marks in the fields.

Perhaps the most beautiful fragments of Sussex both in its setting and in its ruins is the Premonstratensian abbey at Bayham, situated at the extreme northern edge of the county. It was founded in 1208 by Canons from an earlier foundation (1180) at Otham near Hailsham. It was built in the severe, early Gothic style favoured by the Cistercians, and a good deal of the church—particularly of the magnificent central crossing, with its simple but soaring lines—survives. Of the only other Premonstratensian House in Sussex—Durford Abbey near Rogate—nothing whatever is left but a few fragments of carved stone and thirteenth-century encaustic tiling.

Of the smaller establishments, one of the most interesting is the Priory of Wilmington, situated just under the Downs, six miles north-west of Eastbourne. It started as a grange presented by Robert, Count of Mortain, who held the rape of Pevensey, to the Abbey of Grestian in Normandy. By the thirteenth century it had developed into a small Priory, whose Prior acted as the local agent for the estates held by the mother house in half a dozen English countries. In 1414, at the height of the Hundred Years' War, it was dissolved, with other 'alien' houses attached to French abbeys. It was subsequently converted to a manor house and farm; more of the buildings have survived than is the case with any of the monasteries in Sussex dissolved over a hundred years later. The remains are now vested in the Sussex Archaeological Trust and are open to the public.

Of the military orders of the Knights Templars and the Knights Hospitallers, founded soon after the First Crusade, centres were established in Sussex during the twelfth century. In 1125 the Knights Templars were granted the manor and church of Shipley, and later acquired the Church of Sompting (1154), the Manor of Saddlescombe (1228), three miles north of Brighton, and a centre at New Shoreham. In 1312 this great and powerful Order was dissolved by order of the Pope after four years, during which evidence against it was collected by every means available, including the widespread use of torture. In the case of Sussex Templars, the evidence was singularly unconvincing or pure hearsay. When the Knights of Shipley were informed that an apostate brother had accused them of 'spitting on the Cross and denying the Saviour' they refused to believe that

68

'any Brothers had confessed to any iniquity unless compelled by torture, and if they had so confessed, they lied'. It is true that the Templars had become an extremely wealthy and independent organisation, and that their original function had gone with the failure of the last Crusades in the thirteenth century, but the ruthlessness with which they were finally suppressed by the Pope makes the dissolution of the monasteries 230 years later by Henry VIII seem in comparison relatively humane.

The lands of the Knights Templars at Shipley and at Shoreham passed, on the dissolution of the Order, to the Knights Hospitallers, whose headquarters in Sussex was the Preceptory of Poling. The chapel is now incorporated in a dwelling-house, and some of the masonry dates back to the end of the twelfth century, but there is no record of the date of its foundation.

Reliquary, 12th Century, Shipley

Often monasteries were founded with an obligation to perform certain duties for the rest of the community. In the Middle Ages few works were as important as the maintenance of roads and bridges. The Priory of Sele (1080) was responsible for the upkeep of the bridge and causeway across the Adur at Bramber; that of Pynham (often referred to as the Priory of the 'Calceto' or 'the Causeway') was responsible for those across the Arun below Arundel.

Early in the thirteenth century a new movement—that of the Friars—infused new life into the flagging religious enthusiasm of the later twelfth century. Soon after 1225 Franciscan, or Grey Friars established themselves at Chichester, and after that at Winchelsea and Lewes. Not long after, we find the Dominicans, or Black Friars also at Chichester and Winchelsea, and at Arundel. By the end of the century, however, the simplicity, sincerity and dedicated quality which had distinguished the early years of the Friars, had diminished. The Franciscan church which still stands in the Priory Park at Chichester has little in common with the simple wooden temporary structures enjoined by St Francis.

Following the Black Death (1347–50), decay both in ideals and practice continued, and although it is true that at the time of the Reformation the evidence collected by Henry VIII's commissioners to justify the dissolution of the monasteries was likely to be prejudiced, long before that there were sufficient indications to show that in Sussex the whole monastic system was in decline. Recruitment had become difficult, buildings were falling into ruin and duties went unperformed, while in many cases there had been flagrant local scandals. In 1477 the Prior of Sele was summoned to appear at an enquiry held by the Bishop in the Chapel of St Mary, situated on the great stone bridge at Bramber, to answer charges not only of having allowed the bridge to fall into disrepair, but also of virtually embezzling Priory funds in expensive living. In 1478 the Prioress of Easebourne Nunnery, as well as two of her nuns, was accused of gross

Fragment from St. Pancras Priory

immorality and of consuming the Priory's resources in hunting and extravagant entertaining. Similar complaints were widespread.

The tragedy of the Dissolution in Sussex, as in other counties, was that much that was good suffered with the bad. Schools and hospitals maintained by the Monastic Orders were closed. In Sussex the destruction of actual buildings, both at the time of the Reformation and later, seems to have gone further than in any other counties. We have already mentioned the Cluniac Priory of St Pancras as an example, but more recently many buildings which survived the initial wave of destruction or adaptation became quarries for the repair of farm buildings, or were sacrificed for road construction in the eighteenth century, or stood in the way of the development of agriculture and were razed and ploughed over.

Of the sixty-nine establishments marked on the accompanying map, forty-one have completely disappeared and only in eleven is anything substantial left above ground of the domestic buildings. Churches survive in a few cases where they also served the parish, as at Boxgrove, Easebourne, Sele (Beeding) and Wilmington; or were converted to other uses as was that of the Greyfriars at Chichester, and that of the Austin Friars at Rye. Some effort has been made to preserve the remains of domestic buildings, but most are in the hands of private individuals, who have often neither the means nor the will to preserve them. There are, of course, exceptions; Wilmington has already been mentioned. More recently (1960) the remains of Michelham Priory have been splendidly restored and presented to the Sussex Archaeological Trust. They are now open to the public, while a sum of money has been donated for the excavation of the buried portions. In many cases the extent and layout of the buildings, including the church, are conjectural and no reconstruction is possible until the foundations are some day revealed by systematic excavations.

XI The City and See of Chichester from the Norman Conquest

The diocese of Chichester is unique. It has suffered no alteration to its boundaries since the foundation of the Saxon See at Selsey, and it is the only diocese in which an original Saxon kingdom, the See, and the County, have remained coterminous and unaltered since their foundation. The only change is the transfer in 1076 of the Bishop's seat from Selsey to Chichester. This reflected a general policy of centralisation, though it was in part dictated by the encroachment of the sea at Selsey. The transfer had an immediate effect in increasing the importance of Chichester. In the Domesday Survey of 1086 Chichester was described as follows: 'In the City of Chichester in the time of King Edward, there were a hundred houses . . . and three crofts . . . and there are now sixty houses more than there were before.' In other words it had increased by more than sixty per cent in twenty years. It would still be small compared with the Roman city, and most of the space enclosed by the walls would be open gardens and crofts, the houses being grouped roughly along the lines of the four original Roman streets which met at the point where the market Cross was built later. It was on the site, where probably the Roman forum once stood, that the Norman cathedral was built between 1076 and 1140. A Saxon church serving the parish of St Peter already occupied part of the site, and, after its demolition to make way for the cathedral, the parishioners were allowed to use a portion of the nave, and later the north transept for services. In 1187 a disastrous fire destroyed the flat wooden ceiling, the gabled roof, and the clerestory of the Norman building; in the decades that followed these portions were replaced by an early Gothic vault and clerestory, while the original round-ended choir was lengthened, and given a typical English Gothic rectangular east end. Changes and additions were made in the following centuries, including the Lady Chapel and chapter-house at the close of the thirteenth, additional north and south aisles, the great south transept window and the choir-stalls in the fourteenth, and spire, cloisters and bell tower in the fifteenth. Apart from these major additions, innumerable minor changes reflect the whole story of the development of Gothic architecture.

The Bishop's Palace was rebuilt about the same time as the rebuilding of the cathedral after the fire, and the private chapel contains perhaps the most charming example of early Gothic mural painting surviving in this country—a roundel representing the Madonna and Child.

Roundel, Bishop's Palace

71

*Remains St. James's
Hospital, and
inscription*

Early in the thirteenth century, while masons were still at work restoring the cathedral, both Franciscan and Dominican Friars sought a centre for their work within the city. Later the Franciscans were granted the site of the Norman *motte and bailey* enclosure within the north-east angle of the city walls. Today only the church which they built (possibly the chancel of a yet larger building) survives. After the dissolution it served as a Guild-hall, then as an assize court and, finally and most appropriately, it has been converted into a local museum. Of the Dominican, or Black Friars, whose Priory was situated within the south-east sector of the city, not a trace remains.

There were at least three hospitals; that of St James, founded early in the twelfth century for lepers, was well outside the city walls to the east. A fragment of this still survives as a dwelling-house. Another, that of St Mary's built towards the end of the thirteenth century, is the best example in this country of the usual type of general purpose hospital of the period—a great open hall with beds along each side, and a chapel separated from this by a screen at the eastern end. Though the interior has been modified by the building-in of chimneys and apartments, the essential features remain.

The Bishop himself, apart from his palace in Chichester, held various manors in the County directly from the Crown. In days when travel was slow and often difficult, they served as centres from which the Bishop on his visitations and journeys through his diocese could be entertained or hold local conferences. Different manors became at different times the favourite residences of particular bishops—Amberley, for instance, was used by Bishop Rede, who added the great hall, now ruined, and in 1377 the surrounding castellated wall; Cakeham, at Wittering, was chosen by Bishop Sherburne, who at the beginning of the sixteenth century added a look-out tower in early brick. The Archbishop of Canterbury also held some manors in Sussex. One of the largest and most favoured residences was at Mayfield where some of the buildings, including the great hall, have been restored in the present century and now form part of a seminary. A charming sidelight on this aspect of a Bishop's life is shed by letters which have survived from the thirteenth century, written to Bishop Ralph Neville by his steward. In one he says: 'The Archbishop is moving about Sussex. He will stay one night at your manor of Tarring, and thence procede to your manor at Preston. He means to be lodged there at his own cost, but you had better offer to defray it; it will look well, and I know he will not accept.'

It is impossible within the limits of a brief history such as this to deal with the careers and characters of the many outstanding men who served as Bishops of the See of Chichester, but something must be said about St Richard of Wyke, whose tomb in the Cathedral became in the fourteenth and fifteenth centuries an object of pilgrimage rivalling Battle to the east and Glastonbury to the west. St Richard, rather than St Wilfred, came to be regarded as the patron saint of Sussex. This brought considerable wealth and trade to the city.

St Richard was born at Droitwich in Worcestershire, the son of an independent farmer and went to Oxford as a poor scholar to study canon law. From thence he went to Bologna, returning to England to become Chancellor of the diocese of Canterbury, and a close friend of Edmund, the Archbishop. From Saxon times onwards there had been, at various periods, resentment of the tendency within the medieval Catholic Church to treat England as an outlying province in a clerical empire centred mainly on Italy and France—a province providing convenient emoluments for promising continental clerics, and a source of revenue. This provoked a counter-movement in England, and tension of this kind had been growing during the period of Edmund's archbishopric. On the death of Edmund, Richard continued to oppose papal policy in this matter but his position was complicated when he became involved in a conflict of a rather different kind with the King. In 1244 the Canons of Chichester elected, under royal pressure, a favourite of the King, Robert Passilew, but an enquiry into the candidate's fitness proved that he was utterly unsuited for the office. In his stead the Canons chose Richard. The King refused to recognise the appointment, withheld all the manors on which his income depended, and for two years Richard carried out his duties as Bishop virtually penniless—relying on the hospitality of the parish clergy while visiting and administering the diocese. In 1246 the King relented, and seven years later Richard died at Dover, on his way to France to take part in the organisation of one of the last Crusades. He was canonised fourteen years later, and in 1276 his remains were transferred to the newly-erected Shrine in Chichester Cathedral.

From then on he became one of the most popular saints in the English Calendar. Like St Thomas of Canterbury he symbolised to the ordinary people the triumph of spiritual power measured against the secular, of passive resistence successfully defying the armed power of the State. This division between Church and State, between the spiritual and the temporal, was fundamental to the medieval consciousness, and the Middle Ages cannot be understood unless we are fully alive to it. Certainly the interests of Church and State often coincided, but the division of authority was quite real, and the conflicts and tensions this produced were a stimulus to thought, and to an integrity of character, which is typical of the period. It is not surprising that one of the first acts of the Reformation, when Henry VIII was declared Head of the English Church, was the ruthless and utter destruction of the shrines of St Thomas and of St Richard. We cannot even be certain today of the spot where that of St Richard stood.

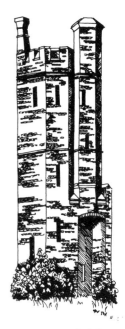

*Brick tower, Cakeham
Manor*

73

Portrait of St. Richard, Norwich Cathedral

Yet for two centuries Chichester had prospered as a pilgrimage centre: so great were the crowds from the villages of Sussex who came on his Feast Day, April 3rd, carrying banners and occasionally fighting for precedence, that special officers had to be appointed to order the processions and preserve the peace.

One of the last pre-Reformation additions to the city was that of the Market Cross. This was the gift of Bishop Storey in 1501, and the Deed of Gift reads: 'To the Sucoure and Comfort of the Poore Peple there . . . a Crosse sett and founded yn the midde of the said cite . . . no housez shoppez nor stallez to be bilded . . . nigh adjoynyng . . . to the lett or dist'baunce of the poore peple to sell their chafer there . . .' More lies behind this gift than appears on the surface, for it established a market free from restrictions. As early as 1135 the Merchant Guild in Chichester received a charter which confirmed 'All its Ancient Rights', and in the next century Chichester was declared a Staple, which virtually gave it a monopoly of the wool trade in this part of the country. Such a Guild exercised powers greater than those of a City Corporation today; particularly in economic matters these were usually restrictive. Throughout the Middle Ages an uneasy balance of influence and control in the city existed between the Guild and the ecclesiastical authorities. With the Reformation the balance shifted finally to the citizens, and it is perhaps symbolic that the Guild, then reconstituted as the Guild of St George, acquired the church of the dissolved Grey Friars as their Guild-hall. A century later, we find the city divided along these lines, with most of the burgesses supporting William Cawley, a wealthy brewer and benefactor who had endowed the Cawley Alms Houses in Broyle Road, while the cathedral chapter and clergy supported the Crown.

During the siege of the city in 1642 the suburb of St Pancras on the east side was destroyed. This almost put an end to a local industry of some importance—needle-making. Yet, in spite of all this, Chichester grew slowly but steadily during the next two centuries. At the time of the Civil War the male population of eighteen years or over was 772, from which we can assume a total of perhaps 3,000. (Today the population residing actually within the line of the walls is somewhat less.) In 1801 the population had risen to approximately 5,000; in 1901, 9,000, and today, 20,000. This expansion has been entirely outside the old walls: within the walls, Chichester has preserved much of the proportion and balance of the medieval city, with its central focus of Cross and Cathedral. But the houses then were of wood. So many were rebuilt or refaçaded in the eighteenth century that it can rightly be described today as a 'Georgian City'.

XII Towns and Villages of Sussex in the later Middle Ages

By the thirteenth century the medieval pattern of settlement of village and town was complete, but within this general pattern considerable development and readjustment were to take place in the later medieval period. The early part of the century found Sussex at the height of its prosperity. Hastings, which had been a foundation member of the Confederation of the Five—or 'Cinque'—Ports, had become its headquarter in the twelfth century, while the Confederation itself had been enlarged by the addition of 'The Two Ancient Towns' of Old Winchelsea and Rye. Thus the dynamic leadership had shifted from the Kentish to the Sussex ports. The Confederation also included among its twenty-seven 'associate' members such important Sussex ports as Seaford, with its harbour on the estuary of the Ouse, which then entered the sea close to the town. The export and import inventories of cargoes included goods of every description but the chief exports were certainly timber and wool, while the principal imports were cloth and wine. In the fifteenth century salt is mentioned increasingly often as an import—an indication that the saltpans, so plentiful in the earlier period, were becoming unworkable.

Borough Seal, Shoreham

Outside the Confederation, ports such as Shoreham, Arundel and Chichester were all thriving commercial centres, while inland the pack-horse trade with, and through, the interior of the county had expanded steadily. We have seen how the Weald itself had been largely settled, and flourishing market towns established at East Grinstead, Horsham and Midhurst. Each of these towns was sufficiently important to be required to send representatives to Parliament in the latter half of the thirteenth century. Thirteen towns in Sussex were represented in these Parliaments as against six for Surrey, eight for Kent, twelve for Hampshire, and approximately 200 for the whole country. The pattern of representation established then became fixed in the following centuries, and it is some measure of the later decline of the maritime boroughs that Camden in 1586 writes of Shoreham, Bramber and Steyning: 'The commodiousness of the Haven by reason of banks and bars of sand cast up at the river's mouth has quite gone: whereas in foregoing times it was wont to carry ships with full sail as far as Bramber, which is a good way from the sea. . . . a little from this lieth Steyning, once a great market and at certain times and set days much frequented.' Of Hastings (he writes): 'The tradition is that the old town of

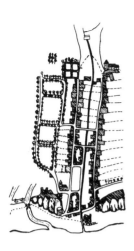

Plan of Hastings
1741

Hastings is swallowed up by the sea. That which standeth now is couched between a high cliff to seaward and as high a hill landward . . . the haven, such as it is being fed but with a poor, small rill is at the south end of the town;' and of Rye: 'It beginneth to complain that the sea abandonneth it . . . and that the river Rother loseth his force to carry away the sands and beach which the sea doth invite into the haven.' Three hundred years, however, before Camden, and long before their final decline, the ports of Sussex were given a terrible warning, had they been able to interpret the signs, in the destruction of Old Winchelsea.

Old Winchelsea had been built on a lowlying island, in what was then the wide estuary of the East Sussex Rother. It rose rapidly to importance, and early in the thirteenth century had supplanted Hastings as the most influential member of the League, when disaster overtook it. It is just possible that the unprecedented storms, which at intervals battered and destroyed walls and houses, were aggravated by a slow rise in the sea-level. In 1250 the town lost 300 houses, and in 1252 the Chronicler Matthew Paris wrote: 'At Winchelsea, a place extremely important to the English, and especially to the Londoners, there was a great inundation, the sea submerging mills and houses, and drowning a large number of the inhabitants.' Plans were already in hand to resite and rebuild the depopulated and half-ruined town on the adjacent mainland, when an even more violent storm in 1287 finally swept it out of existence. So complete has been its obliteration, that it is impossible to say exactly where Old Winchelsea stood. Yet there was evidently no clear understanding of either the natural forces which were slowly but inexorably altering the character of harbours and anchorages, or of the probable importance of Sussex in the changing trade routes of the fourteenth and fifteenth centuries: for it was planned to rebuild Winchelsea on the grandest scale. The town was never completed. Although the streets were laid out and the walls and gates built, before the wharves and warehouses below the walls on the north side had all been constructed, the anchorage was already found to be inadequate in depth, and dredging to be impracticable. Today lush meadows cover the area planned as the harbour.

At Rye the process was slower. As late as the eighteenth century there was still a fairly wide anchorage immediately adjacent to the walls, while an eighteenth-century map of Hastings still indicates a diminutive harbour where the main centre of the town stands today.

The most important industry of Sussex was undoubtedly shipbuilding. The shipwrights were able to draw from the oak of the Weald, which was generally recognised as providing the finest timber in Europe. The iron industry which had existed in the Weald in Celtic and Roman times had been revived, particularly in the area round Battle, and in the Worth and Tilgate forest areas round Crawley. In the north-west corner of the Weald,

76

in the area between Kirdford and the Surrey border, a glass-making industry had been established some time in the twelfth or early thirteenth century. Its centre was just across the Surrey border round Chiddingfold. Like the iron industry it depended on the suitable conjunction of raw materials—in this case (apart from timber for fuel) the right quality of sand, and large areas of bracken, which was cut green and burnt for the production of potash, which served as flux. In 1240 Laurence Vitrearius was given the contract of the stained glass windows at the east end of the abbey at Winchester, and in 1352 John de Alemagne for those in the Royal Chapel of St Stephen. Such contracts indicate the prestige of this wealden industry, while the French and German names associated with it are the beginning of a long succession of immigrant continental craftsmen, who, particularly in the Tudor period of continental religious persecution, settled in Sussex, revitalising other industries including those of iron and clothmaking.

In all this we are witnessing a shift of emphasis from the coast to the Weald, and it is not unreasonable to assume that many of those who found employment in the timber, the glass or the iron industries may have been descended from once prosperous burghers of Shoreham, Hastings or Winchelsea. Another indication of this shift in the relative importance of the Sussex towns can be seen in the location of pre-Reformation Grammar Schools other than those already established in the boroughs. They are at Cuckfield, Battle and Billingshurst, all within the Weald—two in the heart of the iron area, the third on the edge of the glassmaking district.

The period from the end of the twelfth to the middle of the fourteenth century was one of great building activity. More churches were rebuilt or extended in the early Gothic style (which was first introduced in the splendidly reconstructed choirs of New Shoreham church, Boxgrove Priory and Chichester Cathedral at the end of the twelfth century) than in the style of any other period. The principal Norman castles were enlarged, and manor houses were rebuilt in more spacious and convenient form, often in stone. Two of the finest castles in the county (Bodiam and Hurstmonceux) belong to the last phase of the Middle Ages. Bodiam was built in 1385 by Sir Edward Dalyngrigge, a veteran of the Hundred Years' War with France. It was designed as a second line of defence in the event of a French invasion. Rye at the mouth of the eastern Rother had already been sacked in a French raid eight years previously, and Bodiam commanded the upper reaches of the Rother estuary which was even at that date still a quarter of a mile wide where it flowed past the castle. The plan of the castle was itself influenced by French models. As a purely defensive structure (before the development of effective siege cannon) it was one of the most perfectly designed castles in the kingdom.

Still later, towards the close of the Hundred Years' War, the castle of

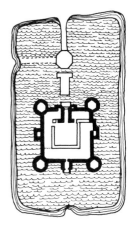

Plan, Bodiam Castle

77

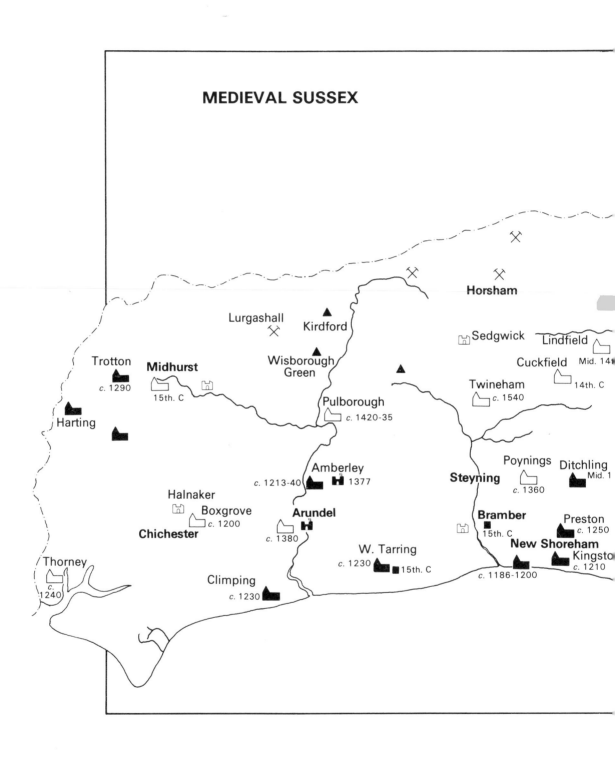

MEDIEVAL SUSSEX

Horsham

Lurgashall
Kirdford

Wisborough
Green

Sedgwick
Lindfield

Trotton
Midhurst
Cuckfield   Mid. 14

c. 1290   15th. C   Twineham   14th. C

Pulborough   *c.* 1540

Harting   *c.* 1420-35

Amberley   Poynings   Ditchling

c. 1213-40   1377   Steyning   Mid. 1

Halnaker   *c.* 1360

Boxgrove   Bramber   Preston

Chichester   Arundel   15th. C   *c.* 1250

c. 1200   *c.* 1380   New Shoreham

Thorney   W. Tarring   Kingsto

c.   *c.* 1230   15th. C   *c.* 1210

1240   Climping   *c.* 1186-1200

c. 1230

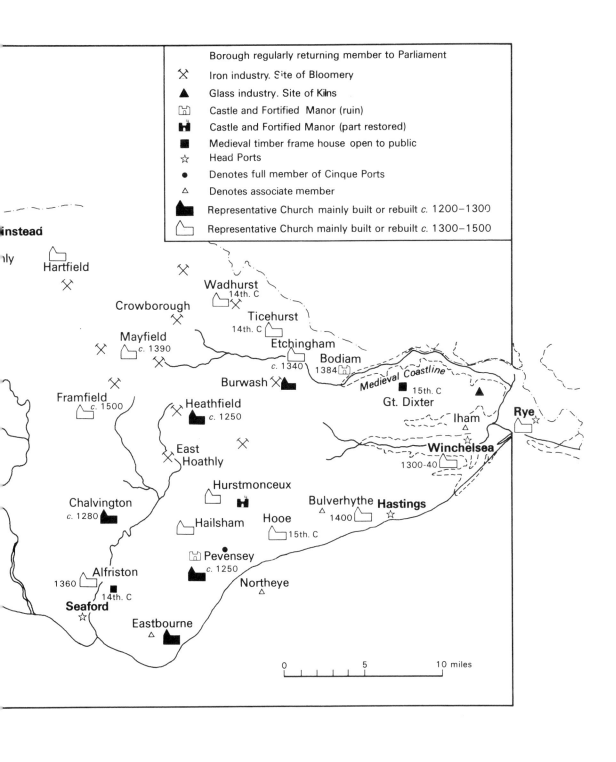

Borough regularly returning member to Parliament

✕ Iron industry. Site of Bloomery

▲ Glass industry. Site of Kilns

⌂ Castle and Fortified Manor (ruin)

▙ Castle and Fortified Manor (part restored)

■ Medieval timber frame house open to public

☆ Head Ports

• Denotes full member of Cinque Ports

△ Denotes associate member

◼ Representative Church mainly built or rebuilt *c.* 1200–1300

⌂ Representative Church mainly built or rebuilt *c.* 1300–1500

instead

Hartfield
✕

Wadhurst
14th. C ✕

Crowborough
✕

Ticehurst
14th. C

Mayfield
c. 1390 ✕

Etchingham
c. 1340

Bodiam
1384

Medieval Coastline

Burwash ✕

Framfield
c. 1500

Heathfield
c. 1250

Gt. Dixter
15th. C

▲

Iham
△

Rye
☆

East
Hoathly

Winchelsea
☆

1300–40

Hurstmonceux

Bulverhythe
△ 1400

Hastings
☆

Chalvington
c. 1280

Hailsham

Hooe
15th. C

Alfriston
1360

Pevensey
c. 1250

Northeye
△

Seaford
☆

14th. C

Eastbourne
△

0   5   10 miles

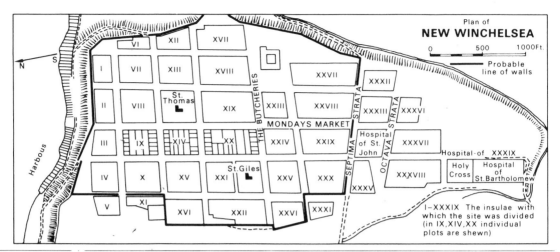

Hurstmonceux was built by Sir Roger de Fienes (another veteran of the war), between 1440 and 1447. As at Bodiam, one motive was certainly defence against a French landing on the flat Pevensey levels which the castle commands. Like Bodiam it was inspired by continental models—in this case the use of brick was copied from the Flanders region. Hurstmonceux was in fact the first building of any size to be built of this material in England since Roman times. Flemish brickmakers and bricklayers had to be brought over to supervise the work.

Some of the changes that took place in the later Middle Ages, such as the decay of the Sussex ports or the decline of the monasteries, were undoubtedly hastened by the universal calamity of the Black Death. This is particularly true of the countryside. In the village communities from the coast to the edge of the Weald Clay the pattern of life established in the Saxon period had continued with little change up to the fourteenth century. Perhaps the effect of the Black Death can best be illustrated from the records of one typical manor, that of Wiston at the foot of Chanctonbury.

For centuries the management and life of this manor had followed the routine laid down in its custumal, which fortunately has survived. The following entry indicates how exactly the obligations of every tenant were defined: 'Henry Calwe holds 1 ferling of land and gives of rent yearly at the feast of St Thomas the Apostle 8d, and at the feast of the Nativity of St John the Baptist 8d, and to the Sheriff's Aid 2d, and to Parksilver 1d. And he shall give at the feast of St Thomas the Apostle 1 cock and 1 hen and at Easter 5 eggs. And he ought to work from the feast of St Michael to the feast of St Peter ad Vincula (1 Aug.) in every week 1 (day's) work, except the 3 weeks at the Nativity of the Lord and at Easter and at Pentecost. And he ought to do from the feast of St Peter ad Vincula to the feast of St Michael 16 works (days' work). And he ought to reap, bind and carry to the lord's grange half an acre of wheat for 1 work . . .', and so on

80

22. A fine 'Wealden' type farmhouse of the fifteenth century, rebuilt at the Weald and Downland Open Air Museum at Singleton. In this example the wing at the service end is jettied at the end as well as on the front (pp. 84–5).

23. A 'Wealden' house in Robertsbridge. When built it would have been very like the house above, and illustrates the kind of alterations made to these houses during the last four hundred years (p. 85).

24. St. Mary, Friston. One of the many small churches scattered over the southern half of the county in which some evidence of late Saxon and certainly early Norman work survives. Mostly it dates from the fourteenth century with a fine crown-post roof. The little tile-hung bell tower is typical of a large number of churches in the greensand belt and in the chalk areas of the county (pp. 82–3).

for more than two pages. What was required in 1 (day's) work was, it will be seen, defined exactly, and whether Henry Calwe did it in person, or whether it took him five hours or fifteen hours was not the lord's concern, provided it was done. The contract was exact and explicit and everyone knew where he was.

This particular custumal dates from the early years of the fourteenth century, yet within a couple of generations the picture had completely changed. Between the years 1349 and 1352 more than half of the tenants had died from the Black Death, their holdings lay vacant and, what was vital from the lord's point of view, the general economy of the manor, as an estate, was jeopardised since the services due were not forthcoming. The resulting competition between manorial lords for such labour as was available led to the rapid substitution of rent and wages in place of the traditional services and payments in kind. Generally speaking, the effect of the Black Death in Sussex was the break-up of the village community as it had existed from early Saxon times. The enclosure by voluntary consent between the tenants of the open fields seems to have been largely completed by the Tudor period, unlike some of the midland counties, where they survived, almost intact, into the eighteenth century. These changes led to the decentralisation of the old, compact village. Tenants now paying rent in lieu of service, rebuilt their houses within their new holdings. The church, previously the focus of the village, often became stranded in open country. In the downland area, where sheep farming had always formed an important element in manorial economy, the lord of the manor was able to make up for his vacant holdings by an extension of grazing, and, in some cases, the village ceased to exist as at Hangleton above Brighton, or Barpham above Worthing.

Brick turret,
Hurstmonceux

XIII Buildings in Town and Countryside in the later Middle Ages

Tower, Cowfold Church

One building, and only one, dominated the village in the Middle Ages—the church. The manor house might be, and often was, close to the church, and also the priest's house, but, relatively, these were unimportant. The church was the symbol of community; with the exception of the chancel it was maintained by the parish and the whole community was involved with its embellishment, its enlargement, or its improvement. It was the one building that reflected in its structure, not the rise and fall of an individual family, but the prosperity or decline of a neighbourhood. The great phase of rebuilding in Sussex during the thirteenth century referred to in the last chapter, was partly the result of continuing prosperity and population expansion, partly a reflection of a new religious consciousness of which the monastic movements of the Cistercians and the Friars were another expression. Of the chancels built by the Normans, with their dim, mysterious and crypt like quality, only a handful were left by the end of the thirteenth century—today only three—Newhaven and the two little churches of North Marden and Up Waltham. The new chancels, had those qualities of lightness and grace which characterised the new Gothic style.

In the fourteenth and fifteenth centuries the picture is rather different. Churches were not so frequently rebuilt or enlarged. In some areas, as in the Adur valley, from Bramber to New Shoreham, churches actually fell into decay. In other places improvements rather than extensions of space were made, and often seem to be motivated by inter-parish rivalry. This is perhaps best seen in the building of bell towers to house the more impressive peals of bells now fashionable. For example, the neighbouring parishes of Cowfold, Henfield, Thakeham and Washington all added towers within a few decades of each other. Only in a few cases were churches completely rebuilt—Poynings, Etchingham and Arundel, towards the end of the fourteenth century, Pulborough, with the exception of the chancel, in the fifteenth century—the first three mainly at the charge of the Lord of the Manor, the fourth through a legacy from its priest. Compared with East Anglia or the West Country, church building in Sussex in the later Middle Ages was relatively modest and reflects its relative decline compared with these other parts of the country. In the towns the differences are still more evident. The decay of the churches of Steyning, Shoreham and New

82

Winchelsea are striking testimonies to the declining population. Following the sack and burning of Hastings by the French in 1337 only two of the previously existing seven churches were rebuilt. Although the churches of Sussex lack the richness of late medieval work found in some other counties of England there is still a great deal of late English Gothic to be found in the form of minor improvements, such as inserted windows.

The county is fairly rich in commemorative tombs and tablets, and is one of the first in which the technique of commemorative brasses was introduced from the continent. The early fourteenth century brass of Margaret Camoys in Trotton Church is probably the finest surviving early brass in England, and those of the Gage family at Firle some of the best from the late sixteenth century; all these are illustrated in marginal drawings.

It is surprising that in a county so rich in timber and with a fine tradition in timber domestic building, there are relatively few late medieval roofs, screens or other forms of decorative wood carving comparable with those of counties such as Somerset or any of the East Anglian counties. Two timber framed churches survived into the nineteenth century—at Plaistow and at Loxwood. Both are recorded in the collection of drawings made between 1781 and 1783 for Sir William Burrell's projected history of Sussex. The one at Loxwood was replaced as late as 1898. It would appear to have dated from the fourteenth century and some of the pews of that period have been preserved in the new stone church, aptly described by Ian Nairn in the *Buildings of Sussex* as 'horrible fiddly neo-Perp'.

It is a different story when we turn to the houses of the period. Only a few houses, apart, that is, from castles and the larger manors, can be dated back to the thirteenth century, and most of these are stone built; but by the fourteenth century there are many, particularly among the farmhouses in the Weald. In this region there appears to have been a continuous improvement and rebuilding of farmsteads both before and after the Black Death. This supports the view that the tendency towards more compact and more efficiently run farms took place earlier in the Weald than in the rest of the county, although the large number surviving may also be partly due to the more plentiful supply of timber resulting in more substantial and more durable buildings.

In timber-framing the most striking development, both in design and technique in the later Middle Ages, was the jetty. It increased enormously the possibility of variations in design. The jettying of one story over the one below, was of course only practicable in a timber structure. It certainly had a practical advantage in towns where the saving of space was important, and where the jetted upper storeys would give some protection from the weather to those using the narrow ways which separated the two

15th Century manuscript drawing, farmstead

83

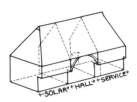

Diagram of 'Wealden' house

sides of the street; and it was almost certainly in London that jetting first became a general practice. It was probably introduced by traders from north German or Scandinavian ports where the jetting of log built wharves and houses dates back at least to the thirteenth century. From London fashion and prestige would be likely to spread the idea quickly in the Home Counties, whether it served any practical purpose or not.

In Sussex the earliest jetted buildings date from the fourteenth century. Apart from the emulation of town by country, which was operative then as now, there must also have been genuine appreciation of the scope which the jetty gave for new and interesting experiments in design: so that before the end of the century there had developed in the Weald an adaptation of the jetty which created one of the most attractive forms of timber building that has ever been conceived—the 'Wealden' house. This is the name later given to describe the kind of jetted house that in the fifteenth century became widely distributed throughout the Weald, spreading into the Downland, and as far as Hampshire to the west. In the 'Wealden' house, the problem of combining a jetted upper floor with the open hall, the walls of which must rise straight from foundations to eaves, was solved by recessing the hall between the projecting upper floor rooms at each end of the hall. By carrying the roof across the recess by means of a massive eaveplate supported by brackets, it was possible to incorporate the jetted wings and the recessed hall under one continuous roof. This is illustrated in the marginal diagram. Although this may seem a simple and straightforward way of solving the problem, it did involve quite complicated structural details, and it is a clear case of the aesthetic appeal, reinforced no doubt by the prestige that soon began to be attached to this type of building, prevailing over considerations of cost or utility, for such a design has no clear practical advantages. In time it became further elaborated, and there are examples where the jetty has been taken right round the building so that the hall was in fact recessed on both sides.

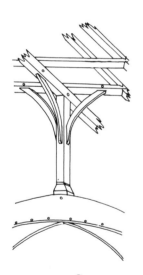

Crown post construction

These 'Wealden' houses represent perhaps the finest expression of medieval house design for that intermediate section of the population lying somewhere between the lesser nobility and the ordinary peasant or villager. They are found as isolated farm houses, in the villages, and in towns, and there are not many parishes north of the Downs where one at least cannot be found. Relatively few were built as manor houses or priests' houses; most appear to have been built by the rising class of yeoman farmers and by successful traders and craftsmen in the larger villages and market towns. A number, perhaps because of their striking appearance, have subsequently been converted to inns, and a few were perhaps originally built as such. Over the county as a whole many have been recognised in recent years concealed behind later façades or additions, or uncovered during actual demolition of what had been assumed to be a quite different

84

type of building. More than any other form of medieval building they have suffered from constant alteration which conceals completely their original appearance, usually by incorporating the hall recess and the space beneath the jetties by a new façade. A recent survey in Robertsbridge has revealed the existence of eight 'Wealden' houses, some quite fragmentary, but four of remarkably fine quality. In a survey of Steyning, of four so far identified, that which became the Poor House retained its external appearance, one had been divided into two cottages with minor alterations (part of the recess being built in). Of the other two, the larger had been converted into two shops, the smaller into one, and both were completely concealed behind later façades. A small early 'Wealden' house which is open to the public is the Priest's house at Alfriston; saved from demolition in 1896 by the National Trust, it was the first building to be taken into care by that body. In this house only the hall is accessible to visitors: but a fine example from the Kent-Sussex border has been repaired and rebuilt at the Singleton museum.

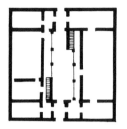

St. Mary's, Bramber, plan and reconstruction

An interesting feature of these 'Wealden' houses is that the interior dimension of the hall, whether large or small, usually approximates to a cube, that is, their height to the collars of their open roof is roughly equal to their length and breadth. This is partly because there were structural weakness if the hall recess was increased in length beyond a certain point. These dimensions, nevertheless, give a surprisingly dignified, spacious quality to the interior, and, as in the case of most medieval buildings, the proportions of brackets, posts, tie-beams and other details, were carefully judged and not dictated simply by questions of stability and strength.

Many houses of traditional design with halls of very different proportions were being built or rebuilt during this period. A few very small halls with width as little as eleven or twelve feet, have been found and may represent the dwellings of the new copyhold class now free from the servile restrictions of villeinhood. A number of priest's houses survive, varying from the tiny hall at Itchingfield to the manor-house proportions of those at West Hoathly and the ancient Prior's at Crawley, or the finely decorated hall of the rectory at Sutton and the massively built Old Rectory at Burwash which was demolished in 1969.

In many of the market towns there would have been inns with closed courtyards. One side of what was almost certainly an inn of this type can be seen in St Mary's, Bramber, a house open to the public. This stood at the end of the great stone bridge over Bramber Water. Built towards the end of the fifteenth century, it was attached to the priory of Sele which had the responsibility of maintaining the bridge and the chapel which stood midway across the bridge. What is left appears to be the east wing of what was once a large enclosed courtyard with arched entries sufficient for the passing of carts which could with their drivers be accommodated within

85

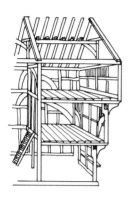

Timber frame of medieval shop, Horsham

the court as in Spanish posadas of the present day. A conjectural reconstruction is given in the marginal drawing. Both the Mermaid and the Flushing Inns at Rye, portions of which go back to the fifteenth century, and the cellars of both to the thirteenth century, were probably of this type, as was the Great George inn at Petworth, which was demolished last century. Contrary to popular belief, inns do not seem to have enjoyed any greater continuity of use than other buildings. For example the most important coaching inns in Arundel in the eighteenth century were The Crown on the west side, and The George on the east side of the High Street. Both probably incorporated parts of earlier medieval hostelries, and both in the nineteenth century were converted to shops and houses. The principal inn today is the Norfolk Arms, a relatively modern building.

Many towns would have had market halls. These were usually in the form of a council chamber or guild hall over a lower, open arcade where traders might have stalls. If they were timber-framed the upper storey was frequently jettied on all sides. The stone built market cross at Chichester provides only an arcade shelter—but at Midhurst a fine timber-framed example with two storeys above the arcade still survives, though very much modified. Others at Petworth and Horsham are recorded in late eighteenth-century drawings, made before their replacement in the early nineteenth century by the present stone built town halls. Their original purpose required a central position, and few could withstand the changing needs of trade and traffic in the nineteenth century.

For the same reason the medieval style of shop disappeared, but at a much earlier date. With its horizontal 'counter' projecting into the street and its unglazed opening above where the craftsmen could be seen at work, few survived even into the eighteenth century. During demolition in 1968 of a shop in the centre of Horsham a remarkable discovery was made. Behind a Victorian pseudo-timber-frame was concealed a genuine medieval town house and shop. This consisted of three storeys, both the first and the second floor being jettied, so that the original gable would have projected some five feet over the street. It consisted simply of three rooms, one above the other, but behind these three rooms was another bay open from the ground to the rafters, providing an enormous open recess to serve as a chimney bay to the shop on the ground floor. This bay presumably formed the general working area, though it has not been possible to identify the actual craft pursued. Similar combined house and shop buildings have been found in other parts of the country, preserving an open hearth under the very high roof necessitated by the three floors on the street frontage. The construction of the Horsham shop is illustrated in the marginal drawing; it may in fact have been a fairly standard arrangement, although few examples have survived.

The continuous terrace may also have been more frequent in towns

86

than has hitherto been supposed. A part of such a terrace can be seen in the old cottages at Tarring, preserved by the Sussex Archaeological Trust, and illustrated in the margin. These cottages were built in the late fifteenth century and are part of a terrace of at least four similar buildings, each of which buildings appear later to have been sub-divided into separate cottages or shops. The original buildings were of a form sometimes described as 'modified Wealden' in which, although the hall was recessed, the roof is in fact continued over the jetty at one side only, the other side being built as a separate wing at right-angles, with the gable end facing the street. An analogous terrace of the same period but in stone can be seen in the Vicars' Close at Chichester. Originally this was twice its present size with a facing terrace enclosing a long central garden area—a kind of modified cloister. The courtyard plan derived from Rome runs in fact like a theme with variations through the medieval scene. Recent excavations at Arundel of the site of the Maison Dieu—a mixture of alms house and hospital founded in 1395, has shown this to have been a large courtyard, quite unlike the completely centralised plan of the great aisled hall of St Mary's hospital at Chichester.

15th Century terrace house, Tarring

These few surviving scattered examples of various types of medieval building help us to visualise something of the Sussex village and townscape towards the close of the Middle Ages, in, say the decade before the dissolution of the monasteries; but it is still necessary to bear in mind the limited extent of our knowledge. Of the smaller houses and cottages in which most people lived, very little remains, and about the general appearance of the buildings there are a number of uncertainties. It is known, for example, that limewash was very widely used as a disinfectant and cleanser both for external and for internal walls, and in the case of timber-frame buildings (and these formed the majority in Sussex), was often applied not only over the wattle and daub infill but over the timber frame as well. The blackening of the timber-frame is a much later fashion, and the medieval village did not necessarily present the magpie black and white contrasts which please the twentieth century. There were even local bye laws stipulating that thatch should be regularly covered with a coat of lime as some precaution against fire. Where such bye laws were actually enforced, many villages and farm groups would have had an external appearance unlike anything to be found today outside certain places in Wales where it is possible to find slate roofs whitened as well as walls.

Another uncertainty is in the matter of roof covering. Broadly speaking it can be said that in Sussex thatch was probably used in the main corn growing areas for most buildings including many of the churches. Clay tiles were, however, used much more generally than is often supposed, particularly in the north and eastern parts of the county, while along the coast the excavations at Hangleton suggest that stone slates imported from

14th Century doorway,
Priest's House,
W. Hoathly

Cornwall or Brittany were to be found even on some of the smaller houses. In the central Weald the laminated sandstone sometimes known as 'Horsham slab' was widely used as roofing in the larger houses and buildings. There is a reference in the records of the Manor of Wiston for the year 1357 'In purchase of one house at Horsham with stone, 66 shillings and 9 pence. In taking down the said stones to Wystneston, 3 shillings and 4 pence; in expenses of divers men carrying the said stones to Wystneston, 3 shillings and 6 pence.' This almost certainly refers to roofing stone of Horsham slab, probably from a decayed timber-frame building, since there was plenty of building stone ready to hand at Wiston and the repairs referred to are in connection with the roof. There is, however, another reference in these accounts to 'one thousand shingles bought, 6 shillings' followed by 'stipend of a roofer with his boy, roofing over the corn grange for three days, 12 pence'. There are many references to shingles in Sussex medieval accounts, and it is clear that wooden slats or shingles, probably of cleft oak, were widely used, but nowhere are there any references to their size. One is therefore left guessing as to the area of roof covered by a thousand shingles, or the relative cost as against tiling or thatching.

Perhaps there are two things at the beginning of the sixteenth century that would strike the observer from the twentieth century most forcibly, the complete absence of glass in windows, which were mostly small in size and positioned on the north and east rather than the south and west, and, except for a few town houses, the complete absence of chimneys, though the use of ornamental coverings to the smoke outlet in the roof may have been more usual and more elaborate than often supposed. It is in these features particularly that revolutionary changes begin to take place within the next half century.

XIV Some Great Tudor and Stuart Mansions

Perhaps the most striking evidence of the shift in the economic and social life of Sussex at the close of the Middle Ages from the coast to the Weald is to be found in the large numbers of country mansions built during the late Tudor and Stuart periods. These are almost all confined to the area north of the Downs. A great deal of this building is, in fact, linked with the expansion of the iron industry described in the next chapter, manor houses being rebuilt or enlarged from profits derived from the sale of timber, or from shares in the new iron foundries. One or two important mansions such as Rowfant, near Crawley, were actually built by Iron Masters, others, such as Slaugham and Wiston were built by families greatly enriched by the industry. Yet others were built by the new class of rich merchants from London, who wished to set themselves up as country gentlemen—a process which has continued ever since. An excellent example of this is the manor of Woolavington, which was purchased in the reign of Elizabeth by Giles Garton, citizen and ironmonger of London. He greatly enlarged and rebuilt the manor house. A most interesting plan and contract made between Garton on the one hand and Henry Hobbs, mason of Arundel on the other, survives, and is probably fairly typical of the type of building contract general in those days.

The contract, dated 1586, specified that all the stone was to be provided by the mason, but Garton was responsible for 'lyme, brycke, sande and nayles . . . spades, bucketts, also scaffold bordes, poles, hurdles, also all flynte, chawke . . . also pyble stones and gravell for roughe costinge of the same . . .' Payment was to be made gradually as the work proceeded, and the last paragraph of the contract reads: 'Fynallye the saide Henry is contented and doth covenant . . . that if any of the saide stone buyldinges after the settinge upp of the same shall by wynde, weather, rayne or otherwise be decayed or for wante of his good workemanshippe then he . . . shall upon requeste to him . . . forthwith at his costes and charges repaire and amend well and substanciallie all suche the decayes and defaultes duringe the space of one wholl yeare nexte after the finishings of the same worke.' This house was entirely rebuilt towards the end of the eighteenth century, but the fine Tudor walled garden, with corner gazebos in moulded brick, still survives.

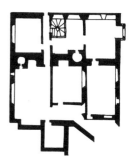

Woolavington, builder's elevation and plan, 1586

Other mansions were built by the growing body of important civil

Great Hall, Cowdray,
1781

servants, lawyers and placemen, a class which proliferated during the Tudor period. Many of these had been rewarded by substantial transfers of monastic land and building after the dissolution of the monasteries. Of the two richest prizes in Sussex, Lewes Priory and Battle Abbey, the first was granted to Thomas Cromwell, a man of this type; the second, Battle, to Sir Anthony Browne, Standard Bearer of England and Lieutenant of the Royal Forests. Sir Anthony razed to the ground church, cloisters and chapter-house and built a magnificent mansion on the site from the materials of the Abbey. His half-brother, William FitzWilliam, Treasurer of the King's Household, acquired the Priories of Shulbrede and Easebourne, and the Abbey of Dureford near Midhurst, and, having purchased the Manor of Cowdray, built there the most splendid of all the Tudor mansions of Sussex.

Some account of Cowdray may be taken as typical, though on a grander scale, of what happened in the case of some dozens of other mansions in the county. It was also one of the first. The original residence, which first gave protection and encouragement to the growing market town of Midhurst, was the Norman castle of Savaric de Bohun on St Anne's hill, which overlooks the town. In the fourteenth century the site was abandoned for a more comfortable, if less strategically defensible, site in the meadow to the north, at the edge of a wood called Le Coudreye. This formed a nucleus for the great mansion to be built nearly two centuries later. In 1528 Sir David Owen, who by marriage had succeeded to the de Bohun estates, sold the property to Sir William FitzWilliam, who completely reconstructed the manor. The existing, asymetrically-placed buildings were incorporated into a balanced courtyard plan in which the older buildings on the east side of the quadrangle were joined by two wings to a great gatehouse on the west side. Later the central court was embellished by a marble fountain in pure Renaissance style, designed, in fact, by Italian craftsmen. In 1543 Sir William died without issue, and the property passed to his half-brother, Sir Anthony Browne. The main building was virtually completed by the end of the reign of Henry VIII, but additions, such as the tall oriel window of the Hall—one of the earliest exploitations of glass on a large scale in a domestic building—and the great staircase, were made a little later. One of the most interesting features of the house consisted of piped water, which was gravity-fed from a pump-house on higher ground some two hundred yards to the north of the mansion. Although in 1793 the house was completely gutted by fire, some surviving details such as the fan-vault in the entrance porch of the Hall, together with the drawings which were made shortly before the fire by the artist Grimm, indicate that the quality of the craftsmanship and the richness of the decorative detail were equal to the best produced in this period anywhere in England.

In more than one way such country houses replaced the monastic

90

establishments of the previous centuries. Although they were entirely secular in their ideals and organisation, and provided few of the services, whether in education, care of the sick, or hospitality, which had been important functions of the monasteries at their best, they nevertheless did become the real cultural centres in the life of this country during the next three hundred years. Music and the arts were patronised, and perhaps flourished by reason of their divorce from the limitations of ecclesiastical control. The greater houses kept open house more effectively than many of the monasteries. The pageants and feasts organised in their halls and grounds were usually shared by the whole community in much the same way as the religious festivals had been. At Cowdray an important officer was the almoner. Another element common to both was the strict ordering and discipline of the establishment, and the paternal conception of the duties of the lord and steward to the community. A book of rules for the household compiled in 1595 by the second Viscount Montague, grandson of the first Sir Anthony Browne, survives. The following quotations give some idea of its flavour, and of the way in which these great houses were managed during their heyday.

Brick staircase,
Laughton Place

'For as much as neither Public Weal nor Private Family can continue or long endure without laws, ordinances and statutes to guide and direct it . . . I have set down the manner and order for the Government of my private house and family . . . what officers and servants . . . with their several charge, office and duty.' There follows a list of thirty-seven principal household officers and servants, after which the duties of each one is set down in detail. Of the almoner he says: 'I will that the Almoner, while he is within the Hall, be at the direction of the Usher thereof . . . that he keep it clean and swept with boughs and flowers . . . I will that he make the fires within the Hall when the fire is there to be used, namely, from All Hallowes Eve at night to Good Friday morning. That he cover the tables when the dishes are laid forth for them . . . that he attend to fetch beer, bread and other necessaries for the gentlemen waiters . . . that he preserve the broken meats, bread and beer for the poor; that he distribute the alms considerately with due regard and respect to the poorest and the most needy: and to conclude that he keep his place at meals with the gentlemen servants and see that table to be well ordered.'

Of the steward he writes: 'The choice of an officer in so high authority shall be such that I will make small doubt of his commendable carriage of himself in his face according to the great trust that I repose in him . . . I will that he do customably dine and sup in the Hall, and that always in a gown unless he be booted for honour or order's sake . . . I will that in civil sort he do reprehend and correct the negligent and disordered persons, and reform them by his grave admonition and vigilant eye over them: the riotous, the contentious and quarrellous persons of any degree, the revengers

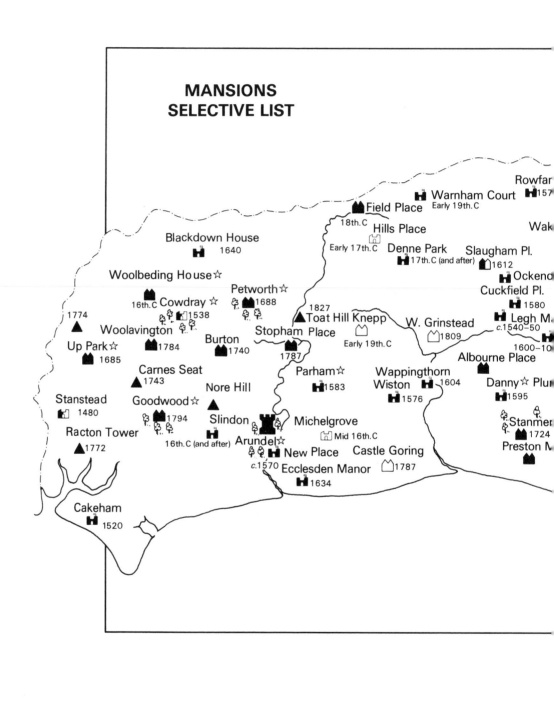

MANSIONS
SELECTIVE LIST

Rowfar

Warnham Court 157
Early 19th.C

Field Place

18th.C   Hills Place

Wak

Blackdown House   Early 17th.C   Denne Park   Slaugham Pl.
1640   17th.C (and after) 1612

Woolbeding House ☆   Ockend

16th.C Cowdray ☆   Petworth ☆   Cuckfield Pl.
                              1688   1580
                     1827
1774   Toat Hill Knepp   W. Grinstead   Legh M.
         Woolavington   c.1540–50
                     1538   Stopham Place   Early 19th.C 1809
Up Park ☆   1784   Burton   1787   1600–10
1685   1740   Albourne Place

         Carnes Seat   Parham ☆   Wappingthorn
         1743   1583   Wiston 1604   Danny ☆ Plu
                   Nore Hill   1576   1595
Stanstead Goodwood ☆
1480   1794   Slindon   Stanmer
Racton Tower   16th.C (and after) Michelgrove   1724
1772   Arundel ☆   Mid 16th.C   Preston M
                  16th.C (and after)
                  New Place   Castle Goring
         c.1570   Ecclesden Manor 1787
Cakeham   1634
1520

establishments of the previous centuries. Although they were entirely secular in their ideals and organisation, and provided few of the services, whether in education, care of the sick, or hospitality, which had been important functions of the monasteries at their best, they nevertheless did become the real cultural centres in the life of this country during the next three hundred years. Music and the arts were patronised, and perhaps flourished by reason of their divorce from the limitations of ecclesiastical control. The greater houses kept open house more effectively than many of the monasteries. The pageants and feasts organised in their halls and grounds were usually shared by the whole community in much the same way as the religious festivals had been. At Cowdray an important officer was the almoner. Another element common to both was the strict ordering and discipline of the establishment, and the paternal conception of the duties of the lord and steward to the community. A book of rules for the household compiled in 1595 by the second Viscount Montague, grandson of the first Sir Anthony Browne, survives. The following quotations give some idea of its flavour, and of the way in which these great houses were managed during their heyday.

Brick staircase, Laughton Place

'For as much as neither Public Weal nor Private Family can continue or long endure without laws, ordinances and statutes to guide and direct it . . . I have set down the manner and order for the Government of my private house and family . . . what officers and servants . . . with their several charge, office and duty.' There follows a list of thirty-seven principal household officers and servants, after which the duties of each one is set down in detail. Of the almoner he says: 'I will that the Almoner, while he is within the Hall, be at the direction of the Usher thereof . . . that he keep it clean and swept with boughs and flowers . . . I will that he make the fires within the Hall when the fire is there to be used, namely, from All Hallowes Eve at night to Good Friday morning. That he cover the tables when the dishes are laid forth for them . . . that he attend to fetch beer, bread and other necessaries for the gentlemen waiters . . . that he preserve the broken meats, bread and beer for the poor; that he distribute the alms considerately with due regard and respect to the poorest and the most needy: and to conclude that he keep his place at meals with the gentlemen servants and see that table to be well ordered.'

Of the steward he writes: 'The choice of an officer in so high authority shall be such that I will make small doubt of his commendable carriage of himself in his face according to the great trust that I repose in him . . . I will that he do customably dine and sup in the Hall, and that always in a gown unless he be booted for honour or order's sake . . . I will that in civil sort he do reprehend and correct the negligent and disordered persons, and reform them by his grave admonition and vigilant eye over them: the riotous, the contentious and quarrellous persons of any degree, the revengers

91

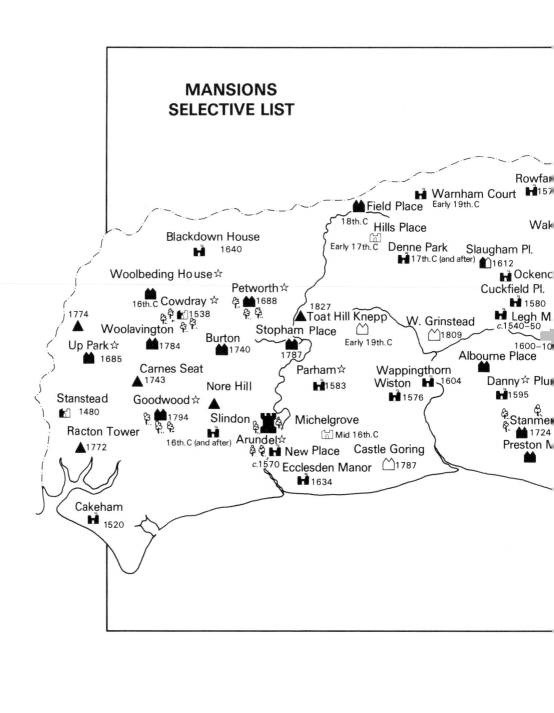

MANSIONS
SELECTIVE LIST

Rowfar

Warnham Court   H 157

Field Place
Early 19th.C

18th.C   Hills Place   Wak

Blackdown House   Early 17th.C   Denne Park   Slaugham Pl.
H 1640   H 17th.C (and after)   1612

Woolbeding House ☆   Ockenc

Petworth ☆   Cuckfield Pl.

16th.C   Cowdray ☆   1688   Legh M
                              1827   1580
1774   1538   Toat Hill Knepp   W. Grinstead   c.1540-50
Woolavington   Stopham Place   Early 19th.C   1809

Burton   1600-10
Up Park ☆   1784   1740
1685   1787   Albourne Place

Carnes Seat   Nore Hill   Parham ☆   Wappingthorn
1743   1583   Wiston   1604
Stanstead   Goodwood ☆   1576   Danny ☆ Plu
1480   1595
Racton Tower   1794   Slindon   Michelgrove   Stanme
                              16th.C (and after)   Mid 16th.C   1724
1772   Arundel ☆   Castle Goring   Preston N
                         c.1570   New Place
                         Ecclesden Manor   1787

Cakeham   1634
1520

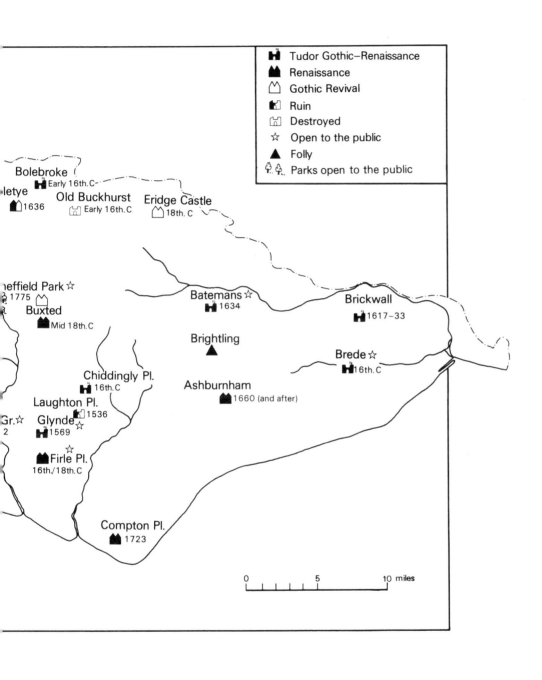

⌂	Tudor Gothic–Renaissance
▲	Renaissance
⌂	Gothic Revival
🏚	Ruin
🏚	Destroyed
☆	Open to the public
▲	Folly
🌳 🌳	Parks open to the public

Bolebroke
letye ⌂ Early 16th.C
🏠1636   Old Buckhurst   Eridge Castle
⌂ Early 16th.C   ⌂ 18th.C

neffield Park ☆
1775 ⌂   Batemans ☆   Brickwall
Buxted   ⌂ 1634   ⌂ 1617–33
▲ Mid 18th.C

Brightling
▲   Brede ☆
⌂ 16th.C

Chiddingly Pl.   Ashburnham
⌂ 16th.C   ▲ 1660 (and after)

Laughton Pl.
Gr.☆   🏚 1536
2   Glynde ☆
⌂ 1569

☆
▲ Firle Pl.
16th./18th.C

Compton Pl.
▲ 1723

0   5   10 miles

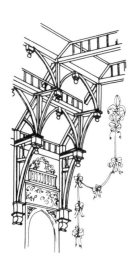

*Hammer beam roof,
Wiston House*

of their own injuries, the privy mutiners, the frequenters of tabling, carding, dicing in corners and at untimely hours and seasons, the conveyors of meat and other matters out of my house, the hunters of ale houses, or suspicious places by day, or by night . . . I will that he do convent apart and after some admonition at his discretion, upon due proof, restrain and forbid their attendance upon me until myself shall otherwise determine.' Considering the laxity and irresponsibility which had invaded so many of the monastic establishments in their later years, it is perhaps somewhat sentimental to assume that the change was necessarily for the worse. It is impossible to forgive the destruction of buildings, libraries and works of art, but these new mansions were at least well maintained, and the estates efficiently managed.

Cowdray belongs to the early and middle years of the sixteenth century. Parham and Wiston, within a few miles of each other, provide an interesting comparison at the century's close. Both were fourteenth-century Manor Houses, rebuilt between 1588 and 1600; the hall at Wiston has a double hammer-beam roof—one of the last open halls of the medieval form to be built in the south of England, while that at Parham, with its flat, decorated plaster ceiling and panelled walls, reflects the Renaissance influences, then beginning to dominate Tudor architecture.

Several of the houses which today present the typical Elizabethan E-shaped façade were originally much larger. Wakehurst, Cuckfield Place and Wiston all enclosed central courts, as at Cowdray, and occupied as much as twice their present area, before being reconstructed in the eighteenth and nineteenth centuries. Other mansions were reduced both in status and in size, as at New Place, Angmering, which is now divided into three cottages.

Danny, near Poynings, Legh Manor near Cuckfield, and Bolebroke near Hatfield, are three of the few remaining mansions built entirely of brick during the late Tudor period in Sussex. Many of the stone-built houses incorporated brick in the chimneys, wall linings and for other details in the manner employed at Cowdray; but it is, perhaps, significant that three of those houses which were the first to be built entirely of brick in the early Tudor period—Buckhurst near Withyam, Michelgrove near Findon, and Laughton Place near Firle—were all later demolished. Should one infer a slight scorn of brick as a building material?

One of the last mansions to be built of timber in Sussex was the Ote Hall at Wivelsfield in 1612. By then, timber for building was already in short supply, thanks to the iron and glass industries: hence brick began, of necessity, to be increasingly used for every type of building during the seventeenth century. This was practicable almost everywhere in Sussex, since good clays for brickmaking are very widely distributed (Map 1).

The seventeenth century is not quite so rich in greater mansions as the

94

sixteenth, but a word must be said of two—Slaugham Place, built at the beginning of the century, and Petworth House at its close. Slaugham Place, like Cowdray, is now a ruin, though for a different reason—the abandonment of a house too large to support, a fate not confined to the present age. Slaugham is of particular interest as one of the first fully Renaissance-style mansions both as to plan and in much of its detail. Unlike Cowdray, Petworth and most of the other great houses, it did not incorporate any part of an earlier building. It was built in 1612 by Sir Walter Covert, one of the most respected figures in Parliament throughout the reign of Elizabeth and for many years 'Father of the House'. In the middle of the eighteenth century the Covert family household at Slaugham is recorded as numbering seventy, yet before the end of the century the house was a ruin and much of the stone was sold for roadmaking. Today the remains of the house, except for two fine, arched arcades, are overgrown, but the surrounding walled garden, with a raised terrace at one side, and charming gazebos at each corner and in the middle of the longer side, is the most complete surviving example in Sussex of this early style of garden planning.

Petworth House, like Cowdray, incorporates part of the earlier house, in this case the thirteenth-century chapel, and is possibly the fourth rebuilding on the same site. Although the side facing the park to the west is a balanced Renaissance design, the rest of the exterior is singularly untidy: an attempt was made in the eighteenth century to reface the remainder of the house, but only the southern end was completed. Both Petworth, and another fine house of the same period, Up Park—south of Midhurst—have recently been presented to the National Trust. Although many great mansions were built during the last two hundred and fifty years—Sheffield Park, Goodwood and Warnham Court to name only three—they do not compare in quantity, quality or variety with those of the sixteenth and seventeenth centuries.

Arcade fragment and plan, Slaugham Place

XV From Open Hall to Inglenook

Chimney c. 1600
Old Erringham

The series of drawings on the opposite page is intended to illustrate two points—first the gradual step by step character of the revolution, or rather evolution, in house plan and design from the medieval to the modern; and second, the most far reaching single element in that change, the disappearance of the open hall with its central hearth. It did not happen all at once; there was a period, roughly that of the sixteenth century, which can only rightly be called 'transitional'. Already towards the end of the fifteenth century the central hall was tending to become smaller in relation to the rooms at either end, with the hearth moved towards the lower end, and the building of a canopy to direct the smoke away from the rest of the hall. The next logical step was to use the space now clear of smoke, more efficiently by inserting a floor. In this way the main bay in a two-bay hall became two rooms, one above the other, and the smaller bay at the lower or service end became virtually a great open chimney. This is, in fact, often referred to as a 'chimney bay'. Within this 'chimney-bay' the hearth could remain open although a funnel-like canopy constructed like the rest of the building of timber frame with wattle and daub infilling, might direct the smoke to a louvre or outlet in the roof. It would still be possible to sit round the open hearth.

In Sussex there is evidence from before the end of the fourteenth century of large canopies of this kind covering a complete bay of the hall, but the period of most rapid change seems to have been in the second quarter of the sixteenth to the first quarter of the seventeenth century. Even this covers more than a life-time. A recent survey of one Sussex parish revealed at least two houses in which a sequence of four successive changes, spread possibly over three or four generations, could be traced before the final insertion of a brick chimney breast and inglenook.

More significantly perhaps, a number of houses have been found in the county which were designed and built to conform to particular stages in this process of change, halls for example with large canopied smoke-bays built at one end, or halls with floors and chambers above except for one bay left open as a smoke-bay, and some with a stone reredos at the lower end with a simple wattle and daub funnel above the hearth to direct smoke through the louvre.

When these transitional stages gave place to brick, or, more often a combination of stone and brick, chimney breasts, these were so built that they still could provide within the brick framework sufficient space to sit

96

1. Open hearth

2. Hearth against reredos under canopy

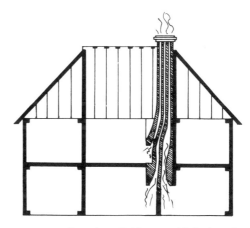

3. Chamber over main bay of hall

4. Insertion of chimney with inglenook

on either side of the hearth. Inglenooks of this kind even in relatively small houses, were sometimes as much as twelve feet across and over three feet deep, and small cottages, numbers of which survive with little alteration, were provided with inglenooks. They were taken as much for granted by the end of the sixteenth century as the open hearth had been in the Middle Ages. A couple of centuries later the majority of these inglenooks were bricked up or converted into cupboards with small grates substituted, as coal gradually took the place of wood.

Windows, however, remained small, and for the most part unglazed. Glass, although general in the greater mansions, was relatively expensive, and a glazed casement remained a luxury to the majority of the population well into the sevententh century. An example which epitomises these changes is to be seen in a small yeoman farmer's house from near Midhurst, which is being rebuilt at the Singleton Museum. This dates from the end of the sixteenth century; although it had a well-built central chimney of

97

*Causeway House,
c. 1600, Horsham*

stone and brick, with three flues, two of which, serviced inglenooks placed back to back on the ground floor, and the third a small fireplace in the best bedroom above; the windows were still unglazed, small, and faced, with one exception, north and east. Yet, within a generation, possibly within the lifetime of the builder, at least two of these windows had been fitted with casements; the two first floor rooms, which had originally been open to the rafters, were given lath and plaster ceilings; and a ladder, which gave access to the upper floor, replaced by a newel staircase. This can be taken as typical of the general pattern of development and change during this period.

Compared with the medieval open hall, these ground floor rooms with their low ceilings must have seemed small and very cosy. It is just possible that a contributing factor was climatic. The period covered by the Tudors and the early Stuarts has been called the 'little ice age', and there certainly appears to have been some worsening of the climate compared with the earlier Middle Ages.

Accompanying these changes in plan was the rapid spread of the use of brick, already referred to in the previous chapter. By the middle of the sixteenth century, brick was in use not merely for the new chimney breasts, but began to take the place of wattle and daub for the infill of timber-frame buildings. One interesting feature of the small yeoman farmer's house just described is that, although the infilling and partitions of the upper floor were all of traditional wattle and daub, that of the ground floor was filled with brick. Brick was also being combined with stone and flint, and its use for corners and the jambs of windows and door openings, enabled rough stone, as well as flint, to be used more effectively. Quite early in the sixteenth century it was also being used for the entire fabric of every type and quality of building, including churches such as those at Twineham and East Guldeford, and it was not considered inappropriate to use it for additions to existing churches as at Egdean, Burton, Warminghurst, Ford and many others. There is no doubt that shortage of timber was a principal cause. Not only was the population in general steadily increasing, but the growth of London was phenomenal, and London depended on the timber of the Weald and the Home Counties for most of its buildings, its shipyards and fuel. At the same time the consumption of timber by the iron and glass furnaces which form the subject of the next chapter, was also increasing. But the question remains unanswered as to why a material which had been used just across the channel ever since Roman times in every kind of building from cottages to cathedrals, had not been developed before in a county rich in clay deposits, and where tile making of many kinds had been practised since the early Middle Ages.

If one considers the kind of activity which must have existed within the Wealden area of Sussex before the replacement of timber by other materials,

98

one is impressed by the amount of labour that must have been continually employed in sawpits, and in the carpenters' and builders' yards, providing timber for houses, ships, barns, waggons, furniture and farm equipment as well as the subsidiary employments of servicing the woodlands—felling and transporting. There is a widely held belief that many houses and barns were built from reused ships' timbers. One reason for this belief is that beams in houses are often found to have mortices or grooves which cannot be explained; but the medieval builder, like his modern counterpart, re-used material which was worth re-using whenever he could. Such timber is more likely to come from the previous building on the site, or from a neighbouring building, than from a ship breaker's yard, miles away. The second reason, and one which can account completely for this universal misconception, is that there are two main varieties of oak which grow in the Weald, one relatively straight, the other spreading with curving branches. The latter was particularly cultivated, and used for the ribs of ships, and was generally referred to as 'ships' timber' whether its destination was a shipyard or not.

Mid-16th Century town house, Midhurst

There are a number of other innovations during this period which affect to a lesser extent both the interior and external planning and appearance of houses, particularly in the towns. One was the introduction of the dormer window, which had been long in use on the continent. The dormer window made it possible to utilise the space within the roof, provided a floor was inserted and an access stair. In towns this would be valuable, but by the end of the sixteenth century attics with dormers are found even in quite rural cottages. New buildings were now more often of three storeys and this was not confined to the towns. An example of a timber framed house of four storeys, if we reckon the semi-basement, is illustrated in the marginal drawing. It was rescued from demolition in Midhurst just after the last war, and is one of a series built in the middle of the sixteenth century; the others were demolished at the end of the First World War. Buildings of a similar plan would be found in most of the towns by the end of the sixteenth century. Quite unsuspected examples were recently uncovered in Horsham and in East Grinstead, one during demolition the other during its reconstruction.

Another innovation was that of the 'semi-detached' paired cottages. This became increasingly general later in the eighteenth and nineteenth centuries, but whereas the latter were almost always mirror versions of each other, identical in every way, those of the sixteenth and seventeenth centuries were more frequently disparate. Often one is slightly larger, with better mouldings and more convenient stairs, or a more commodious inglenook. In the small village of Houghton a number of examples can be seen. Here there are six, timber-framed, paired cottages. Each pair contains a massive central chimney stack dividing the two dwellings, and

99

incorporating large, back to back inglenooks; but one inglenook is slightly deeper than the other, or the cottage slightly longer, giving additional space. Whether these differences reflected minor social or economic distinctions as between, for example, the younger and senior members of a family, or different grades in crafts or husbandry, is difficult to determine. Another feature of these cottages all of which seem to have been built about the same time, is that just as the twin cottages are never identical, so no pair exactly copies any other pair. It seems that the deliberate avoidance, characteristic of the middle ages, of mechanical repetition was still motivating the craftsmen of the early seventeenth century—an attitude quite different from that which lies behind the precisely paired estate cottages of the eighteenth or nineteenth centuries or of a rebuilt and replanned village such as Milton Abbas in Dorset.

A good deal of evidence has also been accumulating since the war of widespread freehand interior mural decoration, mostly dating from the middle of the sixteenth to the first half of the seventeenth century. These usually were painted in black on a lime plaster surface, and in some cases the design was carried over timber-framing. In several examples the entire surface of all four walls were evidently decorated; and a few paintings have been found in polychrome. A point of interest lies less in the general quality of the designs than in the fact that these painted rooms are normally on the upper floor. With the abandonment of the open hall this floor seems to have taken on the importance, almost, of hall and solar.

XVI The Sussex Iron Industry in the Sixteenth and Seventeenth Century

We have seen that in Celtic, Roman and medieval times iron smelting was carried on in various parts of the Weald, but, up to the end of the fifteenth century, it had been a relatively small-scale industry based on a simple furnace, in which charcoal and iron ore were built up in layers to form a circular mound, perhaps three or four feet high, over a central stone hearth. This was then encased in clay, and ignited, air being forced in by bellows at the base. It took two or three days to burn through, and at the end a certain amount of semi-molten 'plastic iron' was formed on the hearth at the base of the mound. This could then be beaten out, cut and shaped in a forge. The lumps of iron were called 'blooms', hence the term 'bloomery' for the furnace. A single bloomery produced a small amount of iron at fairly long intervals, and the work could be carried on by one or two families, with the help of perhaps an equal number of charcoal burners and iron-ore miners. Not more than a few hundred persons would have been engaged at any one time in the industry.

*Cast iron fireback;
Lewes Martyrs*

Towards the end of the fifteenth century a revolution in the technique of smelting was made by iron workers in the forest area of the Ardennes in northern France, and from there the new technique was introduced into the Weald. It involved the building of a permanent structure with a large furnace chamber and a wide chimney. Into the furnace chamber projected a number of great bellows; these, compressed one after another by a rotating wheel which could be driven by water power, oxen or horses, forced air continuously through the furnace chamber; the mixed charcoal and ore burned not only more quickly but at a much higher temperature so that the iron became completely liquified and could be run off from the base of the chamber into moulds. The furnace was fed from the top, and therefore could be maintained almost indefinitely. All these things taken together—the greater size of furnace chamber, the speed of combustion, and the continuity—meant that a large blast furnace, as these new furnaces were called, could produce as much iron as twenty or perhaps thirty bloomeries. This improvement in technique coincided with an increased demand for iron for the production of heavy cannon, which could now be made in moulds, instead of being built up of bands of iron, as were the primitive 'crackys' or 'culverins' first used at Bannockburn (1314) and Crécy (1346). In addition, there was an expanding market abroad for

Primitive banded cannon, Eridge

Cast iron grave stone

these new and improved engines of war. The difference between the banded canon from Erridge made of wrought iron strips bound together with iron hoops and the great cast iron guns of the sixteenth century represents not merely a revolution in the methods of war, but a revolution in technology.

The Sussex Weald was admirably fitted for the rapid development of the iron industry along these new lines. It contained sufficient supplies of excellent iron ore, mostly in layers at the base of the Wadhurst Clay, and very large areas of timber for fuel. Soon a transformation of the Weald took place which attracted national concern. A Royal Commission was set up in 1573 and reported: 'Besides these furnaces aforesaid, there are not so few as a hundred furnaces and Iron Mylles in Sussex, Surrey and Kent, which is greatlie to the decaie, spoile and overthrowe of woods and principle tymber, with a great decaye also of tillage for that they are continuallie employed in carrying of furniture for the said workes, and likewise a great decaie of the highways because they carrie all the wintertyme.'

In 1574 the Privy Council obliged all makers of cannon to enter into bonds not to manufacture or sell without licence from the Queen. In 1581 an Act was passed to check the destruction of timber near London, and prohibited its conversion into fuel for the making of iron within 14 miles of the Thames while forbidding the erection of new iron works within 22 miles of London. Such restrictions no doubt encouraged developments in Sussex, but another Act restricted the cutting of timber within 12 miles of the coast, in order to protect the shipbuilding industry of the Cinque Ports. Other restrictive Acts were passed in the years that followed, but were evidently ineffective since the industry continued to expand. In 1607 John Norden in his *Surveyor's Dialogue* wrote: 'He that well observes it, and hath known the Weald of Surrey, Sussex and Kent, the grand nursery of oak and beech, shall find an alteration within less than thirty years as may well strike a fear lest few years more as pestilent as the former will leave few good trees standing in those wealds. Such a heat issueth out of the many Forges and Furnaces for the making of iron, and out of the glass kilns as hath devoured many famous woods within the wealds.'

In the north-west of the county the situation was aggravated by the expansion of the glass industry referred to in the above extract. As in the iron industry the introduction of new techniques, in this case by Huguenot glass-workers from France, had been responsible for this expansion. One of

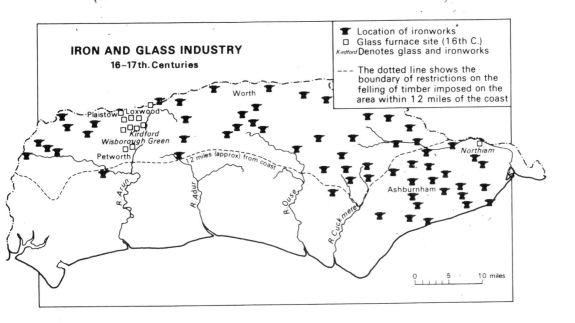

IRON AND GLASS INDUSTRY
16–17th. Centuries

☗ Location of ironworks
□ Glass furnace site (16th C.)
Kirdford Denotes glass and ironworks

--- The dotted line shows the
boundary of restrictions on the
felling of timber imposed on the
area within 12 miles of the coast

Plaistow · Loxwood
Kirdford
Wisborough Green
Petworth
Worth
Northiam
Ashburnham

12 miles (approx) from coast

R. Arun
R. Adur
R. Ouse
R. Cuckmere

0   5   10 miles

these, Jean Carrée, built a large furnace at Farnefold Wood near Wisborough in 1567. Many other furnaces in the Kirdford, Petworth, Loxwood area followed—one was recently discovered as far south as Graffham. For a time therefore there was, in this part of Sussex, keen competition between the iron master and the glass-workers for the available fuel supply, and in 1615 an Act was passed prohibiting the further use of wood fuel for glass-making—a triumph for the iron interests!

Ultimately the rapid expansion of the iron industry ensured its equally speedy extinction. The available forests of the Weald were literally swallowed up by the furnaces. As early as 1547 the accounts of the iron-works at Worth record the consumption during the two previous years of nearly 6,000 cords of wood for the furnace and of nearly 3,000 for the forge—a cord being about two tons of wood. Other factors contributed; many furnaces controlled by families loyal to Charles I were dismantled or destroyed by Parliament in the Civil War. Finally the discovery of methods of coking coal, so that coke could be used in place of charcoal, led to the migration of the industry to the Midlands and the North. By 1717 only twenty furnaces were still active in the Sussex Weald, and only seven in Kent and Surrey combined. In 1809 the last furnace—at Ashburnham—drew its fires for the last time.

It is difficult today to realise the enormous change in the wealden landscape that these hectic years of industrial development involved. The clearing of much of the Weald in Norman and later medieval times had

103

*Glass furnace, 16th
Century drawing*

been relatively slow and unspectacular; while the areas, specifically reserved as woodland, had been carefully tended by those concerned, whether lords of the manor, burgesses, or individual farmers. The system of 'coppice and standard', by which selected oaks were encouraged to grow by adequate spacing, had ensured timber for the building of both houses and ships. There had been continual trade with London and the larger towns, including as we have seen a valuable export trade with the continent. Instead of these carefully husbanded forests, there was now a barren wilderness. Quick and immediate profits had led to a lack of concern for the future. There was little or no replanting at the time. Dotted among the now barren hills and valleys were dozens of lakes, artificially created by dams to provide water power for the hammers and bellows, or washing facilities for cleansing the ore. Today, surrounded by pleasant woods, these form part of the attraction of the Weald; in the seventeenth century they were surrounded by treeless wastes. But this is only one side of the picture; the thousands who had been attracted as labourers when the industry was at its height were now without employment, and a period of distress followed which certainly contributed to the reckless and desperate character of some of the smuggling gangs referred to in a later chapter.

Another consequence was the ruination of the roads. There is no reason to believe that travelling in medieval Sussex was particularly difficult or that the roads were bad; by the seventeenth century they had become notorious. As early as 1585 an Act was passed to compel the iron-masters contribute to the roads which they used. The Act provided that for every six loads of charcoal or ton of iron carried, one cartload of 'sinder, gravell, stone, sande, or chalke' should be laid on the highways and that the Justices of Peace were to see that this was done. This Act seems to have been ineffective and unenforcable, but it is the first attempt to make the user contribute, in proportion to his use, to the cost of maintenance. It is the amplification of this principle, in the first Turnpike Act in 1663, which led directly to the Turnpike System which revolutionised road transport in the eighteenth century.

There was much in the Sussex iron industry of the sixteenth and seventeenth centuries which foreshadowed the industrial revolution of the eighteenth. The new blast furnaces were in part financed by capital provided by London merchants, the landowners receiving shares in the product in return for land and timber concessions—an early form of Joint Stock enterprise. The industry was also dependent on a supply of free mobile labour, and certainly recruited a great part of its labour force from the landless proletariat created by enclosures during the Tudor period in other parts of England. It is one of the paradoxes of history that the earliest large-scale manifestation of those developments, which become the basis of the later industrial revolution, should have occurred in this now rural residential county.

XVII The Civil War and Nonconformity

The cannon foundries of Sussex had an important role to play in the struggle between King and Parliament, but it was not only this which made the control of Sussex of vital importance, and led to a series of campaigns which, although not decisive, played their part in determining the ultimate outcome of the Civil War. Sussex and Kent lay on the shortest route to France, and although the ports were in decline, the kind of assistance which Charles hoped to receive from France—bullion and arms—could be more easily smuggled across the Channel to the shores of Sussex than to any other part of the south coast. For these two reasons, therefore, it was necessary for Parliament to prevent the Royalists gaining control of the county.

As in many other parts of England it is impossible to make any clear distinction of class or location between those who supported the Crown and those who supported Parliament. Among the gentry, families were often divided cousin against cousin, occasionally brother against brother. Although the majority of the older families supported Charles, a considerable number supported Parliament. The following is an extract from a letter written by the Royalist Sir William Campion of Danny (near Ditchling), to his great friend, Colonel Morley of Glynde, principal leader of Parliament in Sussex. 'I did not rashly or unadvisedly put myself upon this service, for it was daily in my prayers for two or three months together to God to direct mee in the right way . . . I believe that you think not that I fight for Popery, God knows my heart, I abhor it. God Prosper me no further than my desires and endeavours tend to the preservation of the Protestant religion settled in Queen Elizabeth's days, the just prerogative of the King, and just privilege of Parliament. However, I heartily thank you for your desire of the preservation of mee and mine, and if ever it lie in my power to do any courtesy to you, it shall not be wanting in your faithful friend and servant.' Such a letter typifies the character of the conflict amd the heart-searching it provoked in all who were involved. Of the fifty-nine signatories to the death warrant of Charles I, seven were Sussex men, three of them great landowners. In the countryside attitudes were very often determined by identification with—or hostility towards—the local great family.

In the towns it is singularly difficult to trace any general pattern. Of the thirteen boroughs returning members to Parliament, five were divided, three had both members supporting the Crown, five had both members supporting Parliament. It might have been thought that the coastal

Cawley almshouses,
Chichester

West gate, Chichester
1781

boroughs would at least have felt strongly about the justice of levying ship-money from inland counties towards the maintenance of sea defences. In fact only Hastings was strongly Royalist. The strange atmosphere of the early months of the conflict was vividly illustrated in Chichester. From the day when the King raised his banner at Nottingham on the 22nd August, 1642, to the first local engagement on the 15th November, when the gentry from the surrounding area entered the city and gained temporary control of it by surprise, supporters of both sides had been drilling daily in different parts of the city, almost within a stone's throw of each other—the Royalists in the Palace precincts, the Parliamentarians in the north-east sector. Chichester was in fact more clearly divided in its loyalties than most of the other towns, The clergy were almost entirely for Charles, and the bulk of the burgesses for Parliament.

The action taken by Parliament on the news of the seizure of Chichester indicates how seriously the control of Sussex was regarded. A large force of 6,000 men was immediately dispatched under General Waller to retake the city. At the same time a subsidiary force made a detour to Arundel to reduce what was, potentially, the strongest fortified centre in Royalist hands: but which, at the time, was garrisoned by only 100 men. Arundel castle fell almost immediately: Chichester held out for six days, during which the suburb of St. Pancras on the east side was almost entirely destroyed by fire. Eventually a breach was made through a bricked-up gate which had been cut through the city wall at the bottom of the deanery garden some two centuries earlier. In the days which followed some damage was done to the fittings of the cathedral by zealots to whom music, stained glass and other imagery was synonymous with popery; but this can be exaggerated, and was little compared with the systematic destruction of stained glass and other ornaments which had been general during the reign of Elizabeth I. We have a vivid description in a letter of Dr. Reeves, the Dean: '. . . Sir Arthur Hazelrigg . . . being entered the place, where the remainder of the Church Plate was, he commanded his servants to break down the wainscot round about the room, which was quickly done, they having brought crows of iron for that purpose . . . Sir Arthur's tongue was not enough to express his joy, it was operative at his heels, for dancing and skipping (pray mark what music that is to which it is lawful for a Puritan to dance) he cried out, "There boys; hark, hark it rattles, it rattles . . ." ' and later 'the common soldiers break down the organs and dashing the pipes with their pole-axes said, "Hark how the organs go!" '

With the occupation of Chichester and Arundel, Parliament had gained complete control of the county, and Royalist sympathizers were unable to continue open resistance without help from outside. This came twelve months later, with a dramatic advance by the Royalist General

106

Hopton, helped by an early frost which made the muddy ways easier for horses and men. Hopton entered the county at the north-west corner via Petersfield on the 5th December, 1643 and arrived before Arundel on the 6th December, after capturing on the way the fortified mansions of Stansted and Cowdray from small Parliamentary garrisons. Three days later Arundel castle surrendered and a garrison of a thousand, including a hundred cavalry, was installed by Hopton.

Meanwhile Colonel Morley of Glynde, the local Parliamentary leader, collected what forces he could and made an appeal for help to Waller who commanded the Parliamentary forces in the Hampshire–Surrey region. Waller, aided in his turn by the continuing frost, responded immediately and crossed into Sussex and Hampshire on the 17th December. Recapturing Cowdray on his way, he reached Arundel on the 19th, with a force of 10,000 men. Then followed a siege which lasted until the morning of the 6th January, 1644, when the whole garrison, reduced partly through the failure of the water-supply, surrendered. To quote a contemporary news writer: 'I never saw so many weak and feeble creatures together in my life, for almost all the common soldiers were half-starved, and many of them hardly able to set one foot before another.'

Bodiam Castle,
'slighted' interior

Both the castle and the town suffered heavily, and that is one of the reasons why so much of Arundel dates from the seventeenth and eighteenth centuries, while the castle itself was almost entirely reconstructed in the nineteenth century—all but the Norman keep and the fourteenth-century Barbican gate being rebuilt in nineteenth-century Gothic with little relationship to the earlier building.

Sussex on the whole, particularly the eastern part of the county, suffered less disruption of its day-to-day life than many of the other English counties. After the second siege of Arundel it remained firmly in the control of Parliament, and, although some families were reduced to beggary by heavy fines, the St. Pancras suburb of Chichester destroyed, and a number of houses and castles in different parts of the county damaged and dismantled, life for most of the population returned to something like normality. As the conflict dragged on, however, there developed a growing resentment among farmers and villagers at the levies of food and the billeting of troops, a resentment not directed necessarily against either side but against the war itself. It was particularly strong in West Sussex where most of the earlier fighting had taken place. On the 18th September, 1645, a meeting of over a thousand villagers and farmers was organized at Rooks Hill (a name then generally used for the Trundle which still had on its crown a medieval chapel dedicated to St. Roc). Other meetings were held at Runcton Down and Bury Hill. The local Parliamentary commanders took drastic action to suppress such protests since they regarded it as a movement of militant non-co-operation.

CIVIL WAR

𝒪 Ifield

Hills Place
(Middleton ☆)

✕July 1648 St. Leonards
𝒪 HORSHAM ▲ Forest

▉ Denne
(Eversfield△)

🏠 Slaugha
(Covert

🏠 Blackdown

WALLER DEC. 17 1643

MIDHURST ★▲

🏠 Cowdray House

▉ Petworth House
(Percy△)

🏠 Knepp
(Burrell△)

𝒪 Nuthurst

▉ Cu

𝒪 Twineham

S.Harting
✕ Nov. 23 1643
▉ Uppark   (Ford ☆)
N.Marden

HOPTON DEC. 1643

W.Dean (Lewkor ☆)

▉ Burton
(Goring △)

▉ Parham
(Bishops ☆)

▉ Albourne
(Juxon ☆)

(Lumley ☆)
▉ Stanstead
(Gunter ☆)
🏠 Racton

Rooks Hill
🏠 Halnaker

© Bury Hill

Houghton

▉ Wiston

🏠 Michelgrove

(Shelley ☆)

𝒪 STEYNING ★

🏠 Rawmere (May☆)(Morley ☆)

ARUNDEL ★▲

⚔ BRAMBER ★▲
✕Dec.12 1643

PRINCE CHARLES' ESCAPE

CHICHESTER ★
✕ Dec.1642   WALLER DEC. 1642

Walberton ©

Star

🏠 Leythorn
(Bowyer ☆)

Southwick

NEW SHOREHAM ▲

In spite of Parliament's control of Sussex, it was from the Sussex port of Shoreham that Prince Charles, escaping after the Battle of Worcester in 1651, secured a passage to France. Disguised as the servant of Colonel Gunter of Racton, whose horse he led, he managed to elude the Parlia-

108

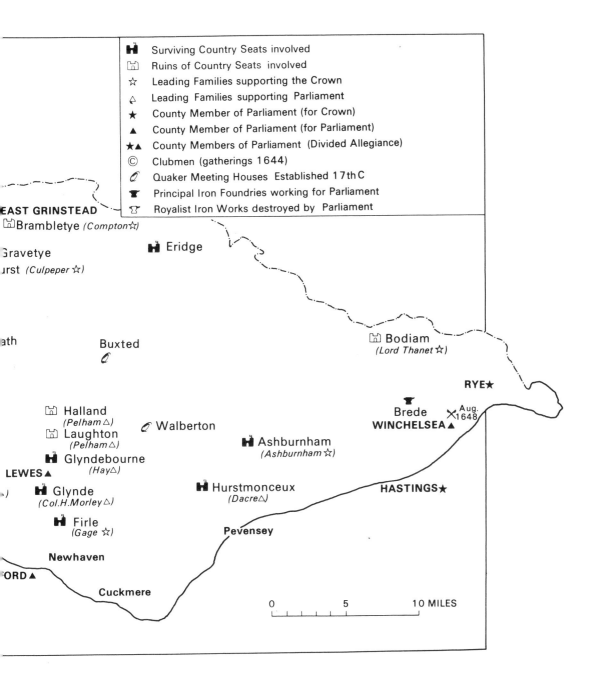

⬛	Surviving Country Seats involved
🏚	Ruins of Country Seats involved
☆	Leading Families supporting the Crown
△	Leading Families supporting Parliament
★	County Member of Parliament (for Crown)
▲	County Member of Parliament (for Parliament)
★▲	County Members of Parliament (Divided Allegiance)
©	Clubmen (gatherings 1644)
ℰ	Quaker Meeting Houses Established 17thC
⊤	Principal Iron Foundries working for Parliament
⊥	Royalist Iron Works destroyed by Parliament

EAST GRINSTEAD
🏚 Brambletye *(Compton☆)*

Gravetye

..rst *(Culpeper ☆)*

..ath

Buxted
ℰ

🏚 Bodiam
(Lord Thanet ☆)

RYE★

🏚 Halland
(Pelham △)
ℰ Walberton
⊤
Brede   ✗ Aug.
WINCHELSEA ▲   1648
🏚 Laughton
(Pelham △)
⬛ Ashburnham
(Ashburnham ☆)
⬛ Glyndebourne
(Hay △)
LEWES ▲
⬛ Glynde
(Col.H.Morley △)
⬛ Hurstmonceux
(Dacre △)
HASTINGS★
⬛ Firle
(Gage ☆)
Pevensey

Newhaven
..ORD ▲
Cuckmere

0   5   10 MILES

⬛ Eridge

mentary controls at the two unavoidable river crossings at Houghton Bridge and Bramber. Many have been the speculations as to how the course of English history might have been altered had he been recognized.

It is not easy to assess the lasting effect of the Civil War in an area like

*Gunter family, 1624
tomb, Racton*

Sussex. The material changes were relatively small and for many of the ordinary countryfolk the attitude of non-attachment to either side was probably fairly general—the political issues were not sufficiently clear-cut in terms that they could recognize. The majority in any case had no representation in Parliament as then constituted. The real effect was indirect and in the sphere of religion. A great many individuals had been forced to reconsider their attitude and crystalize their ideas. These individuals existed in every class and on both sides of the political division. Just as there were many humble folk among the Sussex martyrs, who perished in the flames at Lewes and elsewhere at the time of the Reformation, so in the seventeenth century many of those who joined for conscience' sake one of the many sects such as the Baptists and the Quakers were drawn from the labouring and the smaller yeoman farmer class.

George Fox, the founder of the Society of Friends, visited Sussex in 1655, and wrote in his Journal: 'I passed into Sussex and came to a Lodge near Horsham, where there was a great meeting and many were convinced.' Two years later he wrote: 'I travelled into Sussex visiting Friends, amongst whom I had great meetings; and many times I met with opposition from Baptists and other jangling professors, but the Lord's power went over them.' Before the end of the century more than a dozen regular Quaker Meetings had been established in different parts of the county. Two of the original Meeting Houses, the one at Coolham called the Blue Idol, and the one at Ifield, are still in use. Many of the early meetings were entirely rural congregations. William Penn is reported to have held Quaker Meetings at his house at Warminghurst, ten miles from a town of any size, attended by more than two hundred. In the Quarter Sessions Order Book at Chichester for 1684 is the following entry: 'William Penn being a factious and seditious person . . . doth frequently entertain and keepe unlawfull assemblye and conventicle in his dwelling house at Warminghurst . . . usually are assembled the number of one or two hundred unknowen persons and sometimes more, to the terror of the King's liege people . . .' Terror indeed!

During the early days they suffered a good deal of persecution including much of a petty kind such as the distraint of goods for the refusal to pay tithes out of all proportion to the amounts due, or the interruption of meetings with rotten eggs or stones. But there was also imprisonment and whipping, and between 1665 and 1690 nearly two hundred Quakers were imprisoned for varying periods in Horsham gaol.

The Baptists also were particularly strong in Sussex. In 1669 a survey was made of the Conventicles (or meetings) of the various nonconforming groups in the county. It is probably not complete, but it includes six Quaker congregations, the one at Steyning being estimated at two hundred; eleven Anabaptists, the largest congregation ('fifty to a hundred') being at Trotton; four Presbyterian groups, that at South Malling being estimated at 'at least five hundred'; and three gatherings of independents; there were also twenty-four others, not specifically named. There were, in addition of course, all those who remained loyal to the Catholic faith. These were particularly to be found among the great families. They had for long been used to practise their religion in secret; it was the period of priests' holes and concealed altars. At Slindon House, for instance, an elaborate series of three connected chambers were discovered during alterations in 1874; while at West Grinstead, in the sixteenth-century house adjacent to the new Catholic church, hidden in the roof there was a fully furnished chapel which has now been opened up and restored. With the easing of tension which culminated in the Toleration Act of 1689, secrecy was no longer necessary; it was then for example that the magnificent medieval chapel at Cowdray (which had presumably been carefully concealed during the seven day visit of Queen Elizabeth in 1591) was restored and lavishly redecorated. But many Catholic families were financially ruined by the heavy fines imposed for recusancy; and they suffered particularly during the Commonwealth, when other nonconformist groups were on the whole left unmolested.

*'Blue Idol' Quaker
Meeting House,
Coolham*

XVIII The Eighteenth Century—
Georgian Sussex

Stansted Park and gardens 1708

When the eighteenth century is considered in terms of the changing landscape of this country two things are apparent—first, the tremendous zest with which the landowners vied with one another in an endeavour to shape the landscape according to preconceived ideas of natural beauty: second, the revolution in agricultural methods and techniques which changed the shape of farms, fields and villages in many parts of England. Sussex had its full share of the first, though less of the second.

With the decline of the iron industry nature slowly reconstituted much of the oak forest and mixed woodland of the Weald. Towards the close of the seventeenth century this was helped forward by careful planting. As early as 1664, John Evelyn of Wootton (near the Sussex border in Surrey) advocated in *Sylva* a policy of systematic reafforestation: in fact, quick growing soft woods were often chosen to replace the indigenous woods. At the close of the seventeenth century landscaping was limited to the immediate environs of the great houses—artificial mounts, long terraces, avenues and orchards. All this was merely an extension of the Tudor walled and formal gardens which separated the house from wild and uncontrolled nature. Stimulated by the park at Versailles, and its English reflection in the avenues and canals added to the royal palace at Hampton Court, this developed into an obsession with grandeur and size —with the planting of broader, and taller, and ever longer avenues, which cut across hill and dale, in many cases for several miles. Few of these now remain in Sussex; the best example is perhaps the latest, the avenue at Stansted (1781), now crossed by the main road from Rowland's Castle to Emsworth, but still extending for two miles and providing a vista reaching to the Solent. These great avenues and vistas traversed the landscape but did nothing to mould it. The real triumph of the later eighteenth century was the development of landscaping on principles which followed, but at the same time organized and controlled, nature; and did both on the grand scale. Much of the Sussex landscape, not merely the remaining eighteenth century parks, owes its quality to this considered control, whether in the planting of trees, such as the clump on Chanctonbury or round Singleton, the many lakes, apparently natural but in fact artificial, or the siting of eighteenth-century farms and cottages. The straight line, the dominant element in Renaissance garden planning, was succeeded by the curve, the casual, and the asymmetrical. 'Nature,' wrote Capability Brown, the greatest of the eighteenth-century landscape gardeners, 'abhors a straight line.'

A most interesting example of this change of approach can be seen by comparing the plan drawn up for the improvement of the park at Petworth House, some time early in the eighteenth century, with the park as laid out by Brown later in the century. The main features of the first are the great avenue stretching from the central façade for more than a mile to the west, the conversion of the rounded hill to the north into a series of terraces arranged like giant steps on the east, south and west sides and meeting at right-angles, and finally, beyond the hill to the north-west, a series of exactly similar rectangular fishponds divided by paths—a succession of straight lines reinforcing and reflecting the long lines of the house itself. The park was in fact later laid out with carefully placed but apparently natural clumps of trees, a lake with meandering curves and seemingly natural islands, and an open, turf-covered hillside crowned with trees—not a straight line to be seen. The change in the material environment reflects a change in social attitudes. The pleasant informality at Petworth at the beginning of the last century contrasts with the rigid and somewhat humourless formality of Cowdray two centuries earlier.

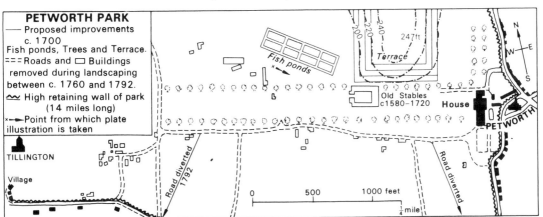

'I really never saw such a character as Lord Egremont. "Live and let live" seems to be his motto. . . . The very flies at Petworth seem to know there is room for their existence, that the windows are theirs. Dogs, horses, cows, deer and pigs, peasantry and servants, guests and family, children and parents, all share alike his bounty and opulence and luxuries. At breakfast, after the guests have all breakfasted, in walks Lord Egremont; first comes a grandchild, whom he sends away happy. Outside the window moan a dozen black spaniels, who are let in, and to them he distributes cakes and comfits, giving all equal shares. After chatting with one guest, and proposing some scheme of pleasure to others, his leathern gaiters are

113

*Toat Tower, built
1827*

buttoned on and away he walks, leaving everybody to take care of themselves, with all that opulence and generosity can place at their disposal, entirely within their reach. Everything solid, liberal, rich and English.' So wrote Benjamin Robert Haydon, in his diary, one of the many artists who were given hospitality.

Although all the great parks in Sussex, such as Cowdray, Arundel, Petworth, Goodwood, Sheffield, Hurstmonceux (to mention some which are open to the public), were reshaped in the eighteenth century under the influence of Capability Brown, in fact only four in the whole county were designed by him personally—Hills Place, near Horsham, Petworth, Ashburnham and Sheffield. Hills Place and Park were destroyed to make way for agriculture early in the nineteenth century, while both Ashburnham and Sheffield have been considerably altered. Sheffield Park in June and early autumn provides, round its lakes and connecting bridges (designed by Brown), a magnificent sequence of exotic flowering trees and shrubs with rich colouring, but these are all plantings of the Victorian period or later, and have little relationship to Brown's conceptions, which were based on the modification rather than the remaking of existing features, and he almost invariably used trees and shrubs native to the locality. The peculiarly English quality of the best eighteenth-century landscaping was often destroyed by the search for the exotic and the unusual in the nineteenth.

This can be seen in one characteristic aspect of the period—the building of 'follies'. There is a world of difference between the elegance and practical usefulness of summer houses such as Carnes Seat in Goodwood park or the now ruined Nore Hill folly in Slindon Park and the quite useless and visually inappropriate structures such as the Sugar Loaf at Brightling built at the beginning of the nineteenth century by the local landowner Jack Fuller to simulate the spire of a nonexistent church, or the narrow chimney like tower on Toat Hill above Pulborough. Somewhere between these two worlds of rational sophisticated leisure and romantic make-believe are the ruined summer house towers in Racton Park and Up Park, dating from the last quarter of the eighteenth century.

Although some of the leading figures in the agricultural developments of the eighteenth century were Sussex farmers and landowners, the Sussex landscape did not suffer the dramatic change by enclosure which transformed the Midlands during this period. In Sussex, enclosure had already taken place gradually and continuously from the time of the Black Death. What Sussex did share with other counties, particularly East Anglia, was an intense interest in new techniques of land improvement which created an agricultural revolution, without which the expanding towns of the North could not have been fed and the industrial revolution would have been frustrated. The leadership came from the greater landowners,

114

and in some cases from the larger yeoman farmers. The latter had increased in number steadily since Tudor and Stuart times at the expense of the smaller yeoman farmers, who had formed the core of the rural population in the seventeenth century and were the descendants of manorial tenants who had enclosed their holdings. These, with an equivalent number of poor cottagers, and landless agricultural labourers depending on wages had formed the great bulk of the population; but by the mid-eighteenth century this class had shrunk considerably. Some had sunk into the growing class of landless labourers, while a smaller number by skill and energy had become large-scale farmers. The Ellmans of Glynde are an excellent example of the latter. They had concentrated particularly on the improvement of the South Down breed of sheep, both in weight and in quality of fleece. By the end of the eighteenth century they had become famous and the South Down breed was known throughout the country. John Ellman, who died in 1832, still preserved an earlier tradition, housing his unmarried workers under his own roof, and dining with them at a common table, and providing them with cottage and stock on marriage—a nineteenth-century version of the patriarchal quality of the medieval manor, but with a totally different and more flexible economic basis.

Racton Tower, built 1772

Perhaps the best example in Sussex of the great landowner devoting himself whole-heartedly to the scientific development of agriculture is that of the third Lord Egremont, already referred to. The landowners by the possession of capital assets could promote large-scale schemes which were quite beyond the means of the wealthiest practising farmers. Lord Egremont financed the Rother navigation, the canal connecting Midhurst and Petworth with the Arun, in the hope of improving agriculture in the Rother area. Arthur Young in 1813 wrote: 'By this most useful and spirited undertaking, many thousand acres of land are necessarily rendered more valuable to the proprietors. Timber is now sent by water. Large falls (fellings) have been exported which would scarcely have been felled . . . an additional tract of country is also supplied with lime from the Houghton and Bury pits. . . .'

The general prosperity of agriculture in Sussex during the eighteenth century is reflected in the number of elegant houses built in towns and villages, and of farmhouses and labourers' cottages in the surrounding countryside. These almost always display that simplicity combined with good taste which was characteristic of the period. They reveal a feeling for the right use of materials—whether brick, stone or flint—and a sense of balance and proportion in the design of window and door space, or in the placing of decorative details. There is hardly a village without one or two good examples, while towns such as Lewes, Chichester and Arundel are probably richer than any other towns of similar size in Britain. In the towns, owners were often content to rebuild the façade only; behind these façades may be found, on examination, buildings which may date from any period from the fourteenth century onwards.

Apart from these many new comfortable houses, the most striking general change that would have struck any traveller in Sussex towards the close of the eighteenth century, if he could have remembered the early or even the middle years, would have been the general increase in the amount of ploughland, the size of many of the fields, the large areas now growing root crops, and the almost complete disappearance of fallow, made possible by more scientific crop rotation.

XIX The Climax and Decline of Traditional and Local Forms of Building

In an earlier chapter the changes in the character of buildings in town and countryside which resulted from the abandonment of the open hall were discussed, and at the close of the last chapter reference was made to the re-façading of earlier timber-frame buildings during the eighteenth century. The present chapter attempts to summarise other developments which took place steadily during the seventeenth and eighteenth centuries, altering the appearance of every town and village—cumulative changes which by the end of the eighteenth century had so transformed village and farmstead as to render them hardly recognisable to a visitor from the fifteenth.

The period from approximately the middle of the sixteenth to the middle of the seventeenth century has been described as that of 'the great rebuilding'. Almost every aspect of the townscape was altered, nor did the farmstead and cottage escape. It is not merely that almost all existing medieval houses were modified—occasionally so much so as to become unrecognisable—with added chimneys, altered windows, inserted floors and partitions, outshots and other extensions, but many more were pulled down and rebuilt in the new style. The new buildings often incorporated materials such as rafters and the main timbers from the buildings they replaced. Sussex, as much as any other county in the south-east, participated in this general revolution. The growth of population over the country as a whole seems to have been in the neighbourhood of fifty per cent, and in Sussex the increase is probably not much below the general level. This meant a tremendous amount of entirely new building, not only the extension of existing towns and villages, but also the building of new farmhouses and cottages away from the village on the now enclosed common fields.

This increase in building coincided with the developments in the use of brick referred to in a previous chapter. In combination with stone such as flint or the upper greensand, it greatly increased the possible uses of local stone. Since Sussex has a remarkably varied geological structure, with many different kinds of stone and clay, greater variety was given to traditional building during this period than perhaps in any other English county. But these variations remained closely tied into, and sympathetic to, the landscape. The transport of heavy materials was no easier in the

Regency cottage,
Brighton

Knapped flintwork,
Slindon Village

seventeenth or eighteenth centuries than it had been in the thirteenth, and in many areas of the Weald was probably more difficult. Once, therefore, timber was no longer the principal structural material the geological pattern in Sussex conditioned much more completely the local pattern of building.

These geological divisions run from east to west so that the belts, though narrow if travelling from north to south, are wide when travelling from east to west. They are still well defined by the visual character of the villages and farms along their length, even though this quality of close relationship to the surrounding landscape has been steadily eroded during the last hundred years. Flint occupies the widest of these belts since it not only includes the whole of the Downland, but the coastal fringe from Selsey to Eastbourne. Along this coastal belt, but rarely extending above a couple of miles into the interior, rounded beach flint, or cobbles, were very generally used for every type of building. It is in the back streets of such towns as Brighton, Shoreham, or Worthing that much of the best remaining work of this kind can be seen, but since the war much of this has been demolished, or else diminished by colour washing.

In the area from Worthing to Eastbourne, where the Downs and the sea meet, so that both the rough nodular flint from the former and the rounded cobble flint from the shore were equally available, many variations in the decorative exploitation of flint-graded selection, coursing, knapping and combination with other contrasting materials such as limestone or brick were developed. Recent surveys in Chichester, Worthing, and Brighton, have shown how much of the buildings in these towns up to the second quarter of the nineteenth century was in flint. A great deal of this, during the Regency period and after, was covered, as far as the façades are concerned, with stucco, some with tilehanging, and still more recently by colour wash, but many inland villages have so far escaped major transformations of this kind—villages such as Stammer near Brighton, Slindon north of Arundel, or Singleton, north of Chichester. Variations also developed in the way brick and flint were combined. In the village of Slindon, for example, the use of brick to divide the flint work vertically is quite different from the more general practice of horizontal string courses.

In the area roughly bounded by Slindon on the west and Worthing on the east, there appeared during the last quarter of the eighteenth century highly elaborate uses of knapped flint. This was often combined with 'galletting', or the filling of the mortar joints with slivers of flint which accumulated in the process of knapping. This seems to have originated, or at least to have been given an impetus locally, during the rebuilding of Goodwood. The lodge gates on the north edge of the park bear the date 1784, and already represent a perfection of this technique, the knapping being so perfect that no brick is used for quoins, door or window jambs or lintels. All are built of meticulously squared flints laid in courses of brick-like precision. Within the next half century this was repeated on the Slindon Estate to the east, and the West Dean Estate to the west, culminating in the flint work to be seen in additions to West Dean House in the eighteen-sixties, which actually has hollow mouldings of knapped flint around windows and doorways. As so often happened, the fashion set by the great estates was copied by other builders in the area, and can be seen in buildings such as the Congregational Schools in Worthing, and in dozens of small houses and even cottages in this part of Sussex.

The great estates have played a large part in helping to maintain and develop local traditions, but their efforts have often been arbitrary, more concerned with the desire to assert their own individuality than to foster a genuine tradition. But in Sussex there is nothing quite comparable with the attempt, for example, of the Dering Estate in Kent to superimpose an estate pattern on villages and houses situated on the estate by a form of moulded brick surrounds for door and window openings. On the whole, in Sussex, the influence of the great estates—particularly in the western region—has been almost entirely beneficial, and has contributed a great deal to the preservation of a relationship between buildings and landscape.

The almost total dependence of the character of building on geological structure can perhaps best be seen in the long line of villages which stretch from east to west along the upper greensand belt just below the escarpment of the Downs. This stone is a very coarse limestone, and for this reason was only used, in preference to the flint obtainable immediately to the south, or the sandstone of the Hythe beds immediately to the north, when it could literally be quarried on the site. It is therefore a very narrow belt indeed in which this stone is employed, rarely more than a mile across; yet it gives quite a distinct homogeneous character to the villages situated along this outcrop. At Amberley cottages can be seen in which it is difficult to distinguish between the walls and the rock on which they are directly built.

The stone from the Hythe beds, which run in an outcrop parallel to the upper greensand some two or three miles to the north, was rather more widely used. It is a hard, warmly coloured sandstone both more durable, and more readily shaped, but even this stone is rarely seen more than a few miles from where it could be quarried. Villages such as Easebourne near Midhurst, or Upperton, near Petworth, were built, or rather rebuilt, in the seventeenth and eighteenth centuries almost entirely of stone quarried on the spot. This stone was often named after a principal local quarry, hence Pulborough stone, or Easebourne stone, (as originally

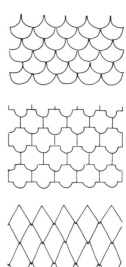

Early patterns of hanging tiles, scallop and diamond

119

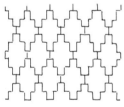

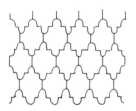

*Later patterns of
hanging tiles*

Hythe stone, which name was taken by geologists in the nineteenth century to cover the whole strata).

The Weald clay was the source of three very different types of stone. One, often referred to as 'winklestone', or by various local names such as 'Kirdford marble' consists of consolidated snail shells; when cut and polished it presents a dark brown finely mottled surface not unlike Purbeck marble. The second is hard sandstone, often called 'Ripplestone' from the ripple-marks formed on the sandbanks and beaches of the then inland sea preserved by an extraordinary coincidence of flooding and petrifaction over a hundred million years ago. Neither of these appreciably affect the exterior appearance of buildings, seldom being used for wall structure—Winklestone was mainly used on internal decorative features, such as fireplaces, and Ripplestone for floor paving. The third, however, is the hard laminated sandstone already referred to in the chapter on medieval building. This was used more consistently than it had ever been used in the Middle Ages in the areas of the western Weald in every sort of building, from church to cottage, during the seventeenth and eighteenth centuries. As in the earlier period it was mainly used for roof covering, but this created something of a recognisably local style, since the weight of these tiles necessitated a lower pitch to the roof, and roof pitch is a very dominant feature in buildings. In the last hundred years a large proportion of these tiled roofs have been stripped, and the tiles replaced with lighter materials in order to reduce the weight on overburdened rafters, often with imported Welsh slate. The resulting hybrid is not only ugly but utterly destructive of the quality of relationship between building and landscape.

Within the area of the Central Weald, stretching from Crawley to Hastings, there are a number of seams of extremely fine sandstone. These, however, do not dominate the local environment to quite the same extent as the more clearly defined areas of the flint and greensand belts, but there are very few villages in the area without a sprinkling of houses built in the eighteenth or early part of the nineteenth centuries from these fine local sandstones.

Brick itself was also given local qualities in its use. The clays in Sussex vary enormously and almost every parish contained a brickyard by the middle of the eighteenth century where bricks were made, often as a part time or seasonal occupation, to meet the needs of the immediate area as they arose. The resulting variations in colour and technique often gave a distinctive quality to the buildings in the locality. In addition there were differences of colour, due to differences of heat in firing; these were also exploited. Just as the Tudor bricklayers had used colour variation to create diaper decorations, the even more striking contrasts, produced in the eighteenth century kilns, between the deep red of the sides and the dark blue ends of the bricks suggested other forms of decoration; string

120

25. The market hall, Midhurst; built about 1520 it still preserves some of the herring bone brick infilling—an early example of this use of brick (pp. 86, 98).

26. St. Mary's, Bramber; almost certainly the surviving wing of a late fifteenth century courtyard inn, a good example of the use of close set vertical timbers (known as 'close studding'), a fashion which became widespread in Sussex at that time (p. 85).

27. Priest House, West Hoathly. Built about 1400, this house is a good example of the normal unjettied type of open hall. The chimney was inserted and the hall divided horizontally and vertically, at about the time the farmhouse illustrated below was built.

28. Pendean farmhouse, near Midhurst. Externally this farmhouse, built about 1600, does not (if we forget the later penthouse addition on the left side) appear very different from the priest's house built two hundred years earlier, illustrated above. The technique of building has changed a little, but the plan and internal arrangements have undergone a revolution. Inglenooks and low ceilings replace the open hall. Threatened by sand quarrying, this house has been dismantled and is now being re-erected at the Weald and Downland Open Air Museum (pp. 97–8).

29. Cowdray from the W. A plan (1737) shows two great avenues converging on the house. The isolated octagonal building on the left is the conduit house which supplied piped water to the mansion (pp. 90–2).

30. Petworth Park and House from the W. This view should be compared with the plan on p. 113. The lake in the foreground covers the series of rectangular fishponds. The hill behind would have been converted into a series of straight parallel terraces (pp. 95, 113).

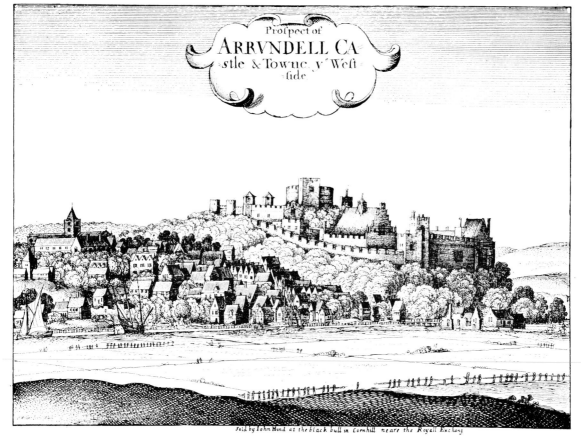

Prospect of
ARRVNDELL CA
stle & Towne, y West
side

Sold by Iohn Hind at the black bull in Cornhill neare the Royall Exchange

31. View of Arundel from the S.E. in 1642. After the siege in the following year the castle became a ruin; its recon-struction in nineteenth-century Gothic bears little resemblance to the building here illustrated, though the central Norman keep was faithfully restored (pp. 46, 50–1, 107).

J. LEWIS F.S.A.

32. Working drawing of Hammer Forge. The Ham-mer (A) might weigh nearly half a ton and the anvil (G) four tons. C is an elastic spring of ash increasing the velocity of the hammer. The latter was raised by knobs projecting from the drum driven by the water wheel. It could strike as much as 150 times a minute (p. 101).

courses and other structural lines could be picked out and emphasised by this method with recognisably regional forms. For example, the use of the blue ends or 'headers' to create large panels of blue within a framing of red 'stretchers' is a feature of both Midhurst in the west and of Lewes in the east of the county, but each in different ways.

In the latter half of the seventeenth century other materials were introduced in the northern parts of the county, the most notable being the development of tile-hanging as a means of wall-cladding. this became elaborated in the eighteenth century by the use of ornamental tiles of various patterns, differing also in colour according to the clay used. These were then used in combination to create many varieties of pattern, and some villages in the north west parts of the county, where most of these ornamental tiles were produced, have been given a quite distinctive character as a result. Here we can see the way in which local traditions of decoration and treatment may develop—the relationship, that is, of villages, or of houses within a particular area, to locally produced material. The process, however, was interrupted by the introduction of cheap and easy transport, before it reached the status of a genuine local style.

Summer House, Rye

Later in the eighteenth century a particular kind of tile hanging which imitated brickwork and came to be known as 'mathematical tiling' was invented. Examples of this exist in almost every town in Sussex, often undetected. The example illustrated in the marginal drawing was the summer house in which Henry James the novelist worked for many years at his home at Rye, unfortunately which was destroyed by a flying bomb. In the Brighton area a particularly striking form was used at the close of the eighteenth century and the beginning of the nineteenth. These tiles have a deep purple glaze and were used on large schemes such as the Royal Crescent at Kemp Town, built in 1806, where the façade is covered entirely with such tiles over a flint rubble wall. In Brighton there are many houses with such façades, although many have been hidden by application of colour wash or stucco.

Parallel with the use of tile hanging in the northern and central parts of the county, was the use of painted weatherboard in the eastern area. This was associated with the growing importation of sawn timber from the Continent particularly from the channel ports, one of which—Deal—gave its name to the type of soft pine woods unloaded there. Painted weatherboard houses of three storeys, built in the eighteenth century, are still in a good state of preservation although framed with pine instead of wealden oak. In other parts of the county it is found sporadically and is probably associated with the introduction of water powered saw mills, as at Blackstone village near Henfield, combined with an increasing supply of locally grown soft wood following the extensive replanting of areas devastated in the period of iron working.

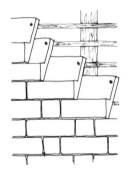

Mathematical wall tiling

Forms of brickwork

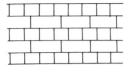

'English bond' general use—c. 1650

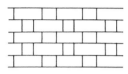

'Flemish bond' general use—after 1650

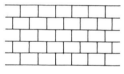

'Headers' only, mainly 18th century

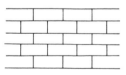

'Stretchers' only, last 100 years

Brick on edge, mainly 1800–1830

In the nineteenth century there were a number of variations in the regional production and use of brick which might have become the basis for recognisably local styles, such, for example, as the use of bricks on edge for a couple of decades at the beginning of the century in a very high proportion of new building within a clearly defined area of the western Weald; or again, towards the close of the century, the use of yellow brick as a patterning element in the north west corner of the county. Developments of this kind based on the local production of new types of brick or tile had, however, only a passing influence and were usually aesthetically deplorable. Apart from the good example of some of the great estates already referred to, perhaps the most valuable contribution during the nineteenth century was the consistent use of local material and occasionally good designs, if we can forget the victorian neogothic windows, of many of the church schools built before 1870, and many of the new Board schools built after that date. In many of these there was a genuine attempt to continue established traditions and they did much to encourage the use of local materials in other buildings erected at the time. These efforts became more and more exceptional towards the end of the century, so that the really close integration of buildings with landscape and its underlying structure ends, virtually, with the eighteenth century.

To sum up, if one were asked to name the period when the traveller through Sussex would have been most impressed, both by the variety of the local scene, and yet, at the same time, to experience the strongest sense of locality and the individual character of village and town, the answer would lie in the half century between 1750 and 1800. By then most of the more attractive regional variations had been developed, the older traditions not yet wholly submerged, and the ultimate dependence in each area on the overall geological pattern still dominant. In addition, since all but the greater buildings still had to depend on materials which could be obtained within a radius of a few miles, local forms were still being evolved, only to be diluted and then lost with the coming of the canals and the railways.

122

XX Regency Sussex

By strict reckoning the Regency period is only the decade from 1811 when
George III became finally and incurably insane, to 1820 when the Prince
Regent ascended the throne as George IV, but it is usually used, as here,
to cover roughly the period of the Napoleonic wars and the reign of
George IV—approximately the thirty years from 1795 to 1825. It was
during this period that the Pavilion, the Regency terraces, the squares and
crescents of Brighton and Hove were built, and when large-scale schemes
of development, not only in Brighton, but in Worthing and Bognor were
formulated, and partly completed.

Brighton, we have seen, was recorded in Domesday as a fishing village.
It possessed a harbour of some importance, presumably where the Steine
and Pool Valley are today, and flourished during the Middle Ages. It was
fortified during the Hundred Years' War, and, at the time of the Armada,
still possessed a 'bulwark' which was renovated only to fall later under the
assaults of the sea. Brighton's decline was, in fact, due partly to the silting
of the harbour (as at Hastings) and partly to the sea's encroachments.
Defoe, in his tour through England and Wales (1724), describes it as:
'A poor fishing town, old built and on the very edge of the sea . . . the sea
is very unkind to this town and has, by its continual encorachments, so
gained upon them (the townspeople) that in a little time more they might
reasonably expect it would eat up the whole town, above a hundred houses
having been devoured by the water in a few years past, they are now
obliged to get a brief granted them, to beg money all over England to
raise banks against the water; the expenses of which will be eight thousand
pounds which . . . would seem to be more than all the houses in it are
worth.'

Such was the town which Dr Russell of Lewes managed between 1750
and 1780 to popularize as a salt-water spa. He advocated sea bathing and
sea drinking as a cure for most ills and established a hydro where the
Albion Hotel now stands. In 1783 the Prince of Wales first visited the town,
returning again the following year, and in 1786 he purchased the site
of the present Pavilion. The following year the Pavilion was built to a
design of Henry Holland in the record time of five months. It was then a
simple Georgian villa which was later to form the nucleus of the building
we know today. For the rest of his life Brighton continued to be the Prince's
favourite residence. This set the seal on the place's growing popularity as
a fashionable resort. In 1780 the population had been 3,600, already a

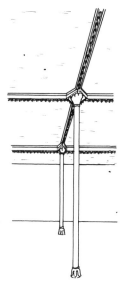

Cast-iron decorative
girders, Brighton
Pavilion

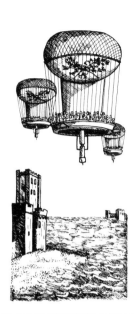

sizable town for the period. By 1794 it had risen to 5,669; by 1801, to 7,337; and by 1821 to 21,429. It was in fact an increase which rivalled the most remarkable parallel developments in Lancashire and Yorkshire, but for entirely different reasons; and so it has continued ever since—for recreation, retirement and commuting from London. The first residential terrace —the Royal Crescent—was built in 1806, the Royal Stables and Riding School (now the Corn Exchange and the Dome) in 1804. Plans for extending the Pavilion and completely transforming it were drawn up first by Repton and finally by Nash, and the Pavilion as we know it was completed in 1821. With the death of George IV Brighton ceased to be the favourite resort of the monarchy. Much of the furniture of the Pavilion was removed to Buckingham Palace, and finally the shell of the building which had cost in all over half a million pounds was bought, as the result of a small majority vote, by the citizens of Brighton in 1850 for £50,000. Brighton has had no reason to regret this purchase: today, refurnished with much of the original furniture, it forms a major attraction.

During most of this period from 1796 to 1815 England was at war with France under Napoleon, and, for at least two years, from 1800 to 1802, a threat of invasion hung continuously over the South Coast. Troops were stationed behind Brighton, and guns had been set up at various points, many on the exact sites used over two hundred years before as gun emplacements against the expected Spanish Armada. Along all the flatter coast from Eastbourne to Kent, where the invasion fleet was expected to land, Martello towers were built; a considerable number of these remain, partly ruined or converted to various uses—an example is the Wish Tower on the front at Eastbourne.

After 1815 for a decade expansion was particularly rapid and grandiose schemes such as that for Kemp town in 1825 on the East Cliff, and that for Brunswick town in Hove were started; both were only half completed, when the tide of popularity turned away from Brighton. By the time it flowed again, after the opening of the Brighton to London railway in 1841, fashion had changed, and the ordered and dignified terraces, squares and communal gardens of the Regency development gave place to the individualism and petty pretentiousness of the Victorian era.

What happened at Brighton was followed, though on a smaller scale, very closely in Worthing and, through the enterprise of Sir Richard Hotham, in Bognor. In 1801 the population of Worthing was approximately 1,000; in 1831, approximately 5,000; that of Bognor in 1801, about 700—in 1831, nearly 3,000.

It is in this period that the turnpike system and the stage coach reach the peak of their development. Cobbett wrote in 1823: 'Brighton is so situated that a coach, which leaves at not very early in the morning, reaches London by noon: and starting to go back in two hours and a half afterwards reaches Brighton not very late at night. Great parcels of stock-jobbers stay at Brighton with the women and children. They skip backward and forward on the coaches and actually carry on stockjobbing in Change Alley though they reside in Brighton.' This perfection of the London to Brighton coaching system led to Brighton becoming for a few years the main cross-channel port of England. Before the development of the railway, there was little difference between the speed of the early cross-channel steam-packets and the stage coach, and Brighton, not Dover or the ports to the east, lay on the direct route from London to Paris. A chain pier, destroyed in a storm in 1896, was built in 1823 to enable passengers to embark directly onto the packet boats from the coaches, without the intermediary of unstable rowing boats and the broad shoulders of the ferry-men. A few years later, the building of the railway in 1847 and the improvement of Newhaven harbour brought this to an end; soon afterwards the Brighton Packet Boat fleet was sold to the railway company. Then, in its turn, Newhaven declined in competition with Folkestone and Dover, for railway speeds became so much faster that the longer land routes with shorter channel crossings became more attractive.

Inland the new canals and the turnpikes described in the following chapters, and the continuing expansion of agriculture, were gradually changing the face of the countryside. In addition the Regency period made itself felt by the widespread imitation in town and village of the stucco used in the fashionable terraces of Brighton and Hove. Innumerable brick, flint, stone and even timber cottages and houses were indiscriminately plastered over and painted. The creeping rot of urban-inspired uniformity had begun.

'*Bowbell*' *milestone*

XXI Smuggling in Sussex

Contraband

Attempts to smuggle goods are inevitable whenever the State, or independent authorities, levy tolls or taxes on the free passage of goods. The greater the tax the greater the incentive, and the larger the number of goods affected the more widespread the traffic becomes. Smuggling, or the evasion of toll and tax, has been rife in Sussex since Saxon times. In the thirteenth century there was continual conflict, for instance, between the merchants of Shoreham and William de Braose concerning the right and extent to which, as Lord of the Manor, he could levy tolls. De Braose, for example, claimed from each ship calling there with wine 'one cask from before the mast and one cask from behind the mast', but the merchants denied the claim to the second cask. Lives were endangered in at least one affray between agents of de Braose and the townsmen. Instances such as this, though widespread, arose from local causes; smuggling on an organised scale began when the Crown first imposed an embargo or a tax on a main article of export—wool-fells. This particularly affected Sussex, which was one of the chief areas of wool production, and in the thirteenth-century wool was a principal export. To control the trade, Wool Staples were established through which all wool destined for export was required to be registered on payment of the export duty. In Sussex the Staples were at Lewes and Chichester. And so the smuggling traffic began—a traffic eventually to be organised on an international scale.

For nearly three centuries wool remained the basis of smuggling in Sussex; although wool is singularly bulky, and the rewards relatively small, the traffic in wool continued right into the eighteenth century. Defoe, in his *Tour through England and Wales* in 1722 observed in the marsh lands round Rye and Winchelsea: 'Dragoons riding about as if they were huntsmen beating up their game . . . in quest of owlers, as they call them . . . often times they are attacked in the night . . . and sometimes killed . . . and obliged as it were to stand still and see the wool carried off before their faces, not daring to meddle, the boats taking it from the very horses' backs . . . are on the coast of France before any notice can be given of them.'

About the time of the first interference with the free export of wool, an embargo was placed on the import of base coin from the Continent. The Statute of Treason in 1351 made this a capital offence, but, as in the case of wool, enforcement proved almost impossible. It is not unreasonable to suppose that those who smuggled wool out from the Sussex coast, safely brought back forbidden coinage, so much easier to handle and dispose of, on their return. Gradually a permanent underground organisation grew up with very wide contacts; thus it was simple to transfer attention to other commodities whenever restrictions were imposed. In the sixteenth century, when the export of cannon without licence was forbidden, there was widespread smuggling of cannon, certainly the most difficult commodity ever to be tackled. In this unlawful traffic many of the great landowners, with their interests in the new iron-works, became involved. The brothers Sir Anthony and Sir Robert Shirley of Wiston combined their activities as official ambassadors, or agents of the Crown, in different parts of Europe and the Mediterranean, with the unofficial sale of armaments from the various iron-works in which they had shares. Sir Anthony even managed to place orders with the Shah of Persia.

In the seventeenth century, during the Civil War, bullion and armaments were smuggled from the Continent on behalf of Charles I. A hundred and fifty years later, during the Napoleonic War, political *emigrés*, or escaped English soldiers were smuggled over from France, while bullion and documents, or escaped French prisoners of war were shipped as contraband from England with complete political impartiality.

Undoubtedly the golden age of smuggling in Sussex was the eighteenth century. It then achieved the position of a major industry, when squire and parson, burgher and peasant, were all involved. During this century the levying of customs and excise duties became a principal element in government finance; national solvency, in fact, in the days before income tax, depended on the increase of indirect taxation. The number of dutiable or restricted articles increased from a dozen or so to several hundred (for a brief period even salt was taxed). Most of these goods were far easier to handle, or conceal, than wool had been. Small barrels of spirits could be dropped overboard, to lie concealed in muddy estuaries: seven pounds of tea, taxed at twenty shillings on the pound, produced a reward quite out of proportion to the older traffic in wool. Since articles such as these were consumed by every section of the population, there was general sympathy with the professional smuggling fraternity. A good deal of casual labour was recruited from the agricultural population. A man could earn 'on the side' one pound a day (considerably more than the equivalent of a week's wages on the land) as a 'runner', carrying the goods from the coast to the secret depots in the vicinity of London.

This highly-organised industry, in which hundreds of men were involved professionally, was opposed by preventive measures which were inefficient and inadequate; this often led to an overweening confidence on the part of the smuggling gangs. In 1747 a notorious Sussex group known as the Hawkhurst gang laid siege to, and broke open, the Customs House at Poole, where goods, seized by preventive officers, had been stored. The fear and hatred of spies and informers also led to drastic measures against

Treadmill, Horsham Gaol

anyone suspected of laying information. The particularly brutal murder of two supposed informers, Chater and Galley, a short time after this led to the capture and trial of several of this particular gang. Seven were condemned to death at the assizes held at Chichester in 1749, two being hanged in chains on Selsey Bill, another on the Trundle, and another on the highway at Rake, as a warning to others. The savagery of the law itself often led desperate men, whose lives were already jeopardised through having been involved in some affray, to further acts of desperation. As late as 1810 a gang of this type, known as the Copthorne gang, terrorized the area east of Crawley.

Since the middle of the sixteenth century assizes had been held almost always at either Horsham or East Grinstead. In 1775 a new gaol was built at Horsham to replace one built in 1640—'the foundations to be three feet deep of hard Horsham stone, the building itself of burnt stock bricks; all timber to be heart oak, tyled roof on heart oak laths'. It was in fact the first 'model' prison in England with separate cell accommodation for the new regime of solitary confinement for all prisoners convicted of felony. Only debtors continued to remain communally housed. The prison reformer John Howard visited the prison in 1782 and highly approved of it. 'This county' he wrote 'has set the noble example of abolishing all fees and also "the tap" (the purchase of drink by prisoners). In consequence I found the gaol as quiet as a private house, the prison as clean, healthy and well regulated'. In 1843 a new county goal was built at Lewes and after that Lewes became the sole assize town in Sussex.

In 1788 a subsidiary prison or 'House of Correction' was built at Petworth to supplement the county gaol at Horsham. This was designed by James Wyatt and for some years shared with the new gaol at Horsham the distinction of being the most up to date prison in the whole country, incorporating also the new system of solitary confinement. It also had an elaborate machine which recorded on a dial called an 'Ergometer' the exact amount of energy each prisoner put into turning a crank. For a time these two prisons served as models for the efficiently planned but utterly inhuman institutions built in almost every county during the next half century. The 'House of Correction' at Petworth was pulled down in 1881, a small section—the governor's house—being incorporated in the present police headquarters.

The assize weeks at Horsham were highly popular events and regularly attracted thousands of visitors who poured in by waggon or on foot, and camped on the great common, north of the town. The last public hanging on the common was in 1820; but there were other public spectacles such as whipping at the cart's tail, standing in the pillory, or sitting in the stocks.

The severity or brutality of punishments however seem to deter less than the certainty of being caught; and the final suppression of smuggling

128

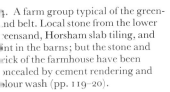The Preacher's house, Ewhurst. The continuous jetty became very popular in the Tudor period. The timber framing of the upper floor is concealed by tile-hanging; the close-studding of the ground floor, however, is well preserved; with the brick oast houses and the weatherboarding it forms a group typical of the north-eastern region of the county (p. 121).

A farm group typical of the green-sand belt. Local stone from the lower greensand, Horsham slab tiling, and flint in the barns; but the stone and brick of the farmhouse have been concealed by cement rendering and colour wash (pp. 119–20).

35. Brighton in 1766 from the N.E. The compact medieval town was bounded by the Steine on the near side and by North Street on the inland side. The parish church of St. Nicholas dominates from the hill on the right. The pavilion was built (twenty years later) beyond, and slightly to the right of, the two walking figures (pp. 123–5).

36. Brighton Pavilion, Repton's design, 1808. Nash reshaped and elaborated Repton's proposals. Repton's designs were in turn influenced by the Royal Stables (now the Dome), designed by William Porden in 1804 (p. 124).

depended on two things—the development of a really effective preventive system, and a lessening of the rewards to be gained by smuggling, by a progressive lowering of taxation on a great many of the highly-taxed commodities. Both these things happened in the years which followed the final defeat of Napoleon. The Navy, released from the task of fighting a major war, was able to turn its attention to the smugglers; and an extremely efficient Coast Guard system was established—an appropriate employment for retired, or now redundant, naval personnel. Along the whole circuit of the English coast, there were set at intervals coastguard stations, each within signalling distance of the next, and each linked to its neighbour by a path which was patrolled every night. Beyond, swift cutters patrolled the sea itself. Within ten years, large-scale smuggling was ended, and though a trickle still continues even today, it is limited to a narrow range of small, but valuable, commodities such as drugs; it has little relationship to the large-scale mass organisation of its heyday when it is reckoned that perhaps as much as one third of the tea, spirits and tobacco consumed in this country had escaped duty.

Portable whipping post and stocks

Just as the decline of the ports in the fifteenth century, or of the iron industry in the seventeenth led many honest burghers or iron-workers to turn to smuggling for a living, so in the 1830's unemployment and distress in Sussex was certainly increased by the successful suppression of smuggling. The following is a quotation from a report on the 'Disturbed Districts of Sussex', published in 1833. 'Since the establishment of the Preventive Service, smuggling is much diminished. This diminution has had the effect of increasing the Poor Rate . . . those who do not directly profit by smuggling consider that it is advantageous as finding employment for many who otherwise would be thrown on their parishes.'

XXII Cobbett's Sussex

Smock Mill, Shipley

Between 1822 and 1825 William Cobbett toured Sussex four times. His vivid account of these journeys is an excellent starting point from which to look at the rural life of the county during the first decades of the last century. Cobbett had been brought up as a farmer, and he saw the landscape with the eyes of a farmer; he judged the changes of the period by how they affected the men who worked on the land, and the kind of crop that the land sustained. He had little sympathy with the Regency developments at Brighton or with the Court: 'This place is a great resort with the "whiskered" gentry. . . . Whence came the means of building these new houses and keeping the inhabitants? Do they come out of trade and commerce? Oh no! They come from the land. . . .' In contrast he says: 'The farm houses have been growing fewer and fewer, the labourers' houses fewer and fewer; and it is manifest to every man who has eyes to see with that the villages are regularly wasting away. . . . In all the really agricultural villages and parts of the kingdom, there is a shocking decay, a great dilapidation and constant pulling down . . .' Although Cobbett tended to exaggerate, we must remember that he was writing in a period of temporary agricultural depression. The high price of corn and the tremendous impetus given to agriculture during the Napoleonic War had led to the ploughing up of great areas previously uncultivated, as well as to general improvements through the use of new machinery and techniques. This boom prosperity had been followed, as after the war of 1914–18, by a rapid fall in agricultural prices, the bankruptcy of many small farmers, and the inability of even the better and more efficient ones to pay adequate wages.

The situation varied a great deal between one part of the country and another; within the county of Sussex there was no uniformity. On his journey via Petworth and Duncton to Singleton and Funtington, Cobbett writes: 'There is, besides, no misery to be seen here. I have seen no wretchedness in Sussex; nothing to be at all compared to that which I have seen in other parts; and as to these villages in the South Downs, they are beautiful to behold. . . . I saw, and with great delight, a pig at almost every labourer's house. The houses are good and warm; and the gardens some of the very best that I have seen in England.' Elsewhere he speaks of: 'The walks and the flower borders, and the honeysuckles and roses framed over the doors and over arched sticks that you see in Hampshire, Sussex and Kent, that I have many a time sitten upon my horse to look at so long and so often, as greatly to retard me on my journey. Nor is this done for show or ostentation. If you find a cottage in these counties, by the side of a bye lane, or in the midst of a forest, you find the same care about the garden and the flowers.' Writing of Horsham (and he writes in a similar vein of Lewes and Billingshurst): 'This is a very nice, solid, country town. Very clean, as all the towns in Sussex are. The people very clean. The Sussex women are very nice in their dress and in their houses. The men and boys wear smock frocks more than they do in some counties. When country people do not they always look dirty and comfortless.'

Describing the wealden area between East Grinstead and Crawley he says: 'The labouring people look pretty well. They have pigs. They invariably do best in the woodland countries. . . .' And again, when comparing the corn country of Thanet with that of Sussex: 'What a difference between the wife of a labouring man here and the wife of a labouring man in the forests and woodlands of Sussex! Invariably have I observed that the richer the soil, and the more destitute of woods, that is to say, the more purely a corn country, the more miserable the labourers.'

Toll Booth, Falmer

Cobbett mentions new enclosures in Sussex in a number of passages; such enclosures were confined almost entirely to the commons and wastes, and in many areas caused hardship and distress. On his ride from Worth to Horsham in 1822 he noted: 'This forest . . . is followed by a large common, now enclosed, cut up, disfigured, spoiled, and the labourers all driven from its skirts. I have seldom travelled over eight miles so well calculated to fill the mind with painful reflections.' This refers to the great common which stretched to the north-east of Horsham and was enclosed by the Lord of the Manor, the eleventh Duke of Norfolk, by an Enclosure Act passed in 1813. Of the 800 acres involved, the bulk was acquired by the Duke, and the cost of the enclosure met by the sale of a small part. By 1911 land thus acquired was fetching £850 per acre. No doubt as a small compensation to the burgesses of Horsham, he rebuilt the Town Hall in a singularly ugly pseudo-Norman style.

On the whole, west Sussex seems to have been more prosperous than the eastern parts of the country. He speaks of the extensive emigration to America of pauperized agricultural labourers from the eastern areas of Sussex; it was in the eastern areas, only a few years later, that distress and unrest reached breaking point.

Cobbett, with the exception of his journey to Battle in January 1822, travelled invariably on horseback, and he has a good deal to say about the turnpike roads. As a farmer his appreciation was mixed with criticism. His attitude is very different from that of Defoe, just a hundred years earlier. Defoe described with enthusiasm the new system by which Turnpike Trusts were authorised to levy tolls on road users to meet the costs of remaking and maintaining the most important highways. Up to then the

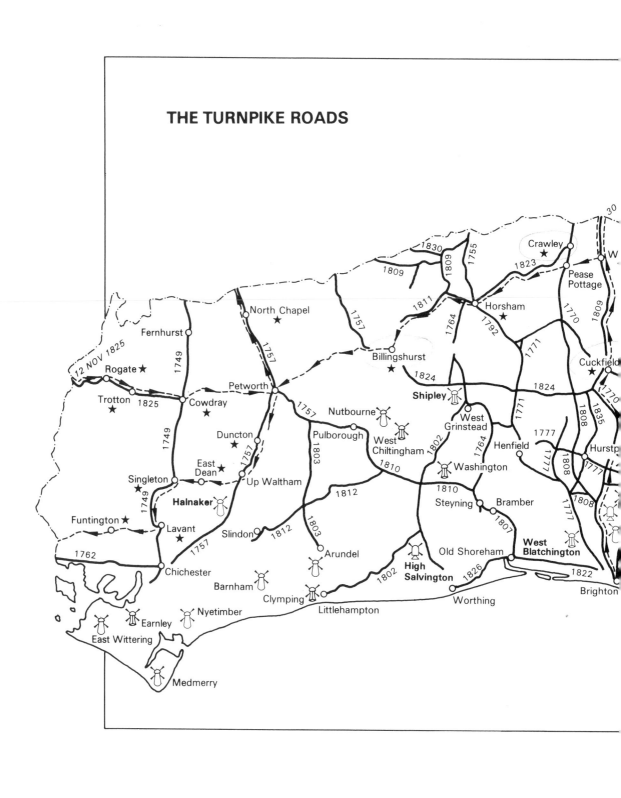

THE TURNPIKE ROADS

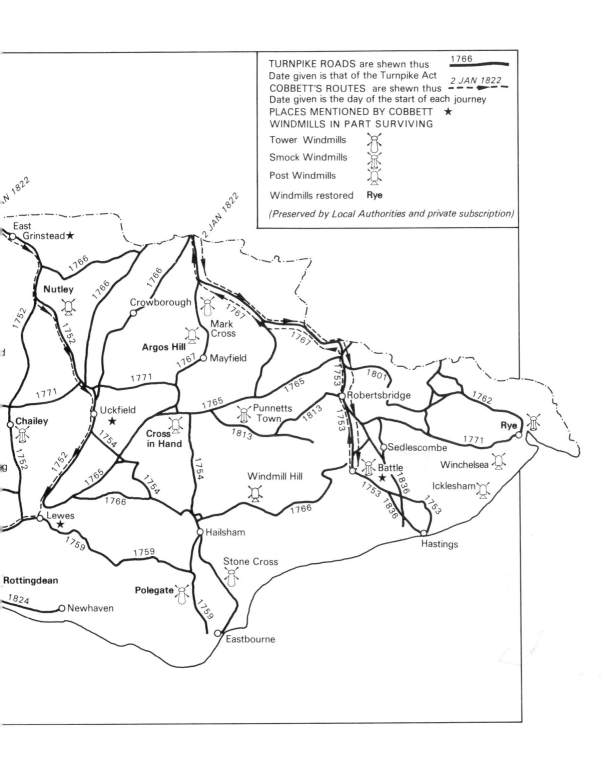

TURNPIKE ROADS are shewn thus — 1766 —————
Date given is that of the Turnpike Act
COBBETT'S ROUTES are shewn thus — 2 JAN 1822 – – – –
Date given is the day of the start of each journey
PLACES MENTIONED BY COBBETT ★
WINDMILLS IN PART SURVIVING

Tower Windmills
Smock Windmills
Post Windmills

Windmills restored **Rye**

(Preserved by Local Authorities and private subscription)

East Grinstead ★
Nutley
Crowborough
Mark Cross
Argos Hill
Mayfield
Chailey
Uckfield ★
Cross in Hand
Punnetts Town
Robertsbridge
Rye
Sedlescombe
Winchelsea
Windmill Hill
Battle ★
Icklesham
Lewes ★
Hailsham
Hastings
Rottingdean
Stone Cross
Polegate
Newhaven
Eastbourne

1822
1766
1766
1766
1752
1752
1767
1767
1767
1771
1765
1765
1753
1801
1762
1771
1813
1813
1753
1766
1754
1754
1765
1752
1752
1766
1759
1759
1753
1836
1753
1836
1753
1824
1759

Section of Britannia Coaching Map, 1671

responsibility had been that of the local parishes. Defoe speaks of the first turnpike in Sussex, which dealt with the road from Godstone to East Grinstead into the central Weald: 'The great Sussex road, which was formerly insufferably bad, is now become admirably good.' But later he writes of the 'appalling conditions of other Sussex roads', in particular of Stane Street 'the old Roman road' which crossed 'a terrible deep country called the Homeward (Holmwood) and so to Petworth and Arundel; but we see nothing of it now; and the country indeed remains in the utmost distress for want of good roads.'

After the Godstone to East Grinstead turnpike, described with such enthusiasm by Defoe, nothing further was done in Sussex until 1749, when the first entirely Sussex Turnpike Trust was set up 'for the repairing the road from Hindhead Heath through Fernhurst lane and Midhurst to the city of Chichester in the county of Sussex'. The preamble to the Act describes 'Many parts thereof so ruinous and deep in the winter season that carriages cannot pass without great danger and difficulty. . . .' The Trustees, mostly local Justices of the Peace, were authorised to let the Tolls 'for any term not exceeding seven years, or to appoint collectors'. The Act also authorised the amount of tolls to be levied, 'For every coach, berlin, landau, chariot, chaise, calash, chair, caravan, or hearse, etc. drawn by six horses or mules, 1/-; if drawn by four, nine pence, if drawn by two, six pence, or by one horse, three pence. For every waggon, wain, cart . . . if drawn by six horses or oxen one and six, if by four, nine pence, and so on for one horse, mule, etc., unladen, one penny for every drove of oxen, ten pence per score. Calves, sheep, etc., five pence. . . .'

This Act represents the general form of the many Turnpike Acts for the county of Sussex which followed in rapid succession. These piecemeal improvements resulted in a rather haphazard system, both of finance and maintenance. Many of the Trusts covered very short lengths of road, only one exceeded thirty miles. In the report on the Turnpike Trusts of the County which was issued in 1857, fifty-one Trusts are enumerated, covering 640 miles of road with 238 toll gates or bars, an average of one gate to every two and a half miles. On the 23-mile turnpike from Mayfield to Wadhurst there were nineteen gates. The longest section under a single Trust was that from Brighton to Cuckfield and West Grinstead, a matter of 35 miles with sixteen gates. Ten of the Trusts covered sections of the road less than five miles in length. The concept of making the user pay was not unsound in theory, but in practice inefficient and costly to enforce. The delays at the gates, the maintenance of the 238 collectors, and the 238 toll cottages and barriers was uneconomic and the system of farming out the collection of tolls by leasing them, though eliminating the need for a great deal of supervision, led also to abuses of other kinds.

The toll cottages were mostly purpose-built, and, though amongst the tiniest cottages built at that time, were often well designed, using traditional local materials. Occasionally an existing building or part of a building—like the one in the centre of Lindfield, illustrated in a marginal drawing, was used. Those which were purpose-built seem invariably to have followed a standard pattern of two rooms, usually separated by a central chimney, each measuring from ten to twelve feet square. Perhaps some forty still survive, but their number diminishes year by year, simply because of their excessively close proximity to the roads which still remain the network of the county today.

Toll House, Lindfield

By Cobbett's time, the Sussex turnpike system was virtually complete, and the organisation of the coaching system on roads such as that from London to Brighton could hardly be carried further, whether in the quality and lightness of coach construction, the grading of inclines and road surfaces, or the perfect timing in the changing of horses at the posting stations. Cobbett admired the perfection achieved, but disliked the ends that it served. They benefited, as he saw it, mainly the wrong people. 'North Chapel is a little town in the Weald of Sussex where there were formerly post chaises, but where there are none kept now . . . the guests at inns are now commercial gentlemen who go about in gigs instead of on horseback.' He resented the differential tolls on the size of wheels, which, as he saw it, penalized the farmer. 'This is the time thought proper to enact that the whole of the farmers in England should have new wheels to their waggons and carts, and that they shall be punished by the payment of heavier tolls.' On the Worthing turnpike, for instance, in 1824, the toll on any waggon, wain, dray or cart with wheels of less than $4\frac{1}{2}$ inches was $3d.$, for waggons etc. with wheels of $4\frac{1}{2}$–6 inches, $2d.$, and for waggons etc. with wheels of 6 inches or over, $1d.$—a threefold difference. In other words, the farmers were encouraged to fit wider wheels to their slow and heavy farm waggons, which would then serve to roll out the ruts created by the swifter narrow-wheeled coaches. Cobbett, instead of regarding this as a concession to the broad-wheeled waggon, saw it as penalizing the farmer for the benefit of the coaching traffic.

Cobbett also regrets the way in which roads which had not been turnpiked was scorned and neglected. On his journey from Petworth to Lavant he wished to avoid going round by the turnpike through Chichester. 'In cases like mine, you are pestered to death to find out the way to get from place to place. The people you have to deal with are innkeepers, ostlers and post boys; and they think you mad if you express your wish to avoid turnpike roads, and a great deal more than half mad if you talk of going even from necessity by any other road. They think you a strange fellow if you will not ride six miles on a turnpike road rather than two on any other road.' In other words, the canalizing of traffic onto the main highways had already begun.

135

Cross in Hand,
Post Mill

Yet this great system of turnpike roads, coaches and coaching inns, in which a vast amount of capital had been invested, began within twenty years to crumble in face of the new transport revolution of the railways. The last turnpike to be constructed in Sussex was in 1841 between Cripps Corner in the central Weald and Hawkhurst. That same year the Brighton to London railway was opened. By 1870 most of the Turnpike Trusts in Sussex had been wound up and hundreds of coachmen, coachbuilders and others put out of business.

Curiously Cobbett makes no reference to windmills. Yet the period at which he wrote was one in which more windmills were under construction than at any other period in our history. All available water-power had long been fully utilised, and steam power was not yet in sight. The rapid increase in population and corn production resulted in the exploitation of wind power to the fullest extent. Hardly a landscape he viewed in Sussex would have lacked its quota. Few villages would be out of sight of at least one or two, and most of these would have been built within his own lifetime. Within two miles of the centre of Hastings there were sixteen windmills, and a number more would have been visible from Castle Hill; within two miles of Brighton there were at least eight, with a dozen more visible from any of the hills in the vicinity. Not only were these new windmills a striking addition to the landscape, but they contrasted with the simply constructed post-mills of the earlier centuries. These new towers, or smock mills as they were called, in which only the cap or top storey, which carried the sails and driving shaft, turned to face the wind, could be very much higher and larger than the post-mills in which the whole structure pivoted on a central post. Their greater size, and the elaborate and delicate automatic devices with which they were fitted for turning the sails into the wind, or adjusting them to the changing wind velocity, represented a technical achievement comparable with the revolution in industrial techniques in the Midlands and the North.

Today only a few survive in ruin or semi-ruin. Of these, eleven are being (or have been) restored by local authorities or by subscription. Those at Salvington, Oldlands near Ditchling, 'Jill' above Clayton are of the older post-mill type; the Cross in Hand and Argos mill (near Rotherfield) are post-mills mechanically turned by geared fantails running on a circular rail on the ground. The mills at Rottingdean and Chailey and the Kingsland mill at Shipley are wooden smock mills. Those at Patcham and Halnaker are brick tower mills, while the mill at Blatchington (above Hove) is built on a platform over the end of a barn. And so there will be preserved a few examples (though probably less than one in twenty) of something which a hundred years ago formed one of the most memorable features of the Sussex landscape.

XXIII The Changing Pattern of Farm and Farmstead since the Seventeenth Century

Previous chapters have dealt briefly with the principal changes in the methods of agriculture and the organisation of the rural community from the time when the first neolithic farmers settled in Sussex up to the end of the Middle Ages.

Terwick Old Mill

During these three to four millenia there were only two periods when changes in the technique of farming and farm management took place so rapidly that they can be described as revolutionary, and both were the result of conquest. The first was the introduction of large scale estate farming by the Romans, which probably affected a good deal of the southern part of the county during the first and second century following the Roman conquest; the second was the introduction of collective farming by the Saxons towards the end of the fifth century. The Saxon system lasted over much of the county for almost a thousand years.

The changes which began to take place towards the end of the Middle Ages with the breakdown of this collective farming system started gradually, increasing the momentum at certain periods. In their totality they have affected not merely the organisation and lay-out of farms and farm buildings, but the whole way of life of the countryside, and it is a still continuing process. The first phase in this development was the consolidation of holdings and their management, the second, the steady improvement in technology involving greater capital investment and thus placing a premium on the increase in the size of holdings. Already, in the later Middle Ages these tendencies were to be seen in the large scale farming practised by some of the monastic establishments, particularly by the Cistercians whose barns astonish by their size, and their sheep farming by its scale. But with the possible exception of some of the estates managed by the Abbey of Battle, and the great Cluniac Priory of St. Pancras at Lewes, there is not much evidence for estate farming of this kind in Sussex. There is, however, considerable evidence to suggest that some of the largest and richest farms of the later Middle Ages were to be found in the mixed farming areas of the Weald where individual holdings had slowly developed from assarts cleared, and brought into cultivation, by pioneer families. Here, judging from fourteenth and

137

Donkey wheel,
Saddlescombe

fifteenth century returns of the woollen trade, sheep farming, as on the Downs, was closely integrated with arable, and land may have been kept in good heart, giving continuous crop production, by the systematic folding of sheep between harvest and sowing. Farming in these areas would also have been combined with the husbandry of timber, providing additional winter employment. This type of mixed economy was still characteristic of the Weald after its slow reafforestation and recovery following the industrial interlude of hammer forge and blast furnace.

Bearing in mind that the enclosure of the great open common fields in the rest of the county had been largely completed by the end of the sixteenth century, it is probable that over the county as a whole there was, by the seventeenth century, the largest number of independent farmers and small holders that the county has ever contained.

The next step was a steady increase in the size of farms in those areas most suited to the application of the improved farming techniques of the eighteenth and nineteenth centuries. These areas were particularly those stretching from the greensand belt through the Downs and over the coastal plain, rather than the more acid and heavier soils of the Weald. The Wealden farmer was therefore, except in a few favourable areas, left behind, and it was possible for Arthur Young writing at the close of the eighteenth century, to describe the Weald as a backward area of relatively small farms compared with the progressive farming by then to be found in the larger farms of the Downland and coastal plain. In his first report on the agriculture of Sussex he writes 'A person viewing the Weald from these hills, would immediately be struck with some degree of surprise at the prodigious proportion of woodland as the country under view appears one uniform mass. This arises partly from the woods being extensive and in part from a most barbarous inveterate practice, when the country was cleared, of leaving a belt of wood several yards wide round every distinct field as a nursery of timber.' He had no reservations as to the desirability of the increase in large scale farming in the Downland and the coastal plain, 'No doubt exists in my own mind . . . from the observation which I have made, of the comparative superiority of great over small farms from every point of view.' He contrasts the traditional farming of the Weald with the new large scale farms, 'In the Weald, although farms sometimes rise to £.200, . . . a far greater number fall very considerably below this . . . the average size is under £.100 a year. On the South Downs they rise much higher. Many farmers occupy the greatest part if not the whole of their respective parishes, as in Bottolph's, Kingston, Coombes, Bramber, North Stoke, Bletchington, Falmer, Piddinghoe, and many others in the neighbourhood of Lewes, Eastbourne and Brighton.' In other words, these villages, once the centre of a collectively organised agriculture, had become single units little

138

differing perhaps from Roman estate farms of the second and third centuries. Yet the mechanisation of farming had in many ways only just begun. 'Thrashing the wheat is everywhere performed by flail-work, and cleaned either with a shovel and broom or by winnowing machines.' He mentions three instances of 'thrashing machines . . . at Bognor, Ashburnham and Petworth . . . the prodigious saving that might be made in the expenses of labour . . . by substituting machinery . . . ought to induce gentleman and large farmers . . . to improve this branch of rural economy.' The steam driven threshing machines of the late nineteenth century might perhaps not have surprised him; the universal employment of the petrol driven combine harvester certainly would.

All these changes are reflected in the farms and farm buildings, built before the present century. The most characteristic and universal of these is the barn, whether for storing grain before threshing, or hay for fodder. With very few exceptions the surviving medieval barns in Sussex are either the barns belonging to the Church, or manorial barns; few are associated with independent farmers, and these are almost all relatively small barns in the Wealden area. Large barns, such as the great aisled barn at Alciston, were mostly associated with the granges belonging to one of the greater monasteries—in the case of Alciston, Battle Abbey. It is not until the sixteenth and seventeenth centuries that we find large barns associated with the new yeoman farmer class. The majority of the greater barns found in the downland and coastal plain appear to have been built during the hundred and fifty years from the end of the seventeenth to the middle of the nineteenth centuries. They are quite clearly the result of the increase in corn yields, coupled with the increase in the size of farms.

Local types of aisled barns

It was during this period that various regional types of barn became established. A form which is widespread in the coastal plain is aisled on both sides and is seldom less than five bays, and very often of nine or ten bays—bays being added when required. They were invariably thatched, with the timbering. mainly of elm, which has been for centuries the dominant tree of the coastal plain—in contrast with the oak of the Weald clay, or the beech of the Downland chalk.

A second type of aisled barn, which is found widely over the south-west area of the county, is quite different in plan. In this the aisles are continued round both ends, and the barns are seldom of more than three bays. The result is a squarish building, measuring on average thirty feet in width by forty-five feet in length. Like the long aisled barns, they seem almost invariably to have been thatched, but the continuation of the aisle round the ends made any extension virtually impossible. Both these types of aisled barn appear to date from the late seventeenth and eighteenth centuries, and it is in this period that they became standardised to meet the needs of increased corn production and larger

139

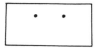

Regional form of single aisled barn

farms. Both are rapidly decreasing in number since, of all forms of barn, the aisled is least adapted to modern needs and the cost of rethatching prohibitive. Within the last five years the writer has noted ten complete demolitions, and ten falling into such dereliction that demolition is certain in the near future.

A third kind of aisled barn has a much wider distribution over the western part of Sussex, extending into Hampshire and northwards into Surrey and is aisled on one side only. The advantage of a single aisle is that the eaves on the non-aisled side are high enough to admit the largest loaded wagon without the necessity for either cutting an entrance through the aisle, or of building a separate gabled roof over the high barn door. These barns are usually of three bays and therefore smaller than the others. Drawings in the margin illustrate these differences in plan and appearance. From their pattern of distribution, and the fact that these single aisled barns are almost always attached to cattle byres or 'hovels' built at right-angles to the ends of the barn, thus forming a sheltered enclosure or yard, it appears that they were principally hay barns associated with the growth of dairy farming, and the majority seem to have been built between the middle of the eighteenth and the middle of the nineteenth century. It is probable, however, that this arrangement of barn and byre has a very early ancestry, and the fact that we have little evidence of this may be simply due to the tremendous rebuilding and enlargement of farms that took place during this period. Another distinguishing feature, and one which reflects the differences in the type of farming is that, whereas the aisled barns associated with corn growing were thatched, the majority of single aisled barns are tiled. For that reason they have, perhaps a slightly better chance of surviving, although equally redundant to the farming economy of the nineteen-seventies.

These aisled barns are all regional and restricted in their distribution within the county. Over the county as a whole the aisleless form predominates. Barns without aisles cannot vary much in plan, but there is plenty of scope for variation in size, or of materials with which they are built (as in the case of farmhouses) and in their relationship to the surrounding landscape. They range from relatively small medieval timber-framed barns with crownpost roof construction and covered with Horsham slab tile in parts of the Weald to the great flint and brick barns in the Downs. They can date, though only a few, from the late Middle Ages to the middle of the nineteenth century, when corn production in the county reached its peak. The unaisled barn is more adapted to conversion to other purposes, and a number have in fact been converted to dwelling houses, thus managing to survive into the twentieth century, but no longer recognisable.

Another development which began in the seventeenth century and which became general in the eighteenth, was the construction of separately designed granaries for the safer storage of thrashed corn. These were relatively small buildings raised from the ground on mushroom shaped staddle stones, protecting the grain from rising damp and vermin. In earlier days, thrashed corn was more often stored on an upper floor in barns, or even in attic stores in the farmhouses; but with the growth of larger farms a specialised building became not only more desirable, but more feasible. In 1815 Charles Vancouver wrote: 'A very excellent practice seems to be fast gaining ground . . . of building wheat barns, . . . upon stands or staddles, the stones, or legs and caps, are supplied from the quarries of Purbeck', and Arthur Young, 'The pleasing manner which the farmers adopt throughout a great part of this county, and especially in the western division, of stacking their corn on circular stone piers cannot be admired too much . . . it most efficiently prevents small vermin from lodging in the sheaves, . . . thereby obviating incalculable losses to the owner.' This seems to refer not only to the building of granaries for grain already thrashed, but for stacking the unthrashed corn also. Later in the nineteenth century it was not unusual for hay to be stacked in this way, and towards the end of the century, cast iron staddles with supporting round or rectangular framework for the base of the rick were being used in the north of the county for this purpose. Although these granaries, like the barns, have little use today and are disappearing, the evidence of their existence remains in the staddle stones which can be seen lining the drives to dozens of farm houses in the county. By the middle of the nineteenth century there must have been few farms in the corn growing areas without one or more granaries mostly built within the previous hundred years.

Granary, Eastergate

Another farm building which since the introduction of the steam engine has had little relevance, but which from the late eighteenth century onwards became a characteristic structure on the larger farms, was the round-house and horse gin. In this a horse or ox by walking round a central turning post transmitted power to a series of geared cog-wheels to drive whatever machinery could be attached within the barn. These round-houses provided shelter for the animals and mechanism, but were usually open at the sides. They were built against the barn, the shaft, geared to the turning post, passing through the barn wall. It is clear from surveys that have been recently made that many more of these existed in the nineteenth century than was previously supposed, but with the development of steam power they became so rapidly obsolete, and were so unsuitable for adaptation to any other use, that very few have survived. For this reason we often fail to realise how important this form of power was in every aspect of rural economy in the past, whether on the farm, in the brickyards, or even for drawing water from a well. Water and

141

*Round House,
Binsted, and interior
reconstruction*

wind power is perhaps better appreciated today than that of horse or ox.

Looking back at the last three hundred years, it is possible to see something like a continuing pattern of change, although within that pattern there have been fluctuations—corn growing, for example, increased steadily up to the eighteen-sixties, to be followed by a switch to dairy farming and sheep: since 1932 a revival of corn production took place, and in the last two decades there has been a rapid development both of intensive and specialised crop production such as mushroom growing or glass-house cultivation and animal husbandry such as that of broiler houses. But underlying all this has been the steady increase in the scale of farming, in the size of farm units and in the amount of capital sunk in farm equipment. This has been more rapid in the last two decades than in any previous period. Perhaps one of the most significant recent developments has been the increasing size not merely of farms, but of fields by the destruction of the hedges and field divisions which the initial process of consolidation by enclosure in the fifteenth and sixteenth centuries had created. In some parts of Sussex—in the south-west region in particular—we may soon have a landscape more closely resembling, in everything except the buildings and the social and economic organisation underlying its use, that of the thirteenth century open fields than at any time since the Middle Ages.

XXIV Canals and Railways

'Soon after quitting Billinghurst I crossed the river Arun, which has a canal running alongside of it. At this there are timber and coal yards, and kilns for lime. This appears to be a grand receiving and distributing place.' So writes Cobbett, in 1823. He is referring to the Arun-Wey canal, which had recently been completed, linking the Arun with the Thames. This canal connected places like Chichester, Littlehampton and Midhurst with the great network of canals which radiated from London to the Industrial North, to East Anglia and even to the West Country as far as Welshpool and Bristol. The burst of canal building, which eclipsed that of the turnpikes earlier, and even that of the railways later, was confined mainly to the years 1790-1815. By 1820 it had come to an end. It may seem surprising that most of our canals were built while we were at war with Napoleon. In fact the war acted as a stimulus, since the canals provided an alternative to the coastal shipping trade—until then the principal method for the transport of heavy and bulky goods and now subject to constant interference by French raiders. One of the Sussex canals—that from Rye to Hythe, skirting the north edge of the Romney marsh—was purely military. Designed to move men, artillery and equipment rapidly and within the coastal area, it also served as a line of defence against any invasion force. Another canal projected for military purposes, but in fact never built, was one which would have linked Portsmouth and Chatham, the two great naval bases. Several alternative routes were considered, one of which, via Chichester and Arundel, would have followed the flat Weald clay through the centre of Sussex, via Horsham and Crawley, to link with the Medway above Tonbridge.

Although military considerations played their part, the main function of most of the Sussex canals was the improvement of agriculture, by the cheaper movement of heavy agricultural products and requisites. To quote Arthur Young: 'Though it be true that Sussex has hardly the shadow of anything that deserves the name of manufacture, yet the advantages which the County has received and is likely still further to gain from increasing her navigation will be very considerable. The principal productions of Sussex are, 1, corn; 2, timber, bark, charcoal; 3, chalk, lime, marl; 4, iron, marble, limestone; 5, cattle and sheep, hides and wool.' The barges were drawn by horses, but also carried sails for use when the wind was favourable.

Lock, Stopham

143

The first canals in Sussex were, strictly speaking, navigations. Their purpose was to make navigable the lower reaches of the rivers, which centuries of neglect had rendered useless as waterways for even small boats. This involved dredging, the removal of sandbars, and occasionally the shortening of the winding course of the river by joining meandering curves with a cut or 'true canal'. This phase did not normally involve the building of locks. The rivers in Sussex made navigable in this way were the Eastern Rother, the Ouse, the Adur, and the Arun.

The 'true canal' was an entirely new waterway, often climbing by means of locks over considerable watersheds, or by means of tunnels maintaining a level course beneath intervening ridges. The canal which linked the Arun Navigation to the Wey Navigation was one of this kind. It climbed by a series of fourteen locks from Stopham near Pulborough to its highest point (in Sidney wood on the Surrey-Sussex border), where it just skirts the 150-foot contour. In places it curved along hillsides some 20 feet above the bottom of the valley.

Other enterprises were part navigation and part canal—such as the (western) Rother Valley Navigation and the extension of the Adur and Ouse navigations by a series of locks and cuttings further into the Weald. The Rother Navigation rose 86 feet from Stopham to Midhurst by a series of eight locks, at intervals of about one-and-a-half miles. A branch followed the little valley of the Haslingbourne to the south-east edge of Petworth built partly on an embankment; it crossed two or three small streams and included two locks.

Apart from the Arun-Wey and the Hythe military canal, the only other true canal in Sussex was the last to be built (1817-23). Its construction was due largely to the initiative and financial backing of the third Lord Egremont, who had financed the Rother Navigation. It linked the Arun above Ford with Portsmouth. One reason for building it was the desire to provide employment during the depression which followed the end of the war with Napoleon. This canal, though it climbs to no great height and contains only four locks between Chichester Harbour (where it enters Sussex) and the Arun, is one of the most interesting in the south of England. It runs parallel to the coast, crossing at right-angles a number of small streams, the largest of these being the Aldingbourne Rife; here the canal runs for nearly half a mile along the top of an embankment some 10 feet above the surrounding meadows, the river running through a tunnel underneath the canal. The canal bed is dry today, and up to a few years ago a humped bridge stood to the south of Barnham in the middle of a farm-track, and, overgrown with thicket and trees, it was apparently as purposeless as the bridge of Croyland.

The Portsmouth-Arun canal was, unlike the Rother Navigation, never a success. In no year did the tolls produce a reasonable return on

LEWES BRIDGE.

37. The bridge, Lewes; a drawing from the Burrell collection (p. 169). This bridge over the Ouse concentrated all traffic to the east at the bottom of Lewes High Street; although enlarged in the nineteenth century it was quite inadequate for the immense increase in traffic in recent years. An inner relief road and a new bridge to the north (completed in 1972) has relieved traffic at this point, but at the expense of the area to the north-west.

38. Brighton and the Chain Pier (about 1850), looking E. from the edge of Pool Valley. The aquarium would occupy the immediate foreground with the Palace Pier on the right (p. 125). The new marina will extend into the sea from below the cliffs on the horizon (p. 155–6).

39. Sea Houses, Eastbourne, about 1840. The village lay nearly a mile inland. The development of Eastbourne was almost entirely between 1850 and 1900. Of all the Sussex resorts it was the most completely Victorian in character, and has grown relatively slowly in the present century (p. 155).

40. Centre of Worthing, c.1850. Worthing still preserved a central open space to the west of South Street, but within twenty years this was built over. Had this open space been retained, Worthing would today have a central garden area comparable with the Steyne gardens at Brighton (pp. 123–4).

the capital invested. By 1855 the canal was virtually abandoned, and in 1888 the Company was finally wound up. A small section at Birdham is still used as a safe anchorage for yachts and motor-boats, while the branch which led from Mundham to Chichester was acquired by the City Corporation, and has recently (1958) been taken over by the County with a view to possible development for pleasure.

The other Sussex canal which would well repay preservation is the Military Canal at the other end of the county. It traverses some of the loveliest and most remote countryside to be found anywhere in England; it contains only two locks and the cost of reclamation, mostly dredging and the clearing of weeds, would not be prohibitive. It is also the widest of the Sussex canals.

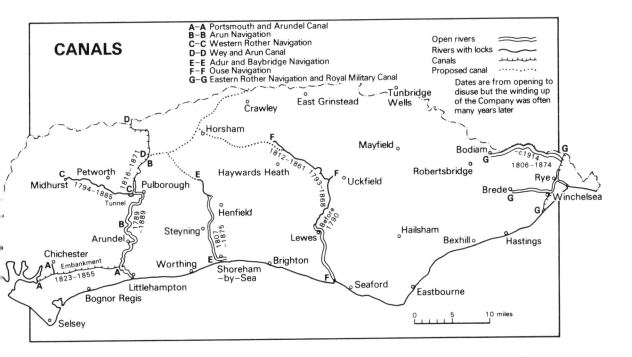

The only canal in Sussex is that which shortened the Arun Navigation by cutting through the ridge at Hardham, along which the ancient line of Stane Street, the railway and the modern motor road run from Pulborough to Coldwaltham. This tunnel, and the lock to the south, was constructed to make it possible for barges to avoid the four-mile tidal loop at Greatham. Barges were propelled through the tunnel by the feet of the bargees who lay on their backs and pushed against the roof. Though the last barge passed through the tunnel in 1885, it was still navigable at the beginning of the century for a small skiff. Today not only are the

145

*Original signal box,
Hardham*

*Funicular, Devil's
Dyke 1890*

entrances choked, but where the railway crosses the canal, concrete reinforcements completely block the canal, making any kind of projected reinstatement virtually impossible.

Of the various schemes put forward between 1800 and 1825 for a ship canal linking the Thames to Portsmouth, that of Cundy in 1824 was by far the most ambitious. To quote from the prospectus, 'This canal . . . is intended to accommodate vessels of the largest dimensions when fully loaded so as to enable them to pass each other; for this purpose twenty-eight feet depth of water will be required and about a hundred and fifty feet in width, with about four locks, three hundred feet in length and sixty-four in depth up to the summit level'. The line of the canal, leaving the Thames at Deptford, would have passed through the Mole gap at Dorking, and thence across the Weald to Arundel. At the highest point approximately three hundred and eighty-two feet above sea level, it was designed to run through a cutting a hundred feet deep. Although nothing came of this and other schemes, they are some measure of the prodigious optimism and confidence of the engineers of the period. Within a little more than a decade these energies were to be transferred to the railways.

The decline of the canals was in fact almost as sudden and dramatic as that of the turnpikes, and for the same reason—the coming of the railways. In the twenty-four years between 1839 and 1863 the main lines in Sussex were completed. Of the secondary lines, the Mid-Sussex from Pulborough to Petersfield was opened in 1867, the section from Midhurst to Chichester in 1885; the Chichester to Selsey line in 1897. The 'Bluebell' line, as it came to be called, which linked the main line at East Grinstead with the main line just north of Lewes, was opened in 1882. The little railway that conveyed visitors from Victorian Brighton to the fun-fairs, cable railway and funicular on the Devil's Dyke was completed in 1887; it had a brief life of less than thirty years before being dismantled to serve in France during the First World War. After the war it was reinstated and closed finally in 1938. The Selsey line followed in 1935; the Chichester to Midhurst line was closed during the last war and the Pulborough to Petersfield section of the mid-Sussex railway was finally closed to both passenger and goods traffic in 1958. The 'Bluebell' line, after being closed by the Transport Commission in 1958, was partly reopened for the summer season by private enterprise

Further to the west plans are being considered for the conversion of part of the Shoreham to Horsham line to a road bypass for Steyning and Bramber, while other sections of this railway, and of the Chichester to Midhurst line, may become a bridle way and nature reserve—changes of use within a century, which would surprise their original builders.

On the other hand, main lines such as the Brighton to London carry a weight and frequency of traffic undreamed of by their original promoters.

146

When this line was first debated in 1863, eight rival schemes were put forward; five of these favoured the devious routes following the Adur valley through Steyning, or the Falmer valley to the east. That the final decision was the direct route through the Downs, necessitating one of the longest tunnels to be made at that time, indicates the foresight, as well as the supreme confidence, of the promoters; while the fact that the magnificent curved viaduct, which takes the Lewes line across the London road and into the hillside terminus at Brighton, can cope with such tremendously increased traffic is a testimony to the quality of early Victorian engineering.

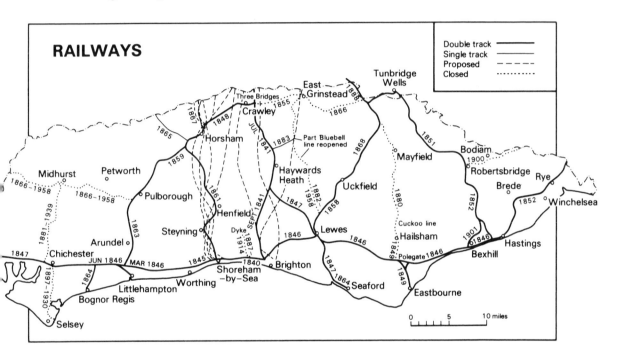

It is, however, well to remember that these skills, as well as the labour force which enabled the railway development to be carried through so rapidly, were the result of the experience gained during the Regency period. Part of the labour then recruited for the equally difficult and occasionally more spectacular task of building the canals, was available for the building of railways. A train can go uphill, water cannot. The canal tunnels, viaducts and bridges all had to be planned with a greater nicety of judgment, and accuracy of measurement than their railway equivalents. This was the achievement of the eighteenth century.

147

XXV The Last 140 Years

'Daddy Longlegs',
Brighton

Considered nationally the last hundred and forty years was a period of almost uninterrupted technological progress. In this, Sussex is regarded as a backwater, bypassed by the developments of the Midlands and the north. This, however, is not quite true. There were no important industries located in Sussex, no new factories using new techniques, and demanding an expanding class of industrial workers; yet it is surprising how many new developments were in fact pioneered in the Brighton area.

In the interior of the Pavilion, Nash had been among the first to use cast iron beams and columns, modelled decoratively and appropriately, not merely in the kitchen, but in principle state rooms such as the saloon and drawing room. The Antheum at Hove, built in 1831 as a great glass and metal dome, antedated, in the boldness of its design and its size, both the Crystal Palace and the Reading Room of the British Museum. It was unfortunate that it collapsed on the day before it was due to open, but even this tragic miscalculation provided data for the later and more successful ventures. The chain pier was again a pioneer work, and first demonstrated the possibility of a suspension system applied to tremendously increased forces of wind and wave. It is true it was carried away finally in a storm in 1896; but this was nearly half a century after it had outlived its original purpose as the main terminus for the cross channel traffic service.

In the eighteen-eighties, the cable car, suspended across the Devil's Dyke, and the cable lift up the steep northern escarpment of the Downs, were at the time among the earliest experiments of this kind, although the visitor to the Dyke today will see nothing to indicate that they ever existed.

In 1883, the first railway to be powered by electricity in the world was built by Mr. Volk along the undercliff at Kemptown: (this still runs). In 1896 a unique railway was laid just above the low tide level. This carried at high tide passengers on a covered platform raised high above the waves on a lower framework. This novelty was popularly nicknamed 'Daddy Longlegs' and is illustrated in a marginal drawing. For five years, until its dismantling at the beginning of the present century it entertained thousands of visitors.

Brighton, however, is not rural Sussex, and during the aftermath of the Napoleonic war, the situation in the countryside was very different. Cobbett wrote his descriptions of Sussex at a time of general agricultural

148

depression, created by falling prices and accompanied by widespread unemployment. A few years later these conditions reached their climax. In certain parts of the county there were outbreaks of violence, mostly rick-burning or window-breaking. At Rye the unpopular overseer of the parish poor, who was responsible for the payment of outdoor relief and controlled the local poor-house, was conducted by a crowd of five hundred along the turnpike road, and deposited outside the confines of the parish. The people of the parish were then regaled with beer by the farmers, whose sympathy was in many instances with the labourers. In these 'riots' which spread to Brede, then to Ringmer, and finally to the area round Horsham, little personal violence was shown. The demands of the labourers were, in fact, singularly moderate. At a packed meeting of nearly a thousand held in the Parish Church at Horsham demands were formulated for a wage of 2s. 6d. per day, and the lowering of rents and tithes. The High Sheriff for Sussex, in a letter to the Home Office wrote: 'I should have found it quite impossible to have prevailed upon any person to serve as special constables—most of the tradespeople and many of the farmers considering the demands of the people but just and equitable.'

Cobden Memorial, Heyshott

From Sussex the demonstrations spread into all the other southern counties. It was as J. L. Hammond describes it in *The Village Labourer*, 'the last Labourers' Revolt'. The measures taken to repress them, and the punishments inflicted, were out of all proportion to the offences committed. Arson was then a capital offence and four men were condemned for rick-burning at the assizes held at Horsham, between 1831 and 1834, and publicly executed in front of the gaol. They included George Wren, a workhouse orphan of nineteen, who was later proved to have been trying to put out the fire.

The distress and agitation of the 'thirties finally came to an end with the return of agricultural prosperity, brought about by the rise in the price of corn due to the steady pressure of population in the Midlands and the North. Richard Cobden, a son of a Sussex yeoman farmer near Midhurst, who for years led the agitation for the repeal of the Corn Laws by which the price of corn was maintained by taxes on imported grain, was vindicated in the years immediately following the repeal in 1846. Farmers were not ruined by foreign competition; on the contrary, the later 'fifties and the 'sixties are often referred to as 'the golden age of English agriculture'. The rural population of Sussex increased steadily without creating any large measure of unemployment; by 1870 more land was under the plough than at any time before or after. Round about the year 1870 however, the tide began to turn again; cheaply produced corn from America, Poland and Russia forced down the price of English grain, and land went out of cultivation. The decline was greatest in those areas

149

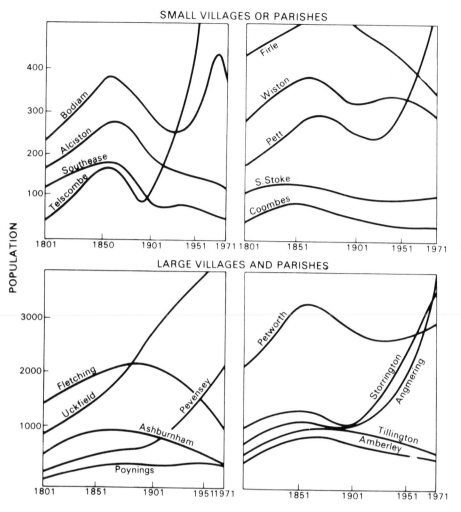

SMALL VILLAGES OR PARISHES

POPULATION

Bodiam
Alciston
Southease
Telscombe

400
300
200
100

1801 1850 1901 1951 1971

Firle
Wiston
Pett
S.Stoke
Coombes

1801 1851 1901 1951 1971

LARGE VILLAGES AND PARISHES

3000
2000
1000

Fletching
Uckfield
Pevensey
Ashburnham
Poynings

1801 1851 1901 19511971

Petworth
Storrington
Angmering
Tillington
Amberley

1851 1901 1951 1971

These graphs of population change, although necessarily selective are typical. They illustrate how universal was the increase in the rural population from 1801 to approximately 1871, followed by a decline except in those parishes affected by the development of the coastal resorts and the railways. It must be remembered that the census figures are based on the parish and that in some cases it is the parish outside the village which may have been subjected to more rapid change.

where land of marginal quality had been ploughed up; large tracts of the Weald consisted of land of this kind. And so, between 1870 and the outbreak of the First World War, the character of the Sussex landscape, particularly of the heavier clay and sandstone areas, was transformed from a checker-board of fields whose colour changed from browns to green and gold with the seasons, to one of unvaried meadowland—from corn growing to pasture and milk production. The climax of this change was reached in 1932. Detailed field maps of several parishes which survive from the sixteenth century show that a far larger area was then under the plough than in 1932. This decline is reflected in the census figures; a great many parishes in the purely rural areas of Sussex had a much smaller population in 1931 than in 1871.

Other changes began in the 1830's which were to have lasting consequences. In 1832 the first Reform Bill changed the traditional system of representation in Parliament, unaltered since the thirteenth century.

150

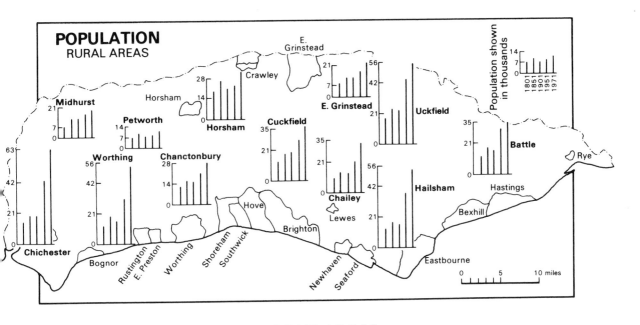

POPULATION—URBAN AREAS

(Figures in Thousands)

	1801	1851	1901	1951	1971
Horsham	3	7	13	17	27
Chichester	5	9	10	19	21
Bognor	0·2	5	13	24	35
Littlehampton	0·6	2	6	14	19
{ Rustington, East Preston	0·4	0·7	1·2	5	15
Worthing	1	6	25	70	90
Shoreham	1	3	4	13	19
Southwick	0·3	1	3	11	12
{ Crawley, Ifield	1	1	4	10	70
E. Grinstead	3	4	6	11	19
Hove	0·1	4	30	70	73
Brighton	7	65	103	156	160
Lewes	4·5	9	11	15	N.A.
Seaford	1	1	3	9	16
Eastbourne	1·7	3	44	58	71
Hastings	3	17	66	66	72
Bexhill	1	3·5	12	26	33

Jubilee Clock Tower,
Brighton

Several of the Sussex boroughs, such as Winchelsea and Bramber, had declined into the worst kind of 'rotten borough', others had become 'pocket boroughs' in which the bulk of the properties, to which votes were traditionally attached, were owned by the local great family. Sir George Trevelyan describes the election of Charles James Fox, then aged nineteen, for whom the constituency of Midhurst was selected in 1768: 'The right of election rested in a few small-holdings on which no human being resided, distinguished among the pastures and the stubble that surrounded them by a large stone set up on end in the middle of each portion. These burbage tenures, as they were called, had all been bought up by a single proprietor, Viscount Montague' (of Cowdray) 'who, when an election was in prospect, assigned a few of them to his servants, with instructions to nominate the members and then make back the property to their employer.'

By the Act of 1832 Bramber, East Grinstead, Seaford, Steyning and Winchelsea lost both their members: Arundel, Horsham, Midhurst and Rye were reduced to single member constituencies. Since then various Acts have modified the parliamentary map of Sussex; new boroughs have been created in Brighton, Hove and Eastbourne, and only Hastings of the thirteen original Sussex boroughs still has, as a town, a representative in Parliament.

The second change introduced in the 'thirties was in the Poor Law. In 1834 the Poor Law Amendment Act altered the whole structure of the system which had been established in the reign of Elizabeth, by which each parish was responsible for the care of its own poor. Parishes varied greatly, but Commissions of Enquiry described appalling conditions in some of the parish workhouses in Sussex. At Shipley a small thatched cottage housed up to twenty children, mostly orphans or illegitimate, verminous and half-starved, sleeping on straw. Many such children were destined, as soon as they were old enough, to be 'apprenticed' to some cotton or woollen manufacturer in the north; by this kind of forced migration, the rural areas of Sussex supplied cheap labour for the industrial towns. In contrast, the workhouse at Easebourne near Midhurst, built through the initiative of the third Lord Egremont in 1798, served as a model for the rest of the country. It has workrooms, handicraft instructors, nurses, and was solid and well designed. It was built under an act of Parliament in 1782 known as Gilbert's Act, which enabled parishes wishing to combine for the maintenance of their poor to do so. In this case twelve parishes co-operated, and what was achieved at Easebourne had some influence on the form of the Act of 1834, in which the parish system was everywhere abandoned in favour of workhouses maintained by groups of parishes or 'Unions'. Under this Act twenty unions were formed and new workhouses were built in various parts of Sussex—bleak, barrack-like structures, mechanically efficient, and though perhaps

152

41. Aisled tithe barn at Alciston, formerly belonging to Battle Abbey; part dates from the fifteenth century, and was extended later (p. 139).

42. Unaisled barn with cattle sheds attached, West Dean. This layout was typical in the dairying and cattle raising areas from at least the seventeenth century until recent years (p. 140).

43. Lock-keeper's cottage on the Western Rother, just N. of the canal tunnel at Hardham. The lock lies immediately to the left of the cottage. The cottage was demolished in 1955 (pp. 144–5).

44. The railway viaduct, Brighton, in 1846 from the W. Today this whole area is completely built over and the magnificent proportions of the viaduct as a whole cannot be judged (p. 147).

45. South Street, Worthing, *c.* 1825. This should be compared with the photograph below taken from exactly the same point in 1960. The houses on the left and in the centre have been transformed by inserted shop fronts, raised roofs, and surface stucco, mostly in the later nineteenth century.

46. A comparison of these two views epitomizes many of the changes characteristic of the last 150 years. The harmony of treatment and simplicity of decoration and design of the eighteenth century has given way to an unco-ordinated individualism, with trivial decoration and ragged roof lines.

47. Crawley New Town. One of the few groups of flats, built in the form of three wings projecting from a central well. Note the preservation of trees, the open shared garden surrounds and curving road. No blocks of more than three stories have so far been built, and there is a strong preference for terraced houses with individual gardens however small (pp. 156–7).

48. This shopping precinct (pedestrians only) connects the new shopping centre with the old High Street. Note the variety of surface treatment (of varied colour), the balconies, the lighting units and, in the foreground, the notice board for the use of local organisations (pp. 156–7).

preferable to the Shipleys, lacking the informality, and sometimes the humanity, of the converted cottage in the village, where at least there would be local ties and contacts. Since then there have been many changes and reforms, culminating in the Local Government Act of 1929 which finally abolished the 'Workhouse System' of 1834. Since then some of the now redundant and over-large country mansions of an earlier age, such as that of the Bartelott family at Stopham, have been converted into old people's homes—a final use which the original builders could hardly have foreseen.

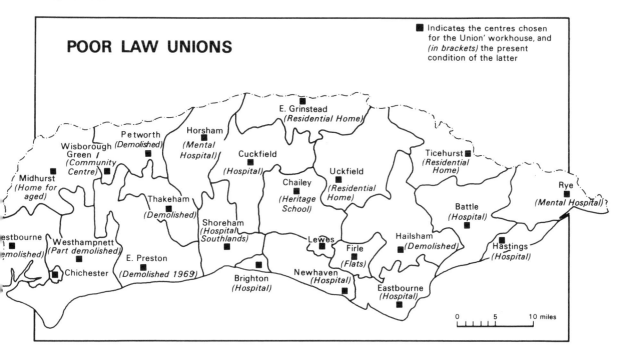

POOR LAW UNIONS

■ Indicates the centres chosen for the Union' workhouse, and *(in brackets)* the present condition of the latter

E. Grinstead *(Residential Home)*

Petworth *(Demolished)*

Wisborough Green *(Community Centre)*

Horsham *(Mental Hospital)*

Cuckfield *(Hospital)*

Ticehurst *(Residential Home)*

Midhurst *(Home for aged)*

Chailey *(Heritage School)*

Uckfield *(Residential Home)*

Rye *(Mental Hospital)*?

Thakeham *(Demolished)*

Shoreham *(Hospital Southlands)*

Battle *(Hospital)*

estbourne *emolished)*

Westhampnett *(Part demolished)*

Lewes

Firle *(Flats)*

Hailsham *(Demolished)*

Hastings *(Hospital)*

E. Preston *(Demolished 1969)*

Chichester

Newhaven *(Hospital)*

Brighton *(Hospital)*

Eastbourne *(Hospital)*

0   5   10 miles

A third development which one can trace back to the 1830's lies in education—then the first grants were voted by Parliament to certain religious bodies to help in the building of schools in areas where there were none. Under this and subsequent legislation, culminating in the Education Act of 1870 by which primary education was made compulsory and universal, schools were built in practically every village in Sussex, two-thirds of them by the Church of England. Since then ideas of accommodation and class management have changed; buildings then erected are out of date; many, under the Education Act of 1944, have been closed, some converted into public halls, some to private houses, while others have been pulled down. They were, in fact, often too well and solidly built, and occasionally we must regret the loss of the small local school on the edge of a common, where the children of the village with their teacher had something of the quality of a happy family.

Village School, North Heath

153

XXVI The Present and the Future

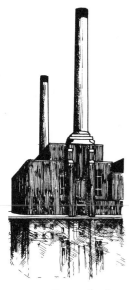

*Power Station,
Southwick*

History is concerned with the past, but one of the reasons why most of us study history is the belief that it can provide clues to the future. During the last fifty years the conditions of life, the distribution and density of population, and the character of the landscape of Sussex, have been changing more rapidly than in any previous period of similar duration. What is more, the tempo of change is accelerating. These developments are due partly to migration into the area for residential or recreational purposes (a process which began in the Weald in the sixteenth century and on the coast in the eighteenth), and partly to changes in agriculture and in the location of industry.

Before the First World War the population of Sussex was increasing steadily, but the rate of growth varied from area to area. It was almost entirely limited to the coast or to the railway routes. Most of the rural villages had, in fact, declined in population since 1870. After the First World War the pattern of new settlements entirely altered, largely owing to the development of road transport. Not only did almost all the villages within easy access of a main road expand, but a general pepper-pot distribution of new houses spread over the county like a rash, destroying the quality of one rural area after another. A few areas, notably the inland parts of West Sussex, escaped this sprawling development through the restrictive action taken by some of the greater landowners. This kind of restriction, perhaps undesirable from certain aspects, became increasingly less possible through the incidence of heavy death duties and the splitting up of the greater estates.

To meet problems such as this, and to give positive direction to the development of town and countryside, the Town and Country Planning Act was passed in 1947. Under this Act every Local Authority of County or County Borough status was required to work out an estimate of the probable rate of future development, and in the light of this to submit development plans designed to regulate urban and village expansion during the next twenty years. Interim revision, where necessary, was provided for at intervals of five years. After twenty years the plans were to be subject to complete revision and reformulation. The main aim of the Act was to produce more compact and integrated villages and towns by restricting development outside certain defined zones; and, by encouraging the building up of undeveloped areas within these zones, to avoid the piecemeal destruction of the rural landscape and consumption of good agricultural land.

154

It was also necessary in the development plan for Education, under the 1944 Education Act, to have some clear picture of the probable population changes in order to decide the size of new schools and the provision of places in Grammar and Technical Schools. Almost immediately the calculations were upset by the rise in the birth rate beyond the anticipated level, so that the original school building programme proved generally inadequate. Secondly, there was an alteration in the trends of migration into the County; the attraction of certain areas—Eastbourne, Brighton and Hove—declined in favour of the coastal districts further to the west. Already in 1960 the Borough of Worthing was asking for a revision of the present development plan since the bulk of the area allocated had been taken up. An inflexible policy by the Planning Authority must result in a more intensive development—the use, for example, of high blocks of flats—or in an actual restriction of any further expansion in the population. Without restrictive measures, most of the coast of Sussex from West Wittering to Peacehaven will, by 1970 or soon after, become an area of linked subtopia.

Tower block, Bognor

The same is true of certain inland areas; villages in Rural Districts such as Chanctonbuty have increased their population, and have already exhausted the areas set aside for residential development, and are clamouring to be allowed to extend into the surrounding farm-land.

This growth in population has intensified for Sussex problems of traffic congestion. An increase within the next ten years of between two and three times the number of cars in the county is probably an underestimate. Yet even a twofold increase will create in all the towns, and many of the villages, traffic and parking problems already intractable. A recent enquiry held at Chichester (January 1960—to quote the Minister's report) posed the dilemma of having 'to make a choice between a larger roundabout at the Market Cross, or a new road across Westgate Fields'. This view from the south-west, across Westgate Fields, is possibly the finest view of any cathedral city still surviving, with much of its original setting of surrounding meadow and walls. The new ring road cuts right across this and destroys much of its quality, yet this was understandably felt to be preferable to the mutilation of the centre of the city. Worthing and Brighton are faced with similar dilemmas, not so great in terms of aesthetic values involved, but greater in terms of cost.

Brighton has maintained its position as a pioneer in the application of technology to the creation of amenities. In 1971 work began on the Marina at the eastern end of the undercliff. The project will use techniques for the building of what will be the largest artificial yachting harbour in Europe based on and developed out of the experience gained from the Mulberry harbours established on the opposite side of the Channel after D-day. At Bognor, plans are in hand for the creation of a new coastal

155

redevelopment involving the reclamation of areas of beach, which like other sections of the coast between Selsey and Worthing, have been lost to the sea during the last two hundred years.

The only new town at present in the county, Crawley, was started in 1947; it is nearer completion than any of the other new towns planned under the New Towns Act of 1946. The original plan was for a population of approximately 60,000, with nine residential 'neighbourhood units' of about 6,000 to 7,000 each. Since then the plan has been enlarged to 65,000 and later to 70,000, with a tenth neighbourhood added in the south-east corner of the designated area. Each neighbourhood has its own shopping and civic centre attractively laid out to create something of the character and informality of a village green. The main town centre has been imaginatively planned; the use of colour and light materials has given it a gay and carefree quality, while pedestrian precincts and adequate car-parks have freed it from the sense of congestion which afflicts the older towns. A great deal of thought has been given to ways of varying the layout of houses by the use of cul-de-sacs, curving roads, and the very careful preservation, wherever possible, of well-grown trees.

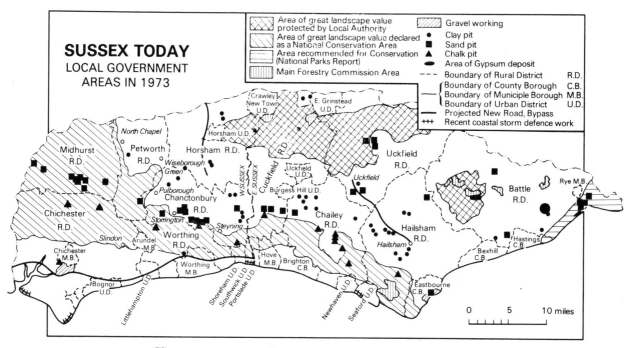

The map on page 153 shows the grouping of parishes into 'Unions' under the Poor Law Amendment Act of 1834. These new units of administration served also other purposes such as the areas for census returns. Several were converted with only minor alterations into the new Rural Districts when the whole structure of local government was recast at the close of the century. A comparison with this map shows the relationship between the 'Unions' and the present Rural Districts, which are now being subjected to a further major reorganization.

156

The factory zone to the north of the town represents the first large concentration of industry in Sussex, employing the bulk of the population of the new town. Some of the most interesting buildings in Crawley, both architecturally and in their general layout, are to be found in this area. They demonstrate how industrial development, if properly controlled, need not necessarily involve ugliness.

The whole plan is, however, essentially one of open development, and the question remains as to whether this type of development can meet the expansion of population which would seem to be inevitable in the future. What will be the position in 1975, or 1980, when the new town, with its present low age structure, and high proportion of children, becomes a more balanced community of old, middle-aged and young? Are the old people of the future, who are the young parents of today, to be pushed out by their married children?

West Sussex Arms

In agriculture, changes since 1939 have restored the landscape in some areas to a pattern very close to that of the mid-nineteenth century; ·but on the downland, farmers, encouraged by subsidies, have been cultivating land which has not been touched by the plough for fifteen hundred years or more. Instead of the great sheep-walks of the eighteenth and nineteenth centuries, much of the Downs is now fenced and enclosed; while, in places, notably in the area north-east of Seaford, they have been planted with conifers—trees utterly alien to the chalk landscape; other areas, unsuited to the plough, but now no longer grazed by sheep, are returning to thistle, bramble and scrub; footpaths have been lost, and land which was once open walking and riding country is tangled with undergrowth or barbed-wire fencing.

The revival of agriculture, and the increase in agricultural production has not, however, because of mechanization, increased the agricultural population. Fewer are, in fact, employed on the land than was the case thirty years ago, and an examination of the Census returns shows many villages in the more remote areas in which the population remains lower than in the 1860's. In places agriculture has been semi-industrialized; near Pulborough has been built what is said to be the largest mushroom-growing and processing plant in Europe, already employing over 700 workers, and in the area north of Worthing there has been a steady increase in the size and number of glass-houses growing tomatoes or flowers.

Possibly the most important industries, in so far as they affect the character of the Sussex landscape, are the extractive ones—sand, chalk and gravel. Here there has been steady expansion since the war; and, in the areas particularly affected, the consequences are sometimes devastating. Planning control has here and there enforced some kind of balance between industrial needs and amenity. The new chalk-pit at Duncton has been partially screened by trees and by a protecting tongue of the

157

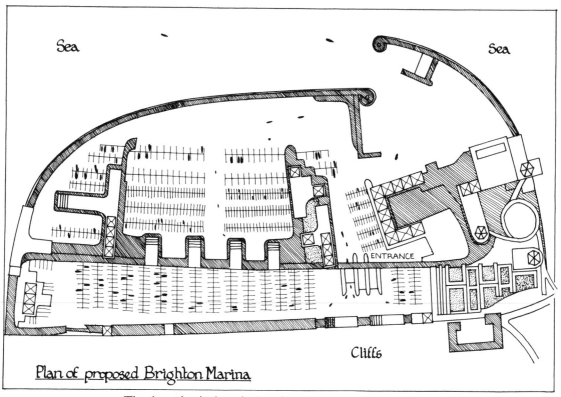

Sea

Sea

ENTRANCE

Cliffs

Plan of proposed Brighton Marina

The above plan is the revised version of the original plan and is now (February 1974) under further discussion. Minor alterations have been made such as the siting of the lock to the inner harbour at the east, instead of the west, side; floating mooring quays are proposed for the tidal (south) side of the central spine.

escarpment, insisted on by the Ministry after a public enquiry. But the scar on perhaps the most beautiful and unspoilt section of the Sussex Downs enlarges yearly. The same is true of the post-war development of the cement works in the Adur valley, north of Shoreham.

Perhaps the most drastic of the recent changes in the landscape, though limited in extent, are to be found in the exploitation of the sand of the Folkestone Beds. These strata of the Lower Greensand, though less than a hundred feet thick, and rarely extending for more than half a mile where it reaches the surface, contain some of the finest building sand in the country. With the increased use of concrete and forms of construction requiring sand, the demand has multiplied spectacularly. Within a decade hills have become holes, and country houses been demolished, for the sake of the sand beneath. Though on a more limited scale, it could be quite as catastrophic as the opencast mining of the Midlands. Again, some checks are imposed by the Planning Authorities, but the need for sand is likely to increase rather than diminish.

Gravel workings are at present limited mainly to the area to the south-east of Chichester; they involve the same kind of problems as that of sand. At least one house of historic and architectural interest, Drayton Manor, is doomed by the extension of gravel working in the next few years, and it is difficult to see where the line between amenity and industrial interests should be drawn. As Thomas Sharp says in *Georgian City* (a plan drawn up in 1949 on the invitation of the Chichester City Council): 'Chichester, maybe, had to have "some" gravel pits. But 800 acres of them is a bellyful indeed.' And he adds: 'The most emphatic action should be taken to stop the new 500 acres being worked.' Yet even within the last two years permission has been given for the extraction of gravel from land north of the city, nearer to the Downs—an area until now not exploited. This new development, it is true, has been limited, but it is difficult to see how arguments which are accepted as valid for the initial exploitation today will not be equally valid for extension in ten or twenty years' time.

In the heart of the Weald, between Netherfield and Brightling, some four miles north-west of Battle, where the Purbeck strata underlying the Hastings Beds come to the surface, valuable gypsum deposits were discovered in 1874. An important local industry has since developed employing nearly 600 workers. The area of possible expansion, even if all the deposits are exploited, is limited to a few hundred acres.

Although some recent developments may seem to threaten much that those who love the county have tried to preserve, these very threats have led to a growing public conscience and to the formation of a large number of bodies, such as the Society of Sussex Downsmen, or the Society of Sussex Wealdmen, or town and village preservation societies, concerned with the protection of landscape and buildings and the improvement of amenities; while the growth of a wealthy residential and retired population has led to the provision of cultural facilities hardly to be found anywhere else in England. Towns like Rye, Hastings, Lewes, Brighton, Hove, Worthing and Chichester have all established attractive local museums, and have fathered excellent studies of aspects of their own history. They have also patronized the arts both in the subsidization of music and exhibitions. At Glyndebourne, private patronage has created a centre for opera which has become internationally famous; while the theatre in the round at Chichester, launched in 1959 and opened in 1962, has fully justified the faith of its founders and plays to full houses drawn partly from outside the county boundaries. At Worthing, a Repertory Theatre, subsidised by the Local Authority, but unfortunately lacking the public support which it deserves, persists in its endeavour to stage significant plays while making some concessions to 'box office' necessities with pantomime and more 'popular' drama. Probably the most important single cultural development within the last decade has been the establishment of the University of Sussex at Falmer. Since 1961 it has proved

*Sussex University
Main Entrance*

East Sussex Arms

to be the most sought after of the new Universities and the building of The Gardner Centre for the Arts, in 1969, has already done much to help to integrate the University with the outside community.

The beauty of the Sussex landscape, the richness of its history and the variety of the buildings which enshrine its past have contributed to its rapid growth in population. There are landscape qualities still to be found in the downland, the central Weald, and in the Greensand areas of West Sussex, which are not to be found in any other part of England, or, for that matter, Europe. A National Park covering the South Downs, and three 'Conservation Areas of Outstanding Landscape Value'—the latter to include part of the central Weald, most of the Greensand area in West Sussex, and the coastal area stretching from Fairlight to Dungeness—were among the recommendations of the Commission of Enquiry into National Parks.

Some of these recommendations have in part been realized, but not all; and it becomes increasingly difficult to strike a reasonable balance between conflicting interests. In this we are all involved, and share responsibility; a satisfactory solution is only likely in so far as we are fully aware of all that we inherit from the past, and if we can set the present in its historical context.

XXVII Conserving the Past

It is just ten years since the final chapter of the first edition of this book was written, and looking back it is possible to assess the gains and losses in the present phase of the county's history. On the whole the pattern has not changed significantly, the tremendous pressures in the south-east which are changing the environment more rapidly than in any previous epoch remain as insistent as they were ten years ago and are likely to persist for at least another two or three decades: but there is now a more widespread understanding of this, and signs of more effective action being taken to cope with the situation. The field of archaeology is a good example.

Reconstructed smithy, Singleton Museum

In January, 1971, a Trust of British Archaeology was formed, appropriately called 'Rescue'. To quote from one of its publicity leaflets, 'The enormous scale of destruction of our ancient sites would, by the year 2,000 have removed a large part of the evidence by which we understand our island's history'. It has been reckoned that at this moment more surviving evidence of the past, whether above or below ground is being destroyed in one decade than in any two centuries in the history of this country. This is probably not an exaggerated estimate; and the position in Sussex is probably neither better nor worse than in most of the counties of the southeast of England, where the pace of destruction is greater than in the north and west. But in spite of some government assistance, the resources of such an organisation as Rescue are simply not adequate to deal with the recording and examination of known sites which are threatened, and one can only speculate on the number of unrecognised and unknown sites which are in fact destroyed without trace.

Reference has been made in several chapters of this history, to some of the more recent contributions of archaeology to our knowledge and understanding of the past, but there is one point which should be stressed; much of the results of the work of the archaeologist is lost so far as the general public is concerned in the pages of learned journals. If the public is to be involved, a more accessible and comprehensible approach is required. This is increasingly recognised by museum and education authorities, and since the war there has been an encouraging co-operation between these services. Even so some of the most significant developments have been through the initiative of private bodies and individuals. The preservation of the site of the Roman Palace at Fishbourne, which easily could have been lost forever, is perhaps the most striking example within

161

The 'Bluebell' Line

the last decade; another example is the Weald and Downland Museum at Singleton, which was opened in 1971. With the help of local archaeologists, it has done something to demonstrate the findings of archaeology and the problems archaeologists face. Two reconstructions—the Saxon 'grubenhaus' and the thirteenth-century Hangleton cottage—have already been referred to in earlier chapters. More recently a replica of a fourteenth-century pottery kiln based on excavations at Binsted has been constructed by a group of potters simulating the techniques and forms of medieval pottery; and a project is now in hand to try to demonstrate some of the problems involved in reconstructions based only on the foundations of early buildings—in this case a Saxon hall, (the actual site of which was infilled and ploughed over as soon as the evidence had been recorded.)

There is another aspect of archaeology which is also attracting increasing public interest—industrial archaeology. This has tended to concentrate on the impact of the industrial revolution and the way new inventions and techniques of production changed the character of life in the eighteenth and nineteenth centuries—changes which are already only half understood by us who participate in the continuing, but in many respects new, industrial revolution of the twentieth century. Sussex may not seem a particularly appropriate county for preservation and conservation of this kind, but a vigorous society—the Sussex Industrial Archaeology Study Group was launched in 1967. It has already done valuable work in research and in the publication of the results of this; and in 1971 a group was formed specifically for the promotion of a museum in Sussex to be devoted to the preservation of early industrial machinery and processes.

The growth of public interest in the recent industrial past is also well illustrated in the way in which the 'Bluebell Line' has been able to develop since its closure by British Railways in 1958 and its re-opening by a few enthusiasts who believed its use would be appreciated. It has now succeeded in recreating the character of the railway as it was during the first four decades of its existence—not merely the engines and rolling stock, but the stations, the advertisements, lighting and other details.

Another example can be taken from the canals of Sussex. Writing in 1961 it would have seemed both optimistic and unrealistic to have suggested that the Arun-Wey Canal might be reconstructed and re-opened as an amenity. The most tentative suggestion one could make was that perhaps the Rye to Hythe Military Canal might be worth consideration. In 1971, however, a group was formed to undertake the restoration of the Arun-Wey Canal, and such has been the enthusiasm and support by volunteer workers that a section of this canal above Newbridge has already been cleared, the repair of one lock undertaken, and another in prospect; on the Surrey side work has commenced on the

162

clearing the canal above Godalming. There are those who are quite confident that within a few years, 'London's lost route to the sea' may be recovered and that it will be possible to take a boat and travel from Arundel, through the heart of the Weald, to the Thames.

Archaeology, however, illustrates only one aspect of the problems of conservation. There are two other facets even more important in the way in which they affect our day to day response to the past and our sense of historic continuity—buildings and landscape.

In 1961 the Sussex Naturalists' Trust was founded. During the last ten years it has grown steadily and is now one of the county's most influential organisations. In 1971 it changed its name to The Sussex Trust for Nature Conservation, in recognition of the fact that it is now involved in wider matters of conservation than that of meeting the interests of naturalists. The properties now under its protection are scattered over the whole county; its latest appeal for the purchase of the Mens and Cut woodland north of Petworth has the generous backing of the West Sussex County Council, and seems likely to succeed in preserving nearly four hundred acres of the last large area of Wealden forest to escape modification during the last three centuries. The widespread support for the Naturalists' Trust in these first ten years of its being is heartening; it now controls several nature reserves, nature trails, and a well placed field centre at Woods Mill near Henfield. Yet, even so, according to the figures for 1972, the two national nature reserves in the county (Lullington Heath in East Sussex and Kingley Vale in West Sussex), plus the four local nature reserves (Pagham Harbour, Chailey Common, Seaford Head and Rye Harbour), plus all those maintained by the Sussex Trust, together amount to only 2,418 acres—approximately one quarter of one per cent of the land of Sussex.

In addition to the rapidly expanding work of the Trust for Nature Conservation, the most important new development in this field is the proposal to establish a centre of the Wild Fowl Trust on the waterside meadows just north of Arundel, similar in many respects to that already established at Slimbridge by the Severn. This has met with considerable local opposition, and the original plans have been somewhat modified as a result. The most cogent of these objections are based on the problems of traffic congestion and the increase in the number of visitors to be expected as a result—perhaps a quarter of a million a year. This conflict of interests epitomises one of the paradoxes of the situation in Sussex. Can the qualities of the countryside be preserved and at the same time public access be encouraged? Given the unwelcome pressure of population, plus the welcome increase in leisure, the only rational solution would appear to be the maximum dispersal of centres for amenity enjoyment, accompanied by landscaping of the areas which have to be disturbed, and the

Proposed restoration Arun Wey Canal

163

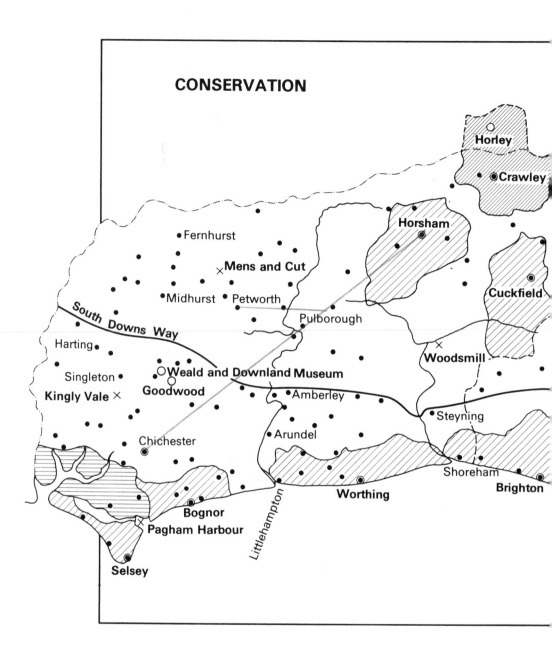

CONSERVATION

Horley

Crawley

Fernhurst

Horsham

Mens and Cut ×

Cuckfield

Midhurst • Petworth

Pulborough

South Downs Way

Harting

Woodsmill ×

Singleton

Weald and Downland Museum

Kingly Vale ×

Goodwood

Amberley

Steyning

Arundel

Chichester

Shoreham

Brighton

Littlehampton

Worthing

Bognor

Pagham Harbour

Selsey

provision of concealed parking sites. The dilemma is a familiar one. Arundel, already possesses in the castle a major tourist attraction, and cannot, it is urged, support further additions to the load it already bears without losing the very qualities which attracted the public in the first place.

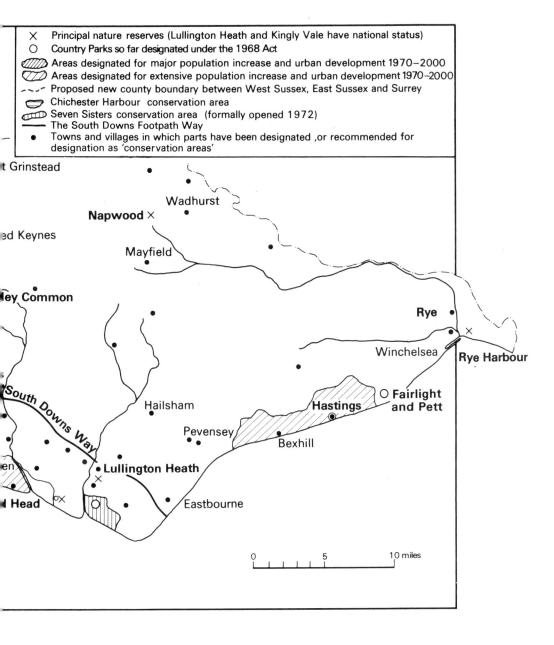

Apart from such specific schemes for the conservation of wild life and the natural ecology of different regions of the county, there has been a splendid addition in 1965 to the already considerable properties held by the National Trust in Sussex—Wakehurst Place, near Ardingly. In addition

165

Nutley Windmill in 1970, now restored

to the handsome late Tudor mansion it includes five hundred and twenty acres of parkland and gardens, the latter now being administered by the Director of the Royal Botanic Gardens at Kew.

The conservation of buildings and landscape must, however, to be generally effective, become increasingly the concern of the public authority; and during the last decade there has been an increase in the powers of action given to the local authorities, and in the readiness of local authorities to use those powers. Particularly important have been the Town and Country Planning Act of 1963, and the Countryside Act of 1968.

For some twenty years after the war there was a general belief that buildings of any historic interest were adequately protected under the Town and Country Planning Act of 1947. Under this Act every local authority was instructed to compile a list of all buildings of special historic or architectural interest. These lists divided such buildings into three categories, those of National importance, those of sufficient importance to be the concern of the Ministry, and those merely recommended to the local authority for protection. Many people recognised at the time that these lists were limited and often misleading, since the compiler had no right of access to buildings, so that the older the building and the more altered or camouflaged by later additions, the less likely was it to be recognised and included in the list. Another weakness was that the third category, which is by far the largest, was made the sole responsibility of the local authority, thus giving no protection whatsoever in those cases, only too frequent, where the local authority was not interested. Increasing pressure during the last decade has at last led to some action being taken to revise these lists by adding buildings which have been overlooked, and by upgrading from the third to the second category where this seems justified. This revision, however, will take many years to complete, and the size of the problem is exemplified by reference to the plan of Steyning High Street in chapter IX. A very careful survey of every house during the last three years by two members of the Wealden Buildings Study Group has revealed rather more than double the number of houses with medieval crown post roof construction than hitherto had been recorded or suspected. A similar house to house survey of a typical rural parish, that of West Chiltington, has produced similar results. These sample surveys can probably be taken as typical of the general situation in Sussex.

Another weakness of the 1947 Act was its concentration on individual buildings, instead of on the grouping of buildings as a whole. A great many of the older towns or villages do not depend on one or two buildings of outstanding interest for their sense of organic unity and historical development, and unless these groupings remain this sense of historical

166

continuity is lost in addition to any purely visual impoverishment. The Act of 1968 has done much to rectify this and local authorities can now designate entire areas or streets in a town or village as 'conservation areas' over which there will be much more effective control. An examination of the map in this chapter will show how many villages and towns in the county contain such designated areas. These lists are not yet complete, but the fact that so many villages within the county have already been designated gives some indication of how much which is worth conserving, still remains. The noticeable difference between East and West Sussex reflects less the relative concern of the two county authorities than the fact that the erosion or destruction of such significant areas started earlier in the eastern part of the county than in the west.

For the conservation of landscape the passing of the Countryside Act in 1968 marks an important new stage. West Sussex was one of the first counties under this Act, to establish a Coast and Countryside Committee, (December 1968), to be followed shortly afterwards, by East Sussex. The Act enables local authorities to establish Country Parks and Amenity Areas of various kinds. So far the most important scheme in West Sussex has been the joint establishment with Portsmouth and Hampshire of a single authority to plan and control as one amenity area, to include boating, fishing and other activities—the whole of the scattered but interconnecting estuaries that lie between Pagham and Langstone Harbour to the northeast of Portsmouth. In East Sussex the most important scheme is that designed to bring the whole of the Downland area behind the cliffs known as the Seven Sisters, between Seaford and Eastbourne, into a comprehensive scheme for amenity use. This includes the charming and as yet unspoilt Cuckmere valley.

These are excellent beginnings, but the action taken by public authorities depends on the pressures to which they are subjected. One of the most encouraging features of the last decade has been the steady increase in the number of amenity societies concerned with the many aspects of conservation. In 1967 a Federation of Sussex Amenity Societies was formed, and within five years the number of societies in this Federation has grown from less than a dozen to over fifty.

In conclusion, perhaps the final sentence of the previous chapter, which was written just ten years ago needs some qualification, namely, that although the balance between conservation and destruction is still overweighted on the side of destruction, the scales now seem to be tilting a little more towards the side of conservation.

Bibliography

Chichester coat of arms

The bibliography that follows is divided into three sections:—

A. Books and source material which relates only to the county and to the county as a whole.

B. Books about individual parishes, towns or buildings or some limited part of the county. These are by now so numerous that a list is bound to be highly selective.

C. General works which, although dealing with an area far wider than the county, nevertheless contain the most complete or authoritative account to date of certain aspects of the county's history.

(A.) Of source material for the county as a whole, by far the most important are the large and rapidly increasing collections of manuscript and other material, in the two county Record Offices situated at Lewes and at Chichester. These range from court rolls, letters and inventories to estate and tithe maps, sketches and photographs. All this is readily available for reference. There is also a growing number of inexpensive paper backed monographs published by the two Record Offices and covering a wide range of subjects; for example a recent publication by the Chichester Office is a 30 page booklet *Local History in West Sussex; a guide to sources* by K. C. Leslie and T. J. McCann, while the latest publication by the East Sussex R.O. is *Rails across the Weald* by S. C. Newton,—very different subjects, and both excellent.

Next in importance to the county Record Office is the reference collection of the Sussex Archaeological Society housed in the latter's headquarters at Barbican House, Lewes. The Society has also published annually since its foundation a two hundred, or more, page volume dealing with every aspect of the county's history, including field archaeology.

It has been the principal vehicle for the reporting of all archaeological work in the county for over a century, the issue for 1972 being the 110th volume. There are comprehensive indexes to every 25 volumes of these collections.

Parallel with these are the publications of the Sussex Records Society, which has now issued nearly seventy volumes including manorial rolls, records of quarter sessions, indentures, parish registers, post mortem inquisitions and so on.

There are also useful secondary collections of documents and prints in the reference departments of several of the larger municipal libraries within the county, notably at Brighton, Hastings and Worthing.

Another extremely valuable collection of source material is the Burrell collection, but as this is housed at the British museum it is not so readily accessible. It consists of material collected by Sir William Burrell between 1770 and 1796 for a projected history of Sussex which he did not live to complete. Particularly valuable are the 8 large folios of drawings made by two artists—Grimm and Lambert—employed by Sir William to record churches, houses, landscapes and ruins to illustrate the projected history. Of these there are nearly 1,200 and perhaps half have by now been published in one context or another, 191 being reproduced, for example, to commemorate the fiftieth anniversary of the founding of the Sussex Record Society, published under the title of *Sussex Views* in 1951. These drawings in the Burrell collection are often the only record which survives to enable us to judge the drastic changes made to churches and other buildings during the nineteenth century. They are supplemented by a useful secondary collection by Edgar Sharpe of drawings of nearly every church in the county, drawn between 1800 and 1820 and housed at The Barbican House, Lewes. An example of the quality of the drawings in the Burrell collection can be seen in one of the plates included in this volume, "The Bridge over the River Ouse at Lewes".

The Burrell collection has been an important source for later histories of the county, commencing with Cartwright and Dalloway's *History of the Western Division of the County* which was published in three volumes between 1815 and 1832.

More recent and more comprehensive are the six volumes so far published of the Victoria County History. The first three deal with general aspects of the county's history and topography, the last six (of which three so far have been published) deal with the county parish by parish, each volume covering one of the six rapes into which the county is divided. Those so far completed are the rapes of Hastings, Lewes and Chichester. For the archaeological history of the county E. C. Curwen's, *Sussex*, in the County Archaeologies series, is likely to remain the standard work.

For the buildings of Sussex, the volume by Pevsner and Nairns in the *Buildings of England* (Penguin) series is definitive and not likely to be superseded. It deals, however, almost exclusively with the ecclesiastical buildings and the greater houses, very little being said about the vernacular buildings of the county.

For the Civil War, Thomas Stanford's, *Sussex in the Great Civil War* is definitive.

For a comprehensive survey of agriculture and rural conditions at the beginning of the nineteenth century the Rev. Arthur Young's *General View of the Agriculture of the County of Sussex* is invaluable. As a supplement to this the Sussex volume of the Land Utilization Survey of Britain provides a general account up to 1934.

There are a number of books dealing with special topics such as:—

E. A. Fisher, *Saxon Churches of Sussex*. (1970).

G. P. Elphick, *Sussex Bells and Belfries*. (1970).

P. Hemming, *Windmills in Sussex*.

E. B. Poland, *The Friars in Sussex 1228–1928*.

R. B. Manning, *Religion and Society in Elizabethan Sussex*. (1968).

H. R. Mosse, *The Monumental Effigies of Sussex 1250–1650*.

A. Mawer and F. M. Stenton and J. E. B. Glover, *The Place Names of Sussex*, in 2 volumes.

An extremely useful collection of facsimiles of Sussex maps from 1575 to 1825 has been recently published (1972) by Phillimore.

For general guides to the county ranging from the anecdotal to the straightforward topographical, and published within the present century, no county has been better served. It is invidious to make a selection but the following should be mentioned for their general attraction and abiding interest:—

E. V. Lucas, *Sussex*, in the Highways and Byways Series.

E. Meynell, *Sussex*, in the County Books Series.

Lastly there are the monthly volumes of the *Sussex County Magazine* published from 1926 to 1956. These contain many articles of lasting interest, recording the archaeology and history of the county, and much of this material cannot be found elsewhere.

(B.) Books dealing with individual parishes, towns, buildings, etc.

There are so many that any list must be very selective indeed. The two towns most completely covered are Worthing and Chichester,—Worthing in the 'Pageant of Worthing' Series, edited by Henfrey Smail, every volume of which has been splendidly illustrated,—Chichester, by the series of monographs, edited by F. W. Steer, under the general heading *Chichester Papers*. Over fifty have now been published, an equivalent of four large bound volumes.

A fair number of books have been written about Brighton. The following embrace between them a wide range of interests:—

A. Dale, *A History of Architecture in Brighton*.

———— *Fashionable Brighton 1820–60*.

C. Musgrave, *Life in Brighton*.

E. W. Gilbert, *Brighton; Old Ocean's Bauble*.

C. Volk, *Magnus Volk of Brighton*. A biography of the pioneer electrical engineer.

Horsham is well covered by W. Albery's *Parliamentary History of Horsham*, and his *Millennium of facts in the history of Horsham and Sussex (947–1947)*.

Arundel by G. W. Eustace, *Arundel; borough and castle*.

Hastings by L. F. Salzman (in the *English Towns* series).

Rye, by L. A. Vidler, *A New History of Rye*.

Shoreham by H. Cheal, *The Story of Shoreham*.

Parish and manorial histories range from monumental works such as L. Fleming's *History of Pagham*, in three Volumes, or a more specialised study such as Lord Leconfield's *Petworth Manor in the Seventeenth Century*, to condensed accounts such as *Cuckfield—an Old Sussex Town*, by M. Wright, or the more anecdotal such as *Round about Old Storrington*, by F. M. Greenfield, being an account of changes within living memory, both recently published. A number of books deal with the history and topography of special areas such as:—

R. H. Goodsall, *Arun and the Western Rother*.

I. Done, *Looking back in Sussex*, (an account of the early history of the Manhood peninsula).

There are also many delightful and revealing memoirs such as:—

M. Robinson, *A Southdown Farm in the Sixties*.

The Memoirs of Gaius Carley, a Sussex Blacksmith, (edited by F. W. Steer).

Old Sussex Diarists, (edited by J. H. Rees).

A great number of buildings have been described in detail from both their architectural and their historical aspects:—for example,

B. Cunliffe, *Fishbourne; A Roman Palace and its Garden.*

A. Ponsonby, *The Priory and Manor of Lynchmere and Shulbrede.*

R. A. E. Roundell, *Cowdray House.*

A. S. Duncan Jones, *The Story of Chichester Cathedral.*

Rev. E. Crake, *The Castle of Hurstmonceux.*

C. Musgrave, *The Pavilion*, (Brighton).

(C.) Books which cover a wider area than the county, but which contain the best—sometimes the only—account of one aspect of the county's history:—

S. W. Woolridge and F. Goldring, *The Weald* (New Naturalist Series).

C. Copley, *Archaeology of South East England.*

I. D. Margary, *Roman Ways in the Weald.*

H. C. Darby, *The Domesday Geography of South East England.*

E. Straker, *Wealden Iron.*

G. H. Kenyon, *The Glass Industry of the Weald.*

R. T. Mason, *Framed Buildings of the Weald.*

R. and F. Jessup, *The Cinque Ports.*

H. N. Shore, *Smuggling Days and Smuggling Ways.*

D. Stroud, *Capability Brown.*

P. A. L. Vine, *London's Lost Route to the Sea (the history of the Arun Wey Canal).*

C. Hadfield, *The Canals of South and South East England.*

J. L. Hammond, *The Village Labourer.*

C. D. F. Marshall, *A History of the Southern Railway.*

It is hardly necessary to add Cobbett's *Rural Rides* or Defoe's *A Tour Through the Whole Island of Great Britain 1724–6*, as both are referred to repeatedly in the text, but mention should be made of *The Journeys of Celia Fiennes (c. 1685–1702)* edited by C. Morris.

Index

172